WINGS!

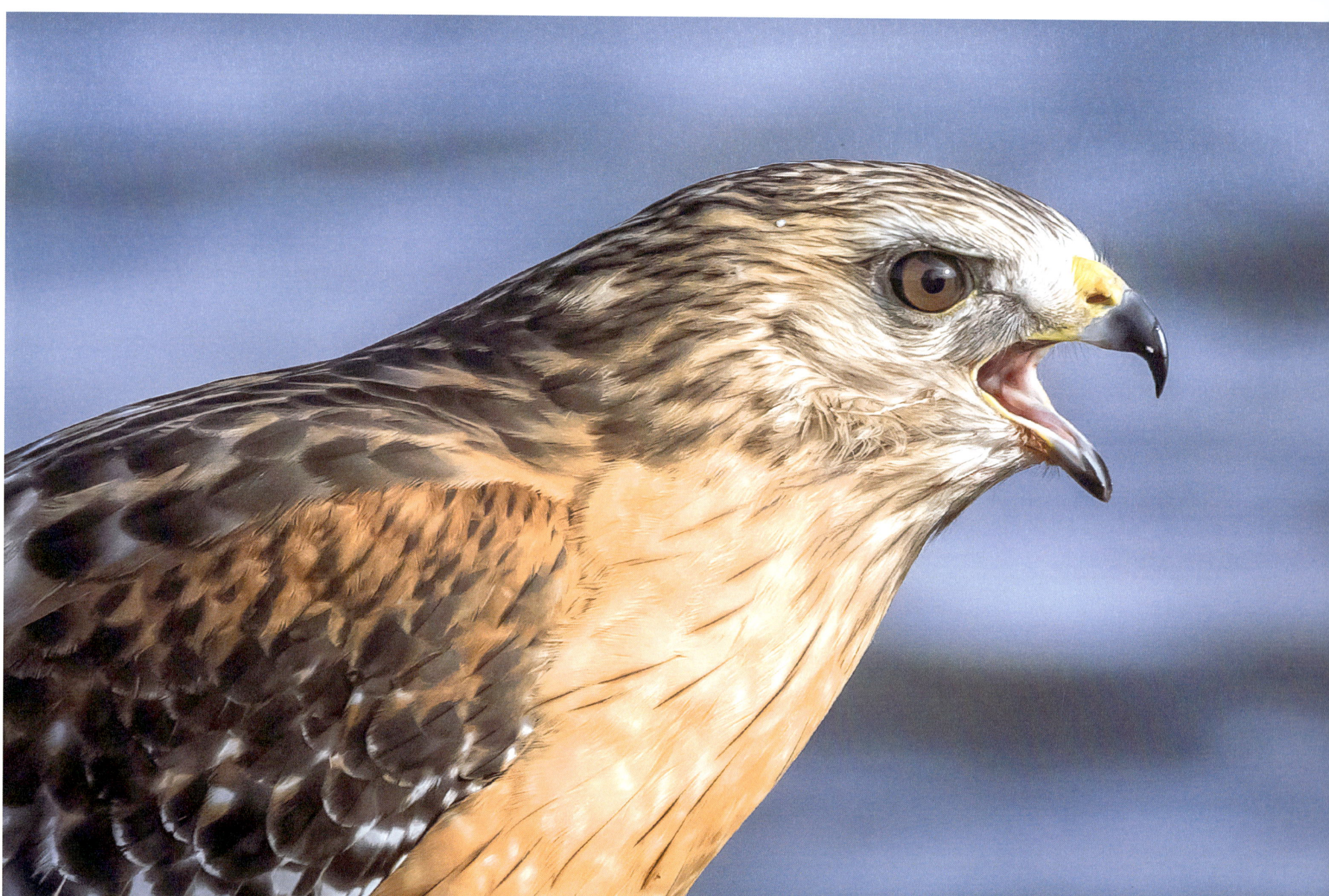

Wings!

A Collection of Bird Photographs

Richard Smith

WINGS!

A COLLECTION OF BIRD IMAGES
Richard Smith

SINGULAR IMAGE PUBLICATIONS
http://singular.myrsphoto.com

Copyright © 2020 by Richard Smith

NOTICE OF RIGHTS
All rights reserved. No part of this book may be reproduced or transmitted in any form by any means, electronic, mechanical, photocopying, recording, or otherwise, without prior written permission from the publisher.

NOTICE OF LIABILITY
The information in this book is distributed on an "As Is" basis, without warranty. While every precaution has been taken in the preparation of the book, neither the author or Singular Image Publications have any liability to to any person or entity with respect to any loss or damage caused or alleged to be caused directly or indirectly by this book or by the photographic software and hardware products described in it.

TRADEMARKS
Adobe Lightroom, Adobe Photoshop, and Canon are registered trademarks. All trademarks are the property of their respective owners. All product names and services identified throughout this book are used in editorial fashion only and for the benefit of such companies with no intention of infringement of the trademark. No such use, or the use of any trade name, is intended to convey endorsement or other affiliation with this book.

ISBN: 978-1-0879-2284-3

"How countless are Your works, LORD!

In wisdom You have made them all;

the earth is full of Your creatures."

- Psalm 104:24

Preface

Some years ago, I was visiting our local zoo with a friend. As we were leaving, I remarked about the wonderful variety of animals and wondered why God had made them all so different and fascinating, each in their own way. My friend suggested that maybe God just wanted to reveal his great creativity and spark a sense of wonder and joy in us at the same time. It struck me as a beautifully simple reason. It is my hope the reader will experience a similar sense of joy and wonder while viewing these photographs.

My first interest in photographic art was in the landscape and the great black and white photographers. Then I began to introduce birds as elements in a larger landscape. As my experience grew, and my equipment became more capable, animals began to be a larger part of my work. Birds, in particular, present an interesting photographic challenge. They are not easy to photograph, but the challenge is intriguing, and their beauty and variety is never-ending.

Richard Smith
Oklahoma City, 2020

Acknowledgements

No book could be completed without significant support from others. Making photographs of wild creatures often requires getting up before the sun, staying late, and taking long drives to distant locations. My wife, Debbie, and my family have been extraordinarily patient with such things and I thank them. Debbie has also provided invaluable help in the preparation of this book and in reviewing its content.

I am also grateful to my daughter, Alison Laing, for reviewing the book and making several important observations and corrections.

Thanks to Callen Clarke for encouraging me to prepare this book and for helping with the editing.

Thanks to Michael Anderson for his incisive comments on the text as well as his help and expertise with the typography and his frequent sharing of valuable photographic knowledge.

Introduction

This book is a collection of my photographs of birds. It is not intended as a comprehensive view of many species or a reference work of any kind. I have not tried to document endangered species or birds from distant parts of the world. In fact, many of the birds are quite ordinary, but they are interesting to me for their appearance or their behavior.

The photographs were made primarily in Oklahoma with the addition of several from Colorado, New Mexico, and Texas. These states are part of what is known as the Central Flyway, a busy migratory route, so a good variety of birds pass through at various times of the year.

This work is about the photographs and the birds who are the subjects of the photographs. As such, text is minimal. It is hoped that the images speak for themselves and few words are needed.

A technical note for those who might be interested: All the images in this book were made with Canon cameras – usually a 7D Mark II. Most were also made with Canon lenses. ISO tends to be 640 and by far the most common aperture is f8. All are edited and catalogued in Adobe Lightroom with additional work in Adobe Photoshop as needed.

Table of Contents

Preface .... *vi*

Acknowledgements .... *vii*

Introduction .... *viii*

Scissor-tailed Flycatchers 1

Egrets 7

Herons 21

Shorebirds 35

Birds of Prey 49

Small Birds 65

Pelicans 101

Index of Birds *110*

x

Scissor-tailed Flycatchers

As athletic as it is beautiful, this gymnastic little flyer seems like a good way to begin. That long tail is a perfect rudder for aerial acrobatics, and it seems like there is little they cannot do in the air. They are common in Oklahoma (where they are the official state bird) and the people never tire of watching them. Even people who normally pay little attention to birds will comment on the magnificent scissor-tailed flycatcher.

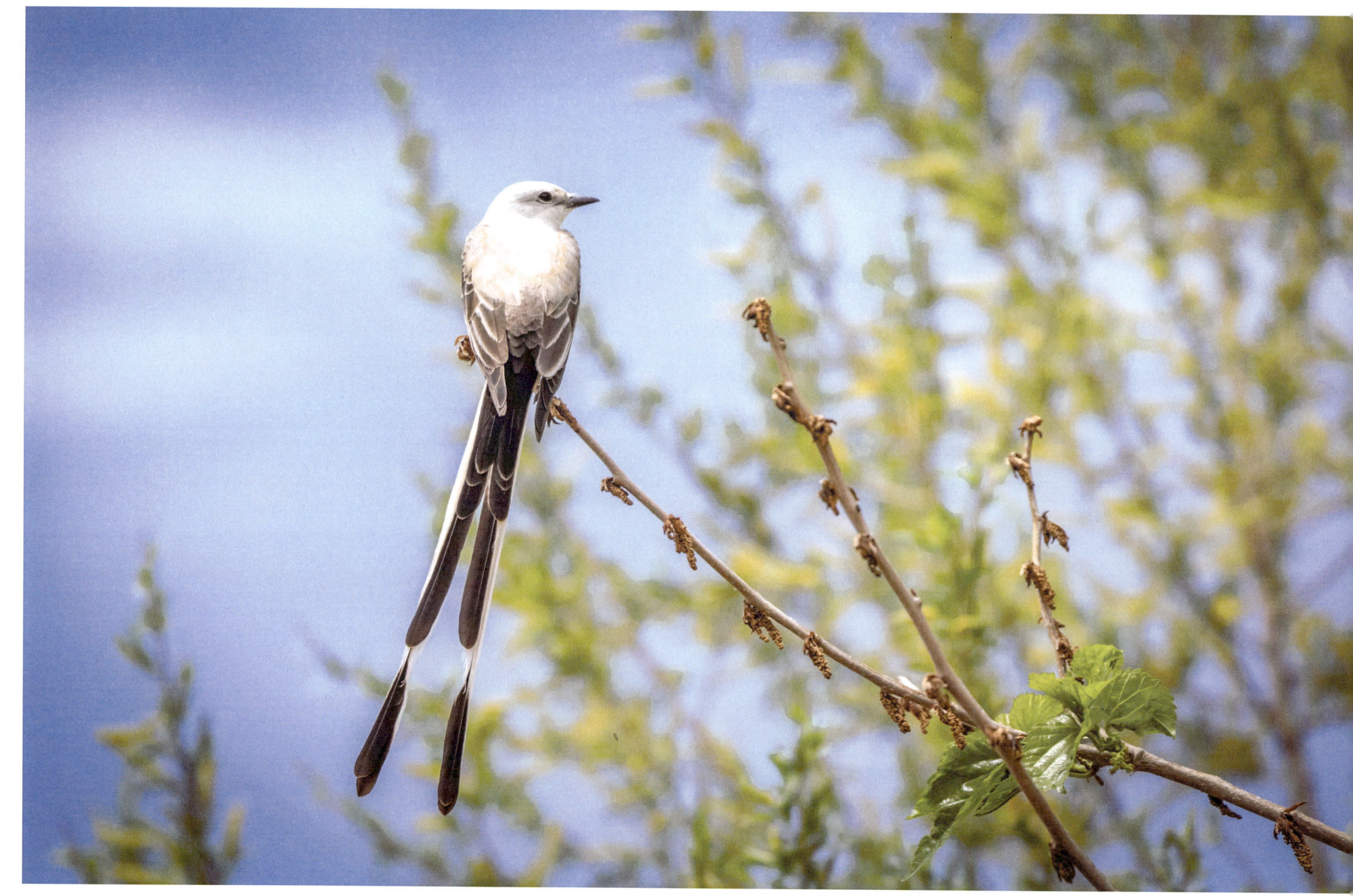

Scissor-tailed Flycatcher Showing Off the Tail

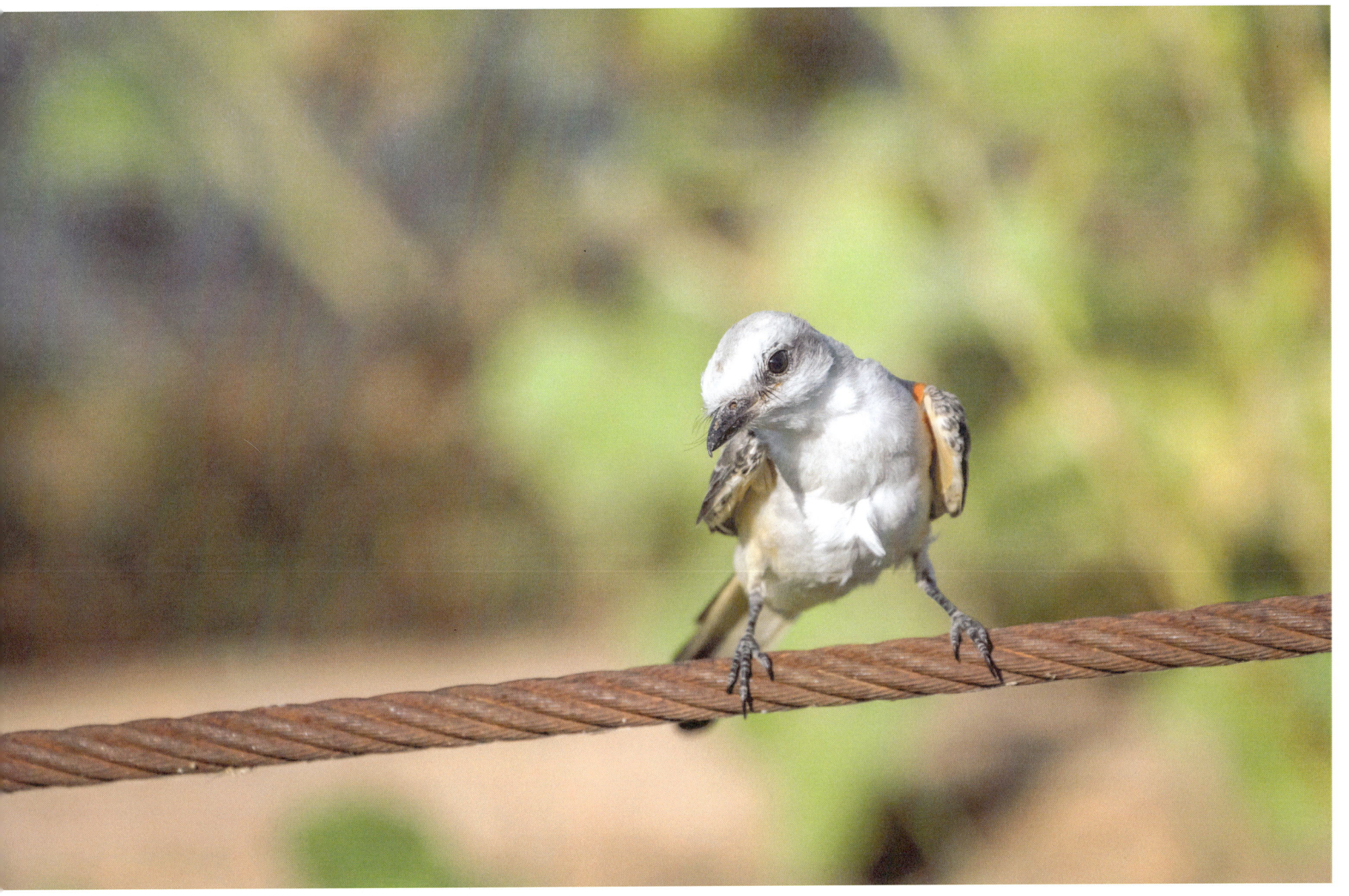

Scissor-tailed Flycatcher Looking Quizzical

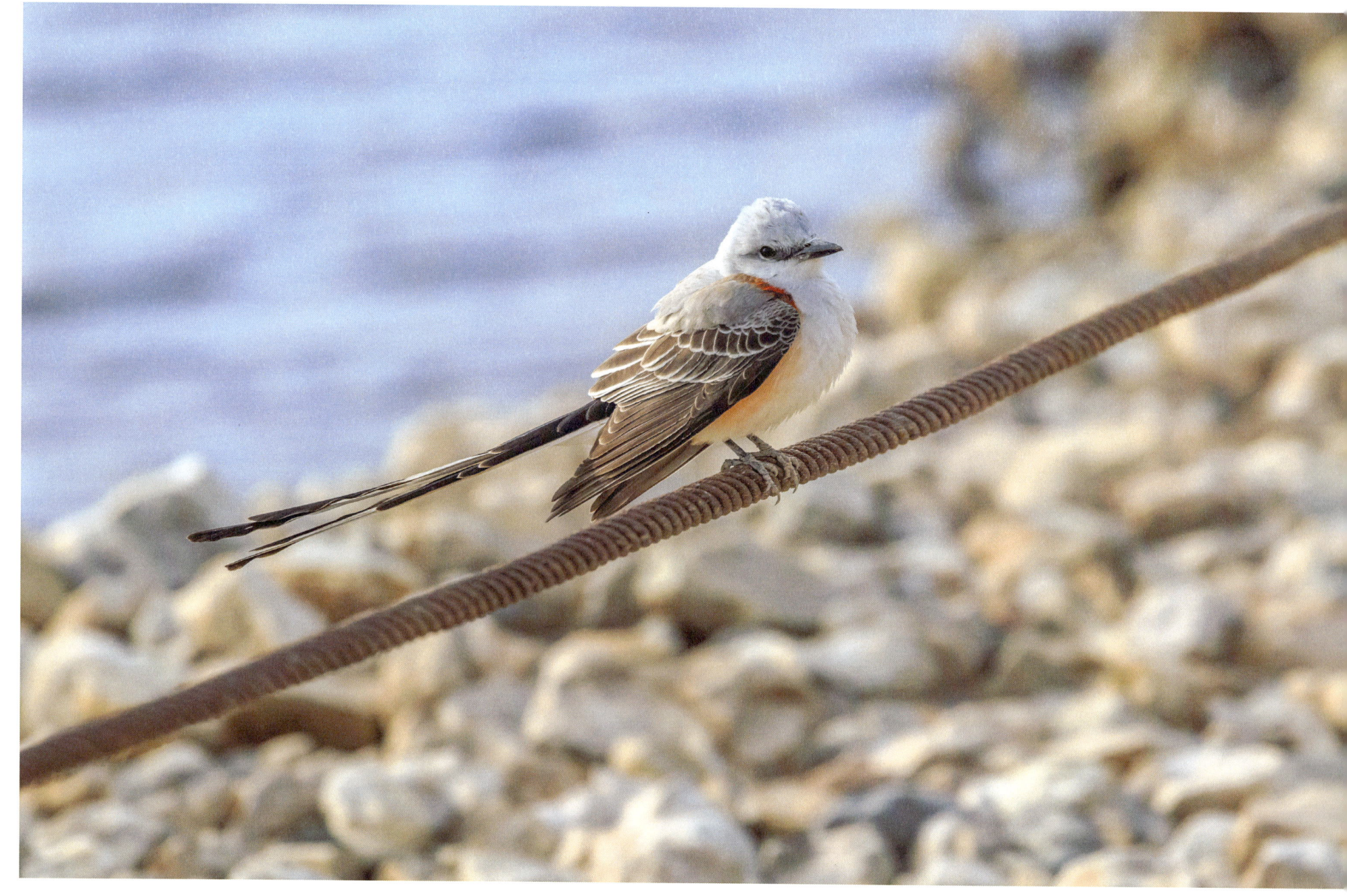

Scissor-tailed Flycatcher on the Shore

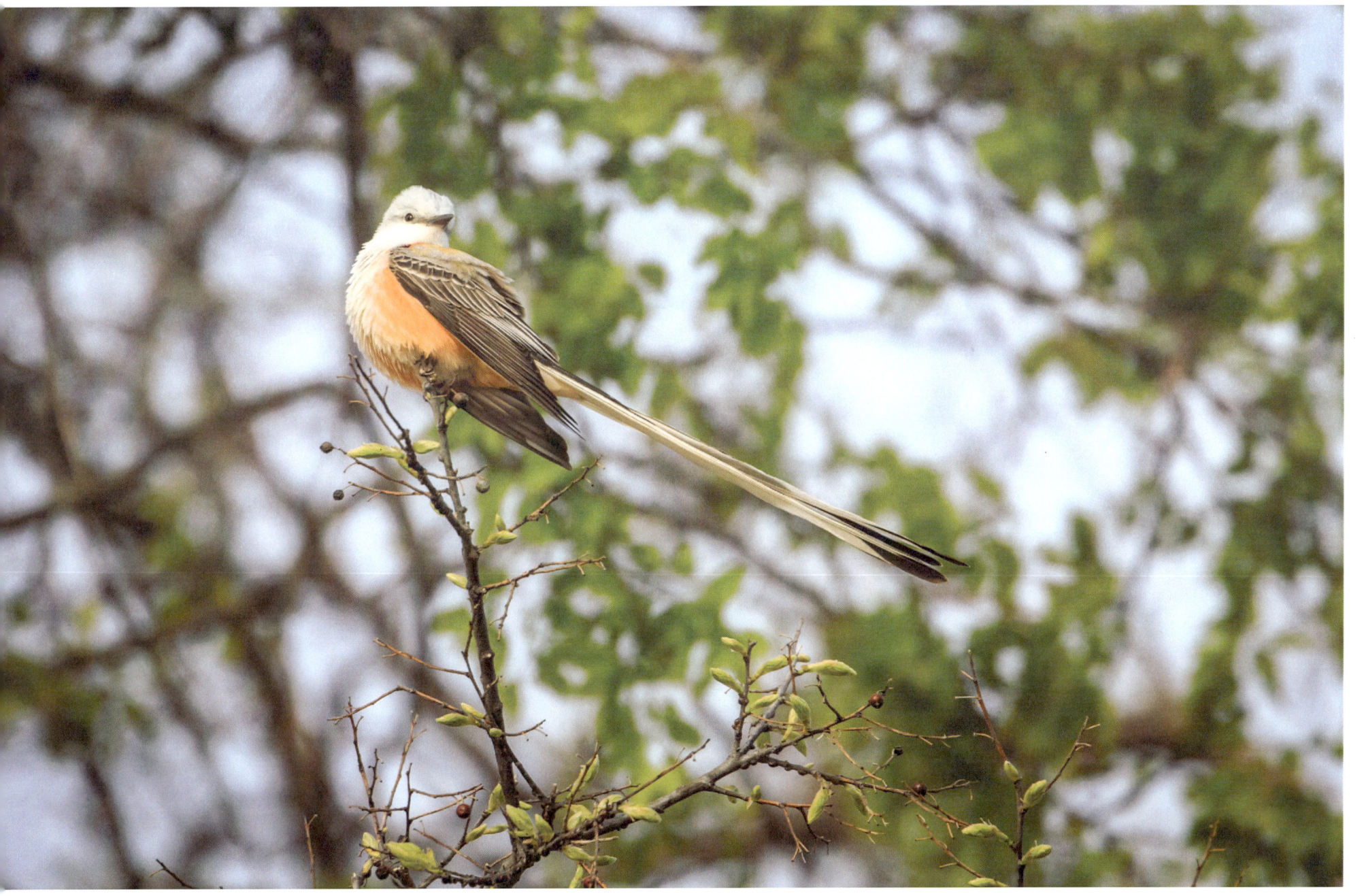

Scissor-tailed Flycatcher

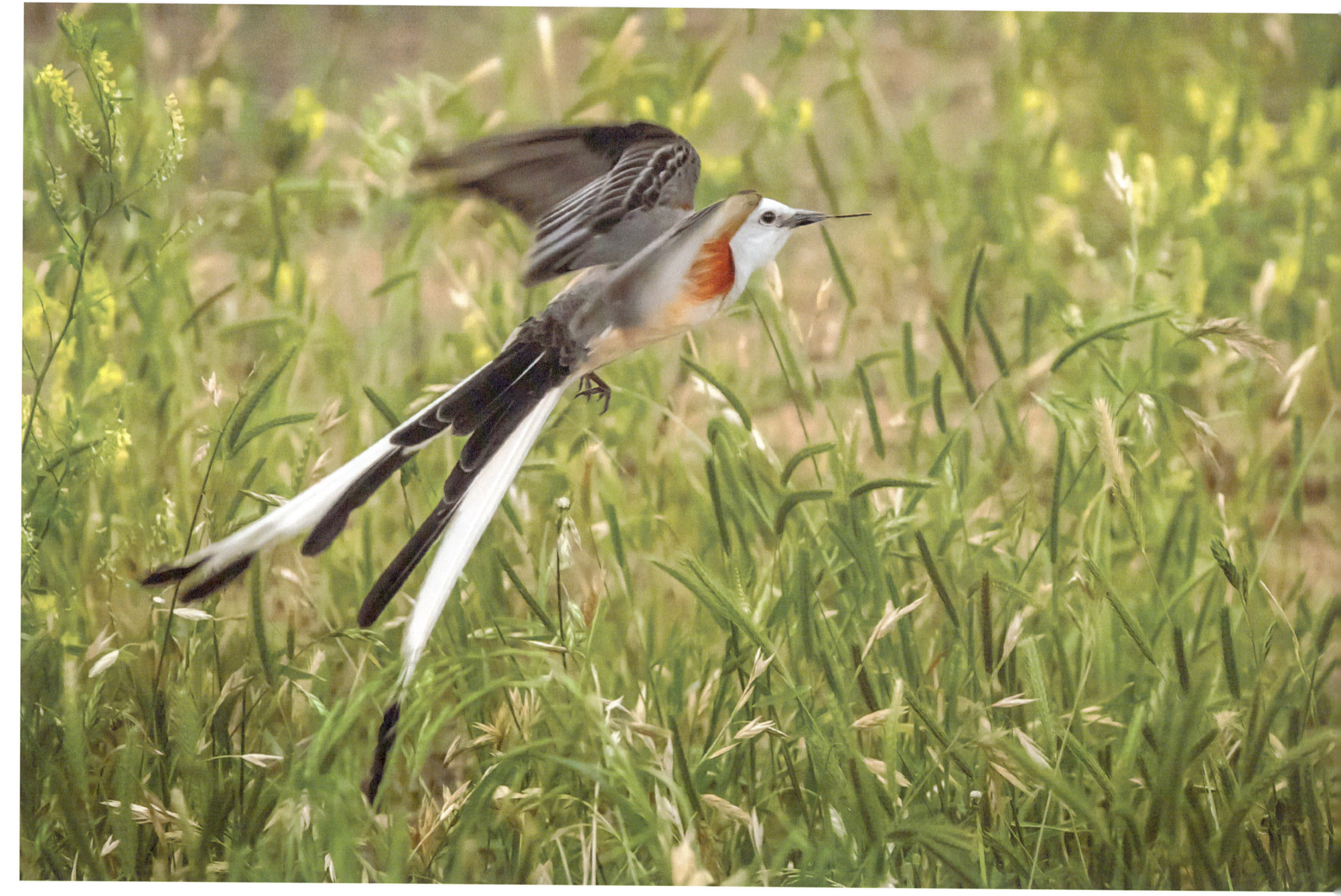
Scissor-tailed Flycatcher in Flight

Egrets

With slow, powerful beats of its massive wings, the great egret gracefully rises from the shallow water near the shore where it often stands, nearly motionless, or strolls slowly, waiting for fish to come to it. It rarely swims. The great egret is a large, brilliantly white bird with a dignified bearing - unless seen at a nesting area where loud disputes and territorial squabbles abound.

By contrast, the smaller snowy egret lacks the great egret's size and elegant bearing. It even seems a bit plain when seen standing near the shore, but it has an animated character and is a resourceful fisherman. The fly/dive technique seen on the following pages is one of the more creative approaches to bird fishing.

Neither of these two can match the little cattle egret for beauty. With a bit of subtle cinnamon color on its head and chest and matching beak, this one is not pure white.

Egrets do not hide. They stand out by their bright white color and their commanding presence on the shore.

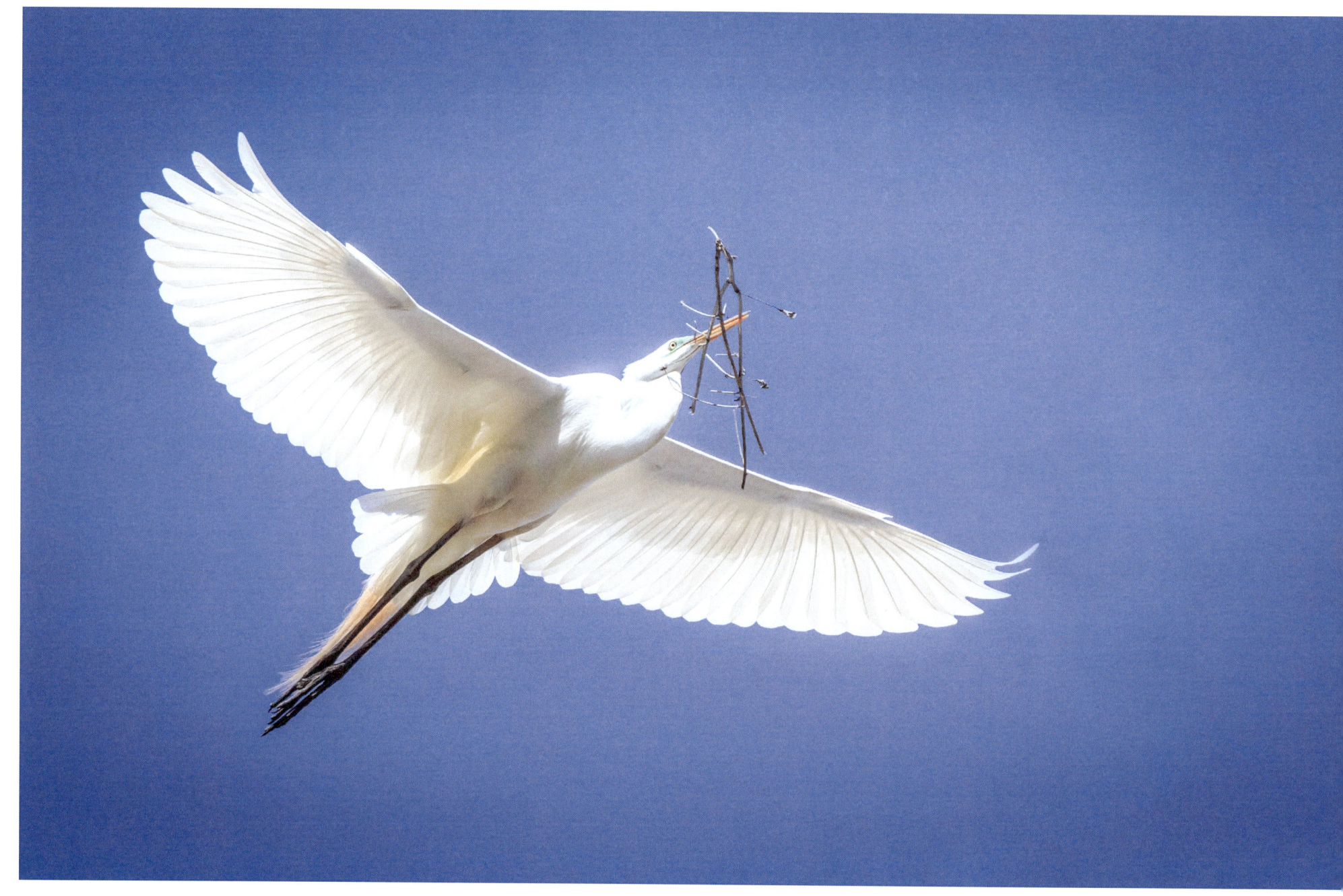

Great Egret in Flight with Nesting Material

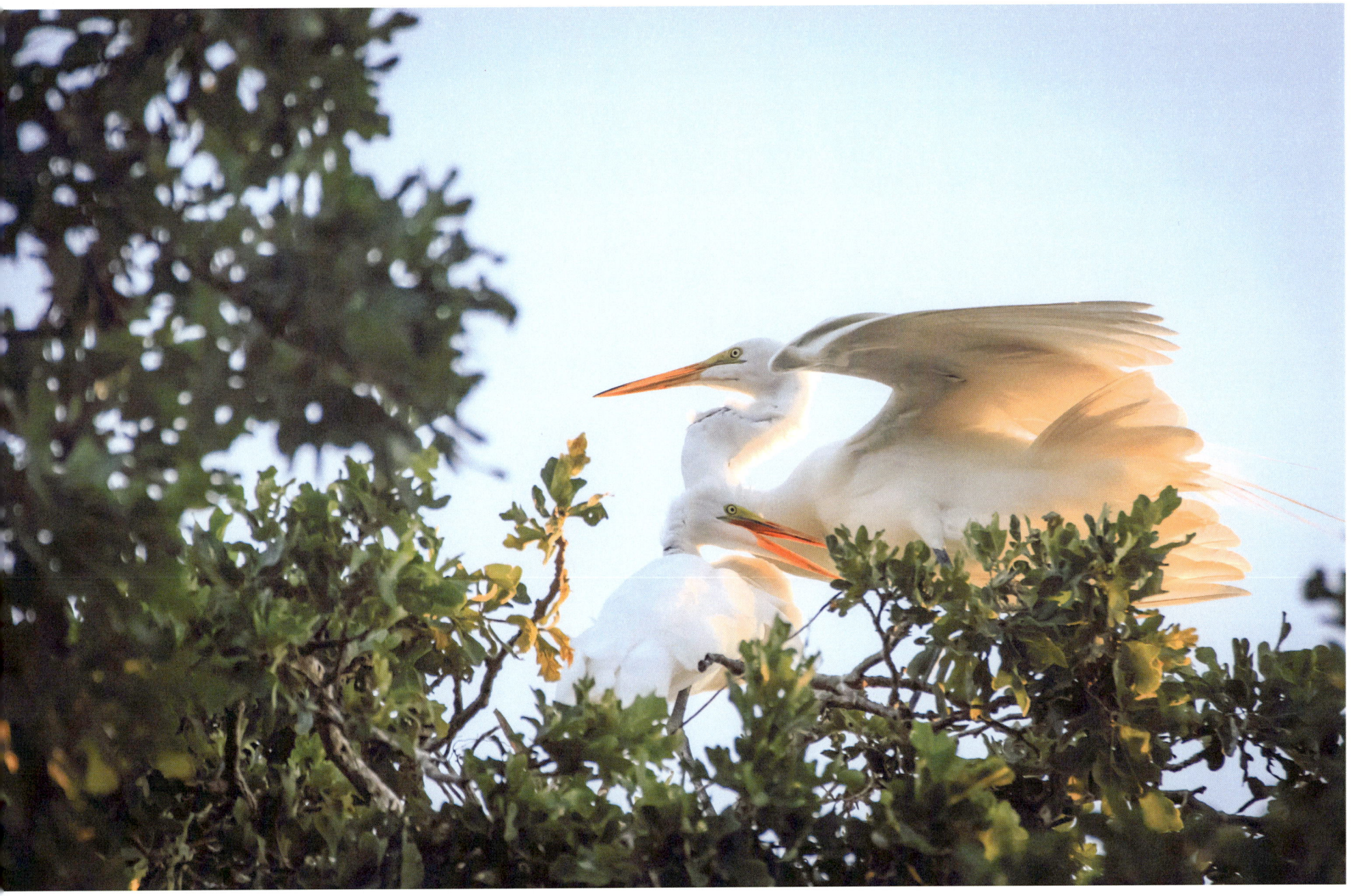
Great Egret in the Tree Tops at Sunset

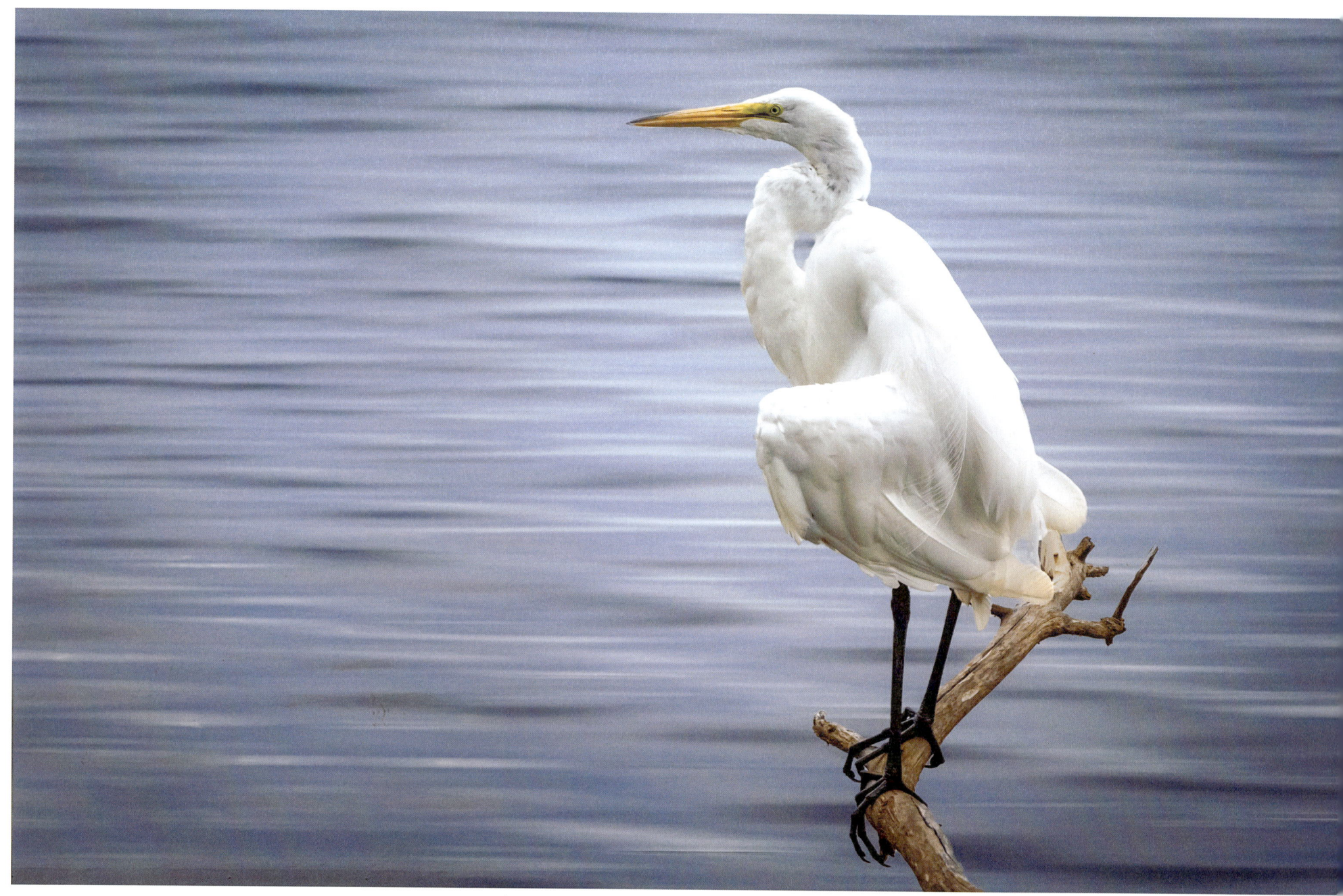

"The Thinker"
Great Egret Relaxing on a Branch Over Water

A Sequence
"Welcome Home"

A great egret returns to his nest only to be greeted by an interloper. An argument ensues, followed by threats of violence, before the new arrival decides to find another tree.

(Photographs begin on the next page)

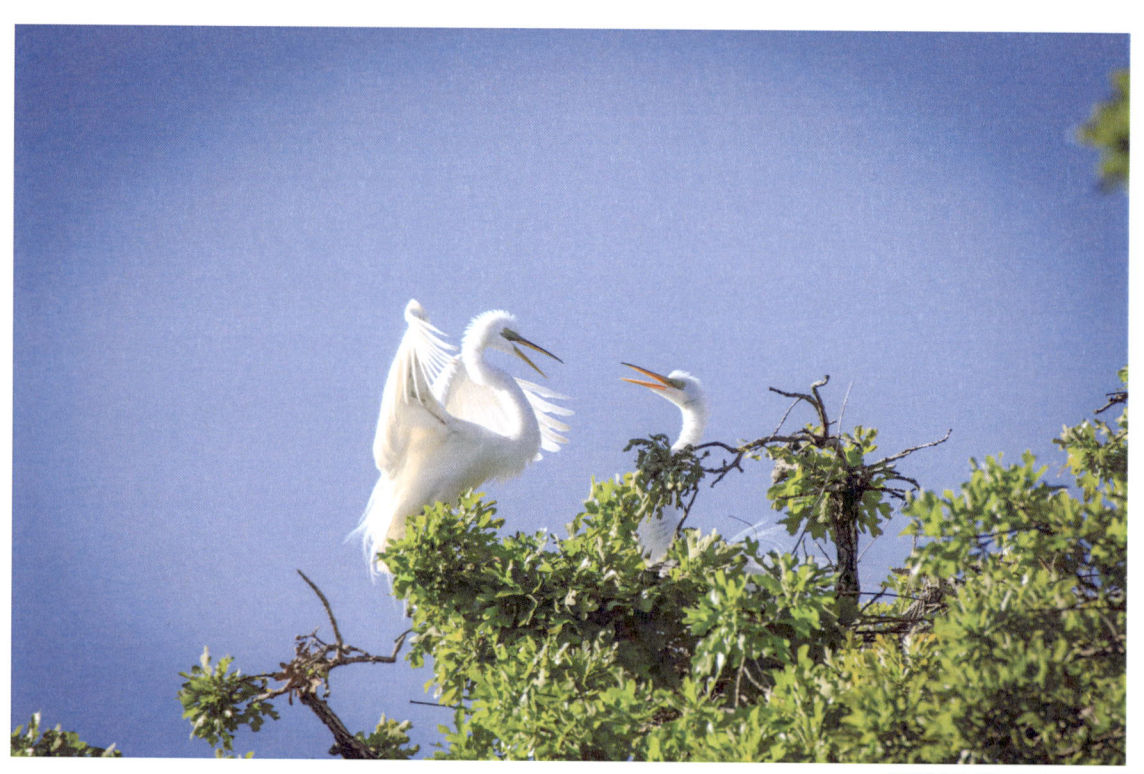
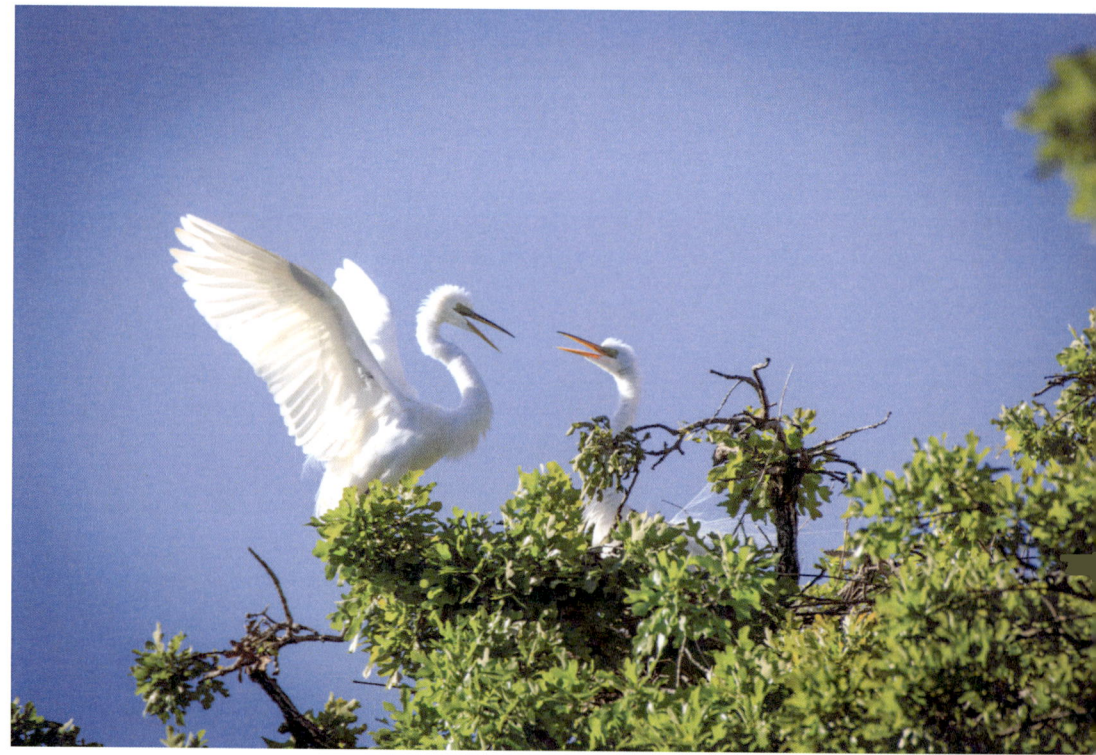

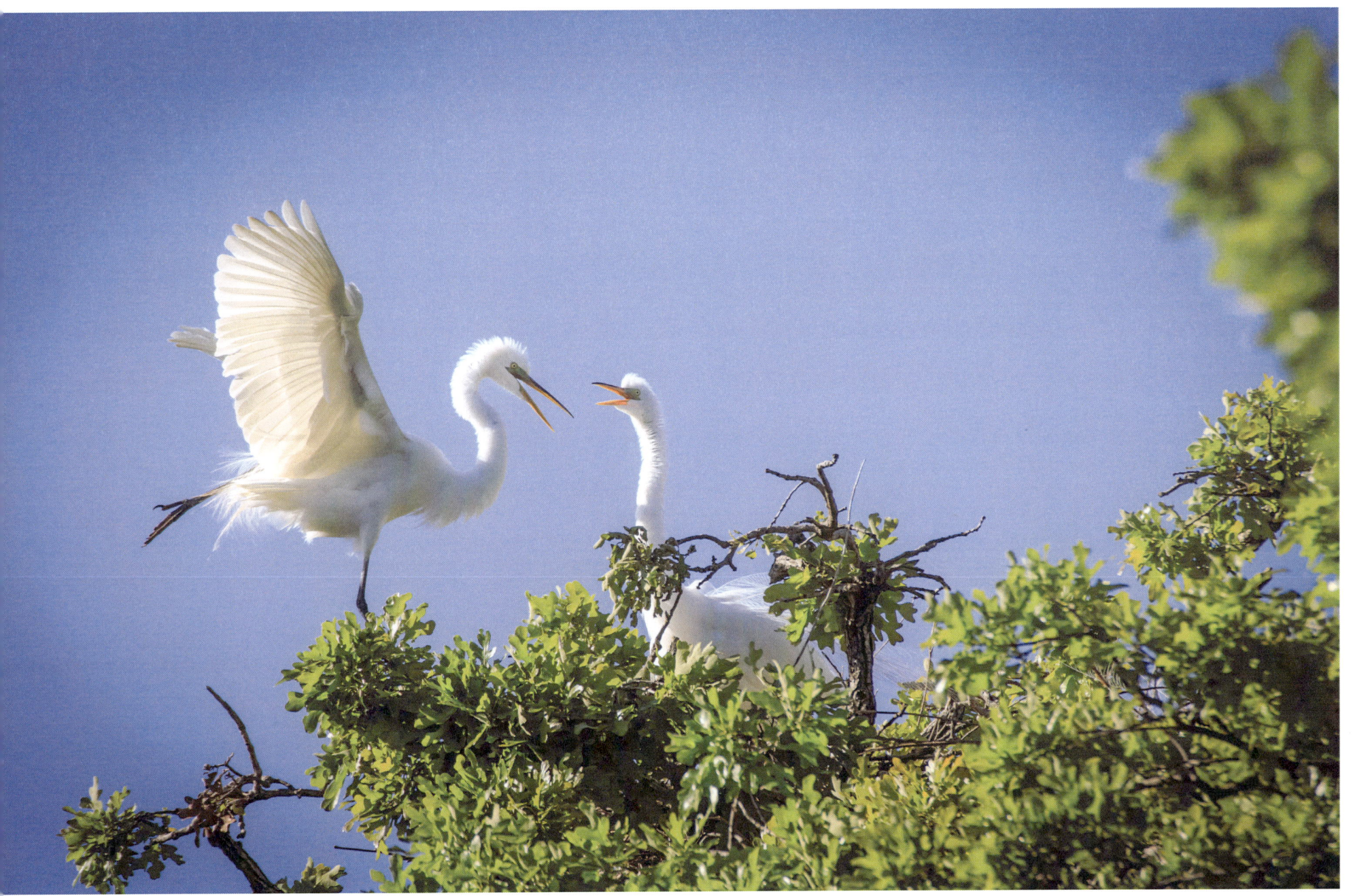

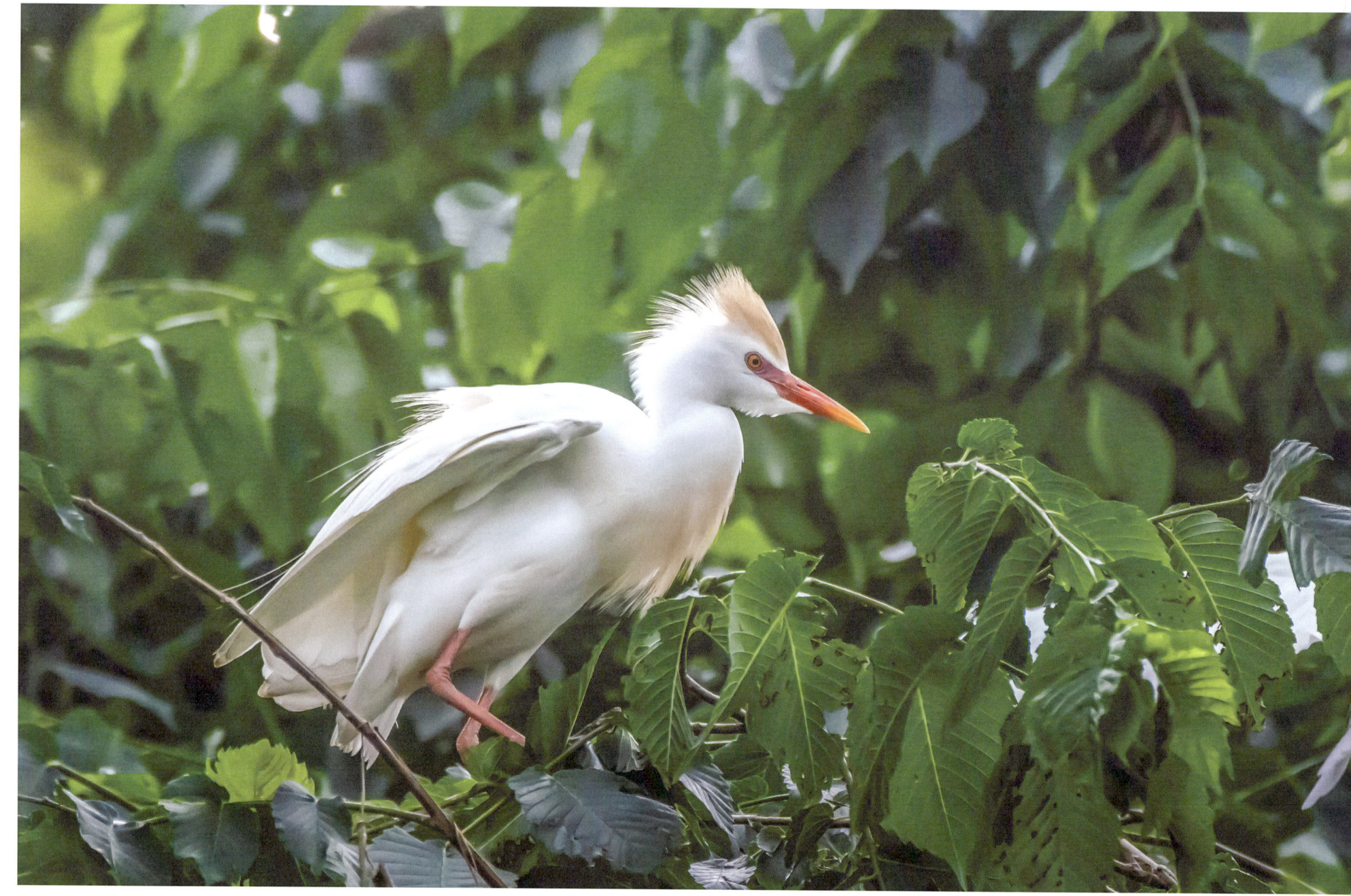

Cattle Egret Deep in the Woods

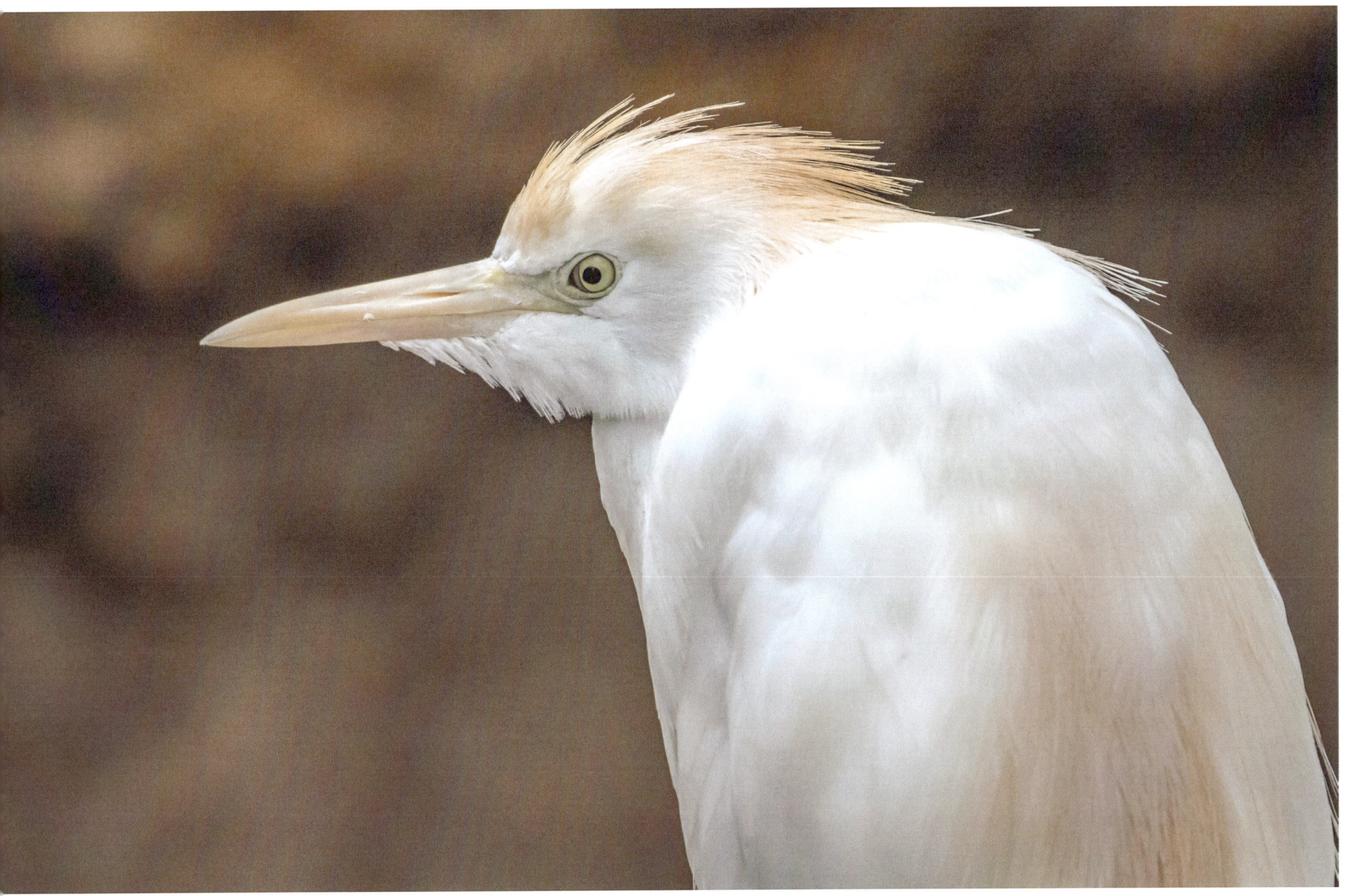

Cattle Egret

A Sequence
"Snowy Egret Fishing"

The small but highly animated snowy egret is exuberant in its search for food. After finding its prey, the little white bird uses its wings to spring a few feet into the air and then hit the water forcefully and capture the target.

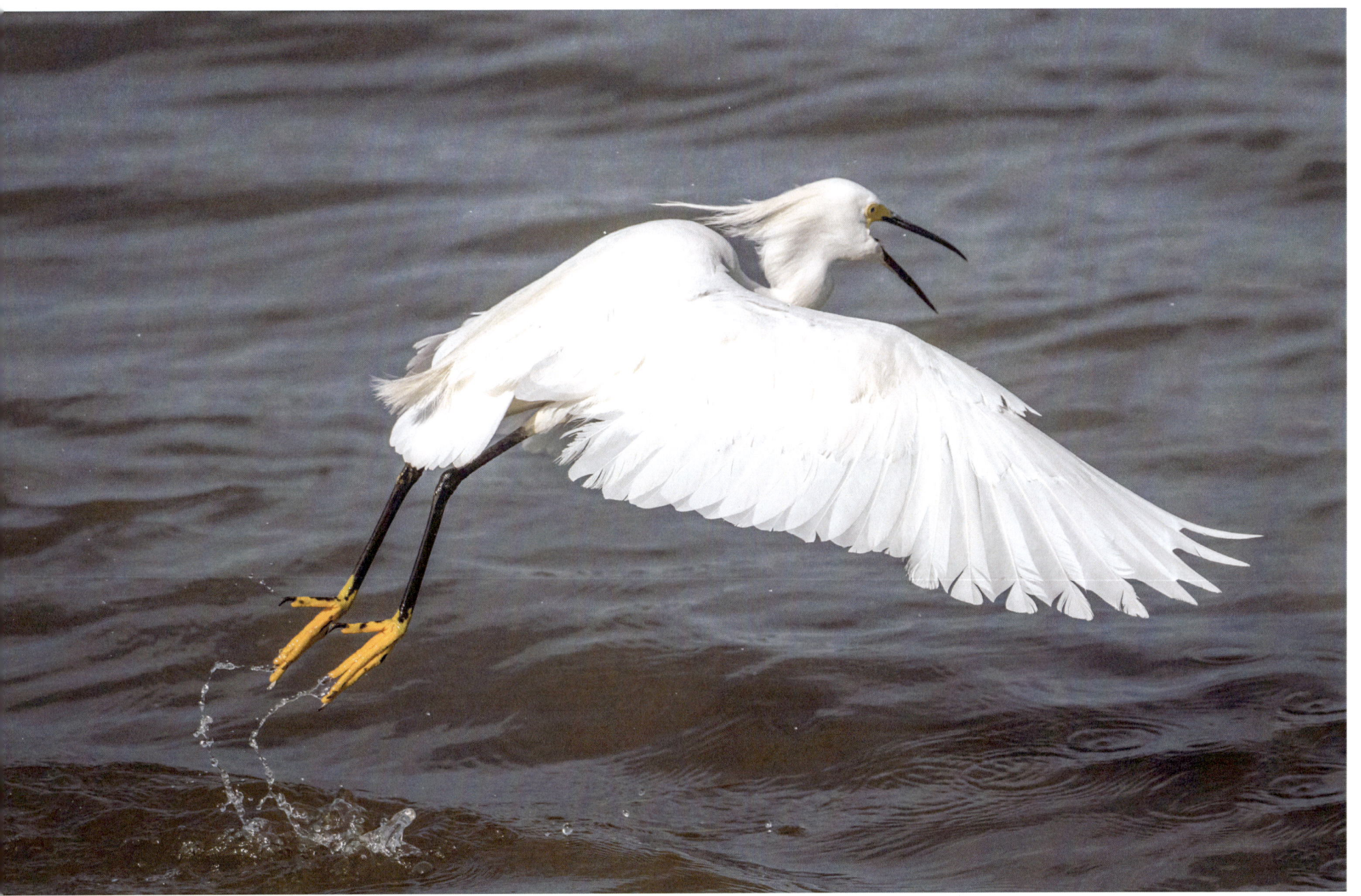

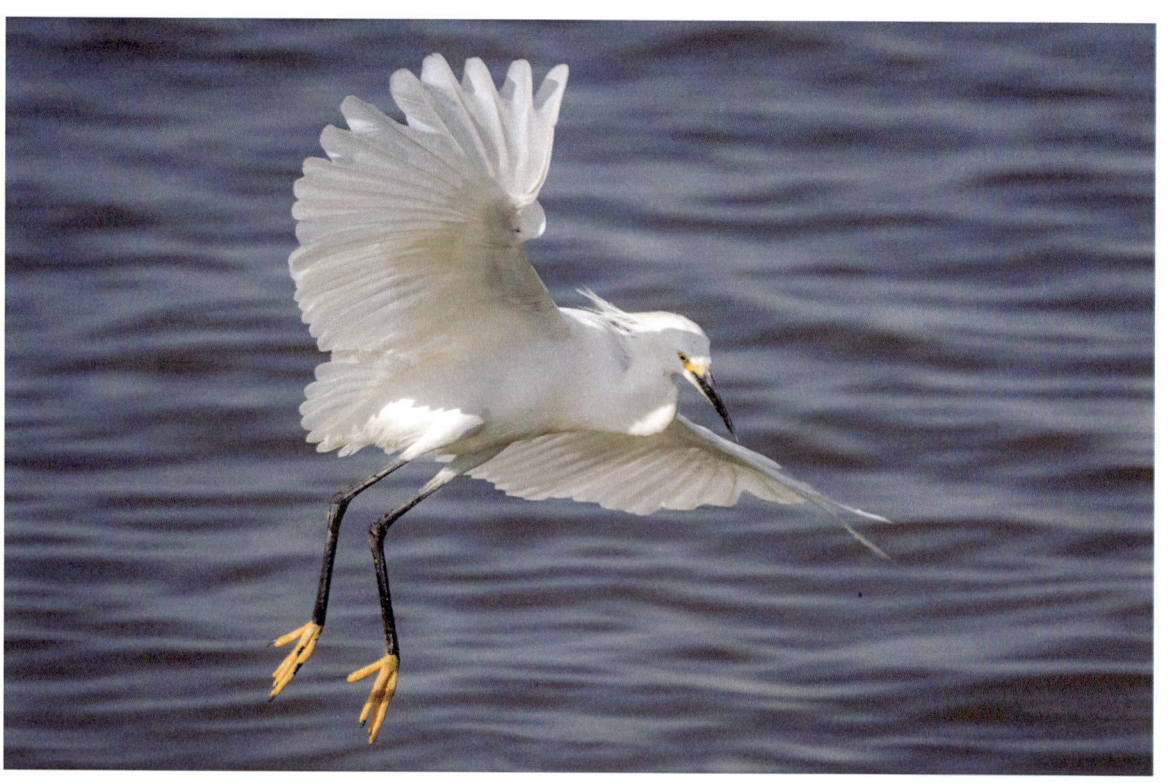
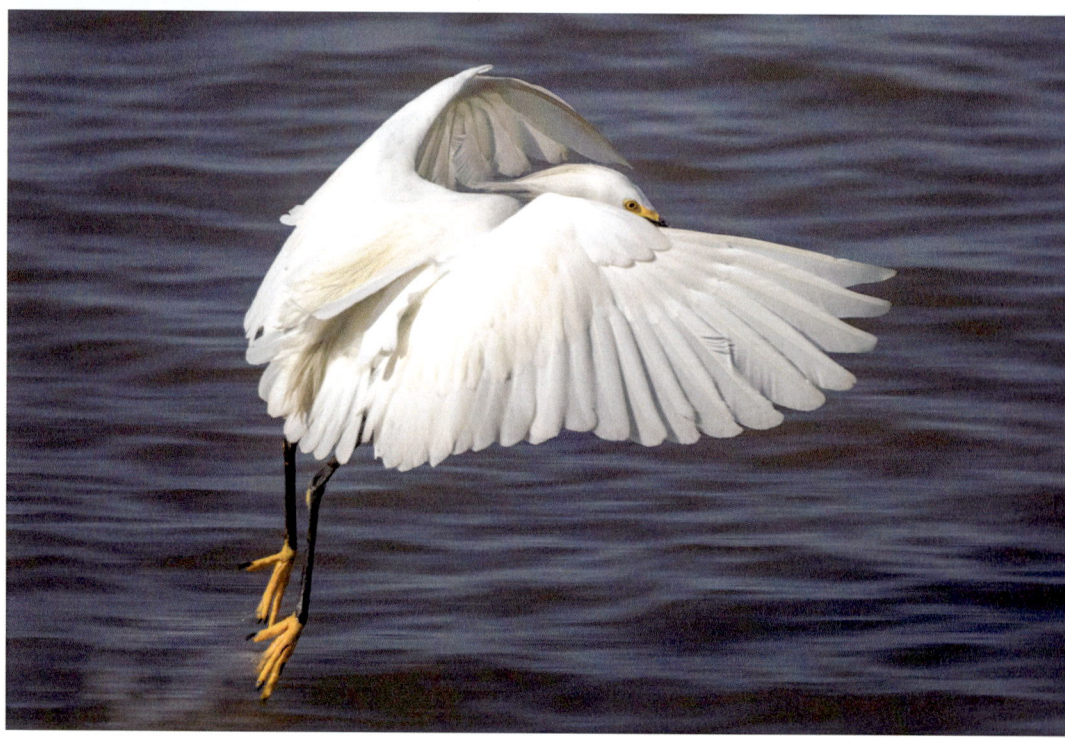

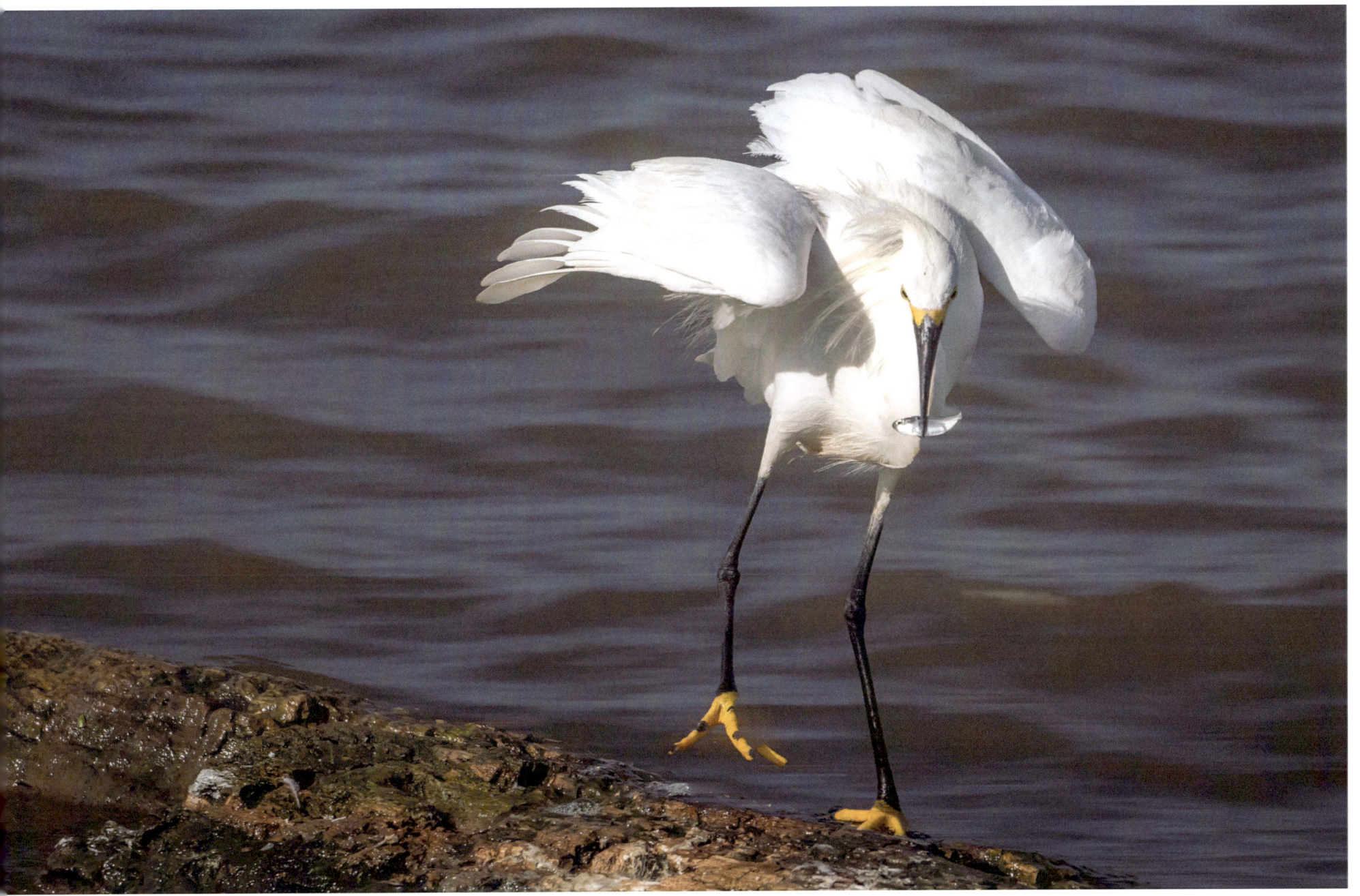

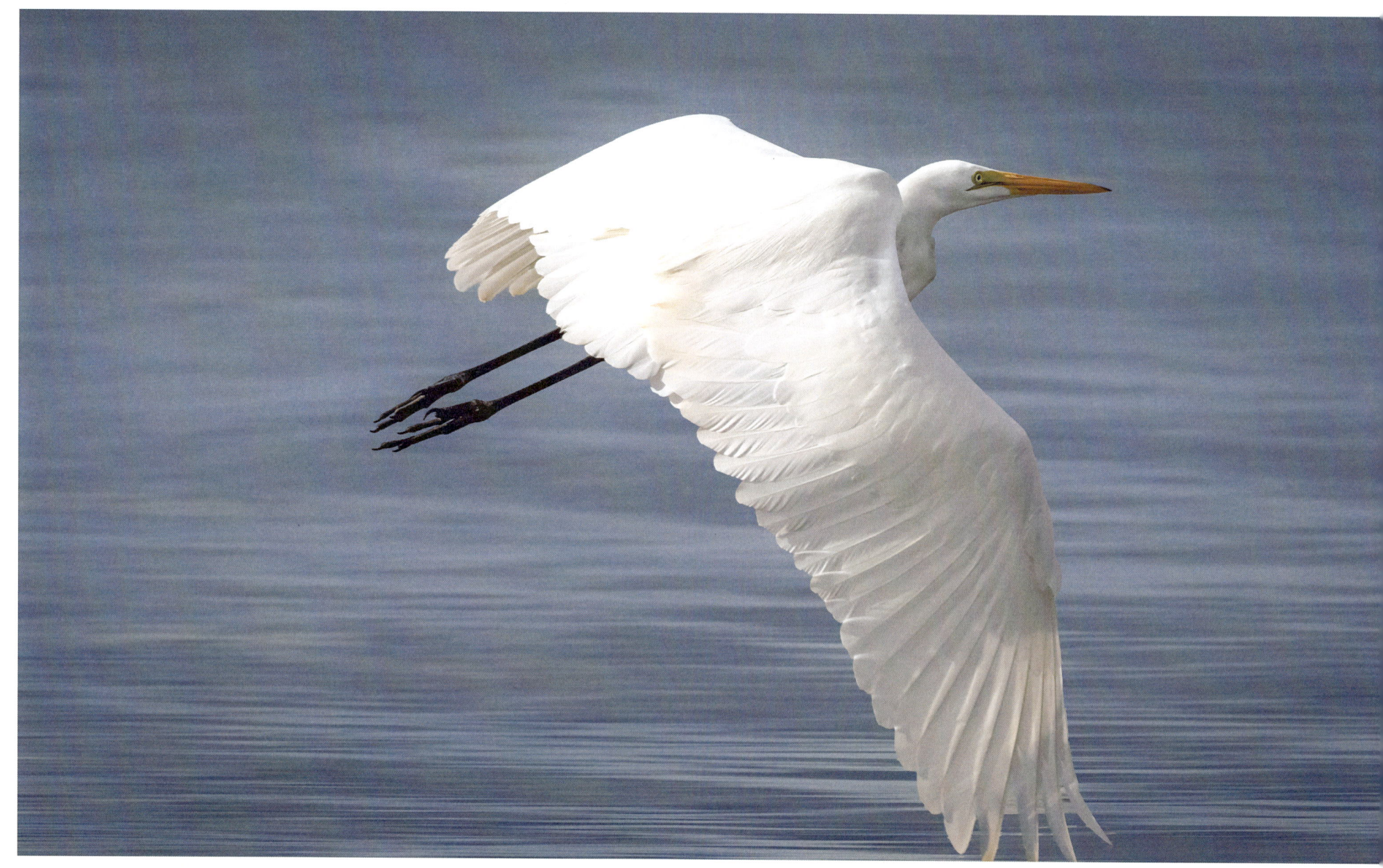

Great Egret In Flight

Herons

As you wander along a quiet shoreline, you are surprised by the rush of great wings and a large blue-gray bird giving voice with a loud, primeval squawk. You have just startled, and been startled by, a great blue heron. Sometimes standing nearly four feet tall, this giant bird often hides quietly in plain sight along the shore until it suddenly takes flight. One of the largest of all wading birds, the great blue heron's beauty is extravagant. They are hard not to like and almost irresistible to a photographer.

By contrast, the small and reclusive green heron – not much larger than a crow – is not often seen. The yellow-crowned night heron is a bit bolder than other herons. The secretive black-crowned night heron has intense red eyes and stealthy habits. All herons are fishing experts. Watching them catch a fish and skillfully toss it around until it is oriented correctly to be swallowed whole is intriguing (it goes down headfirst). Even more interesting is the heron's technique of using scraps of bread to lure fish within striking range. Herons are interesting birds indeed.

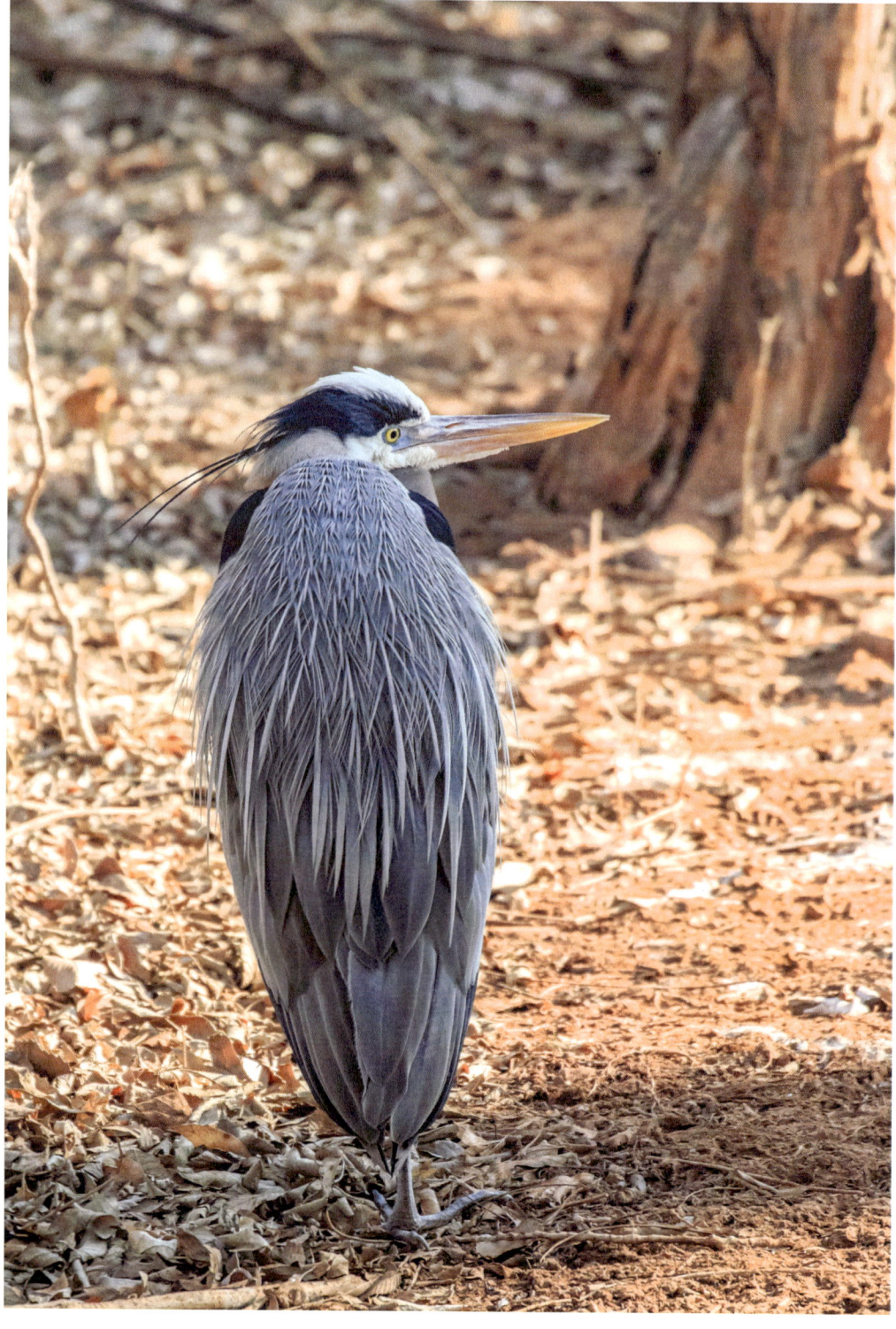

Great Blue Heron Standing in a Forest Clearing

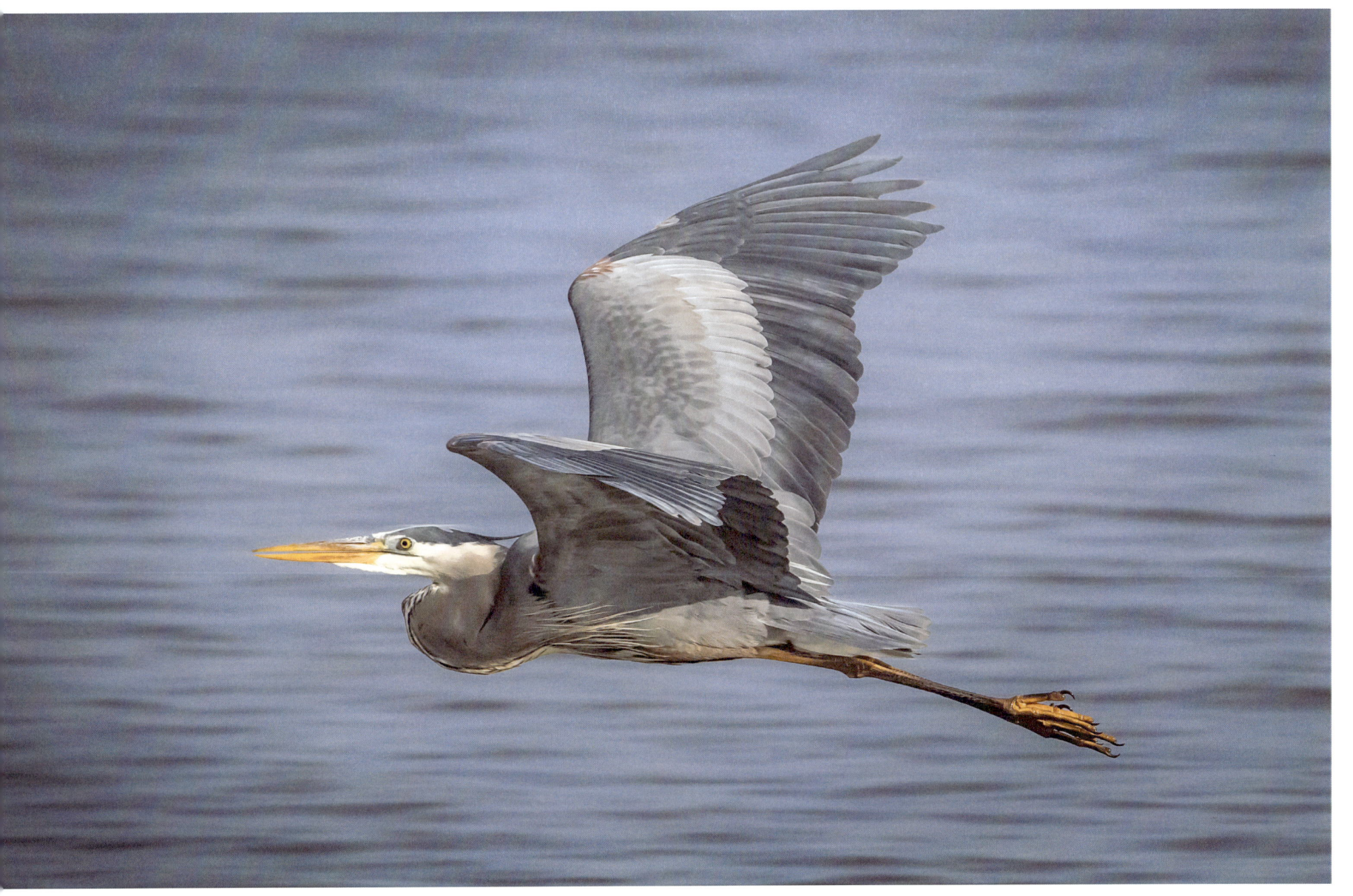

Great Blue Heron in Flight

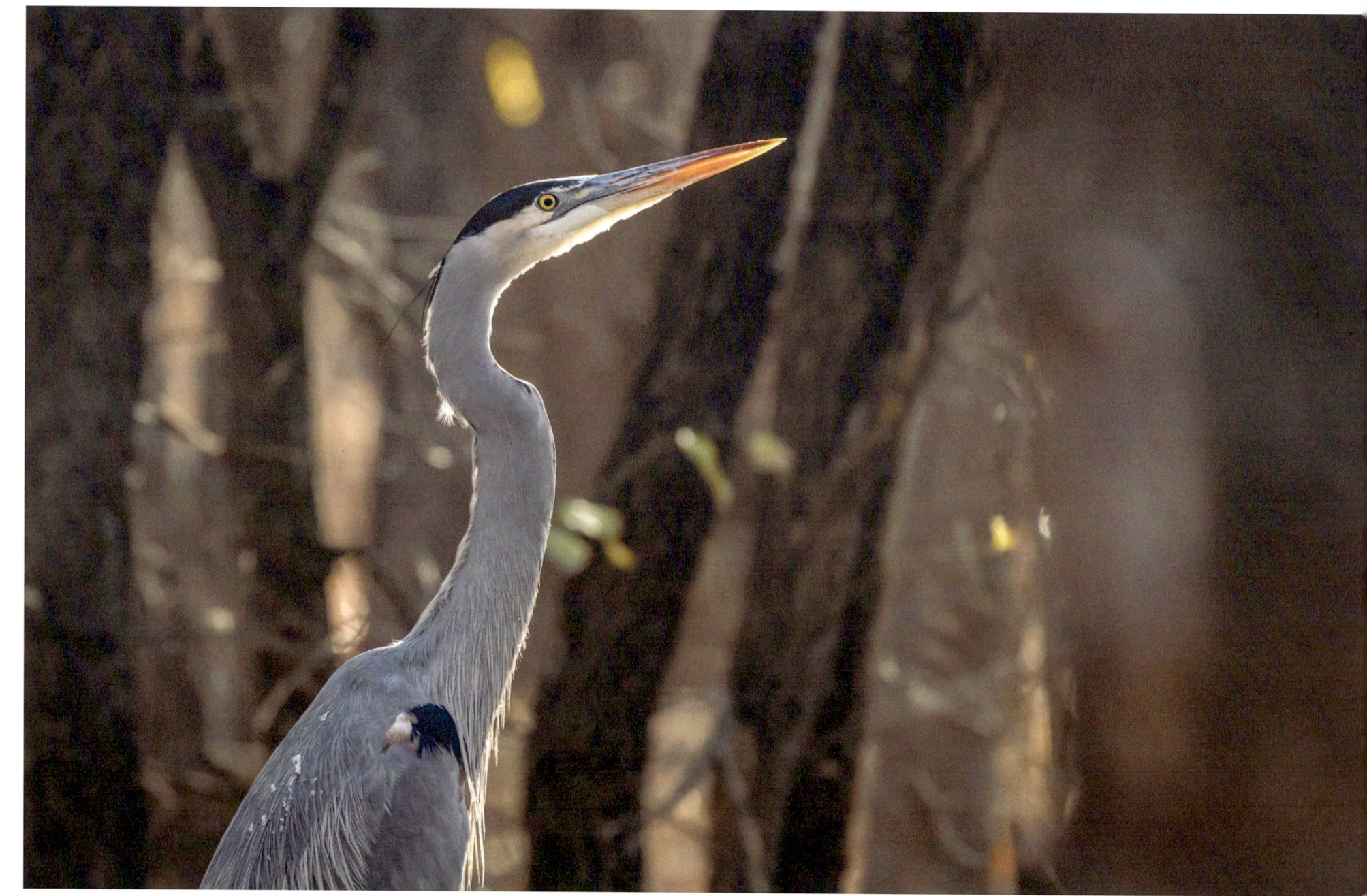

Great Blue Heron Profile

Black-crowned Night Heron
Hiding in a Blooming Tree in Early Spring

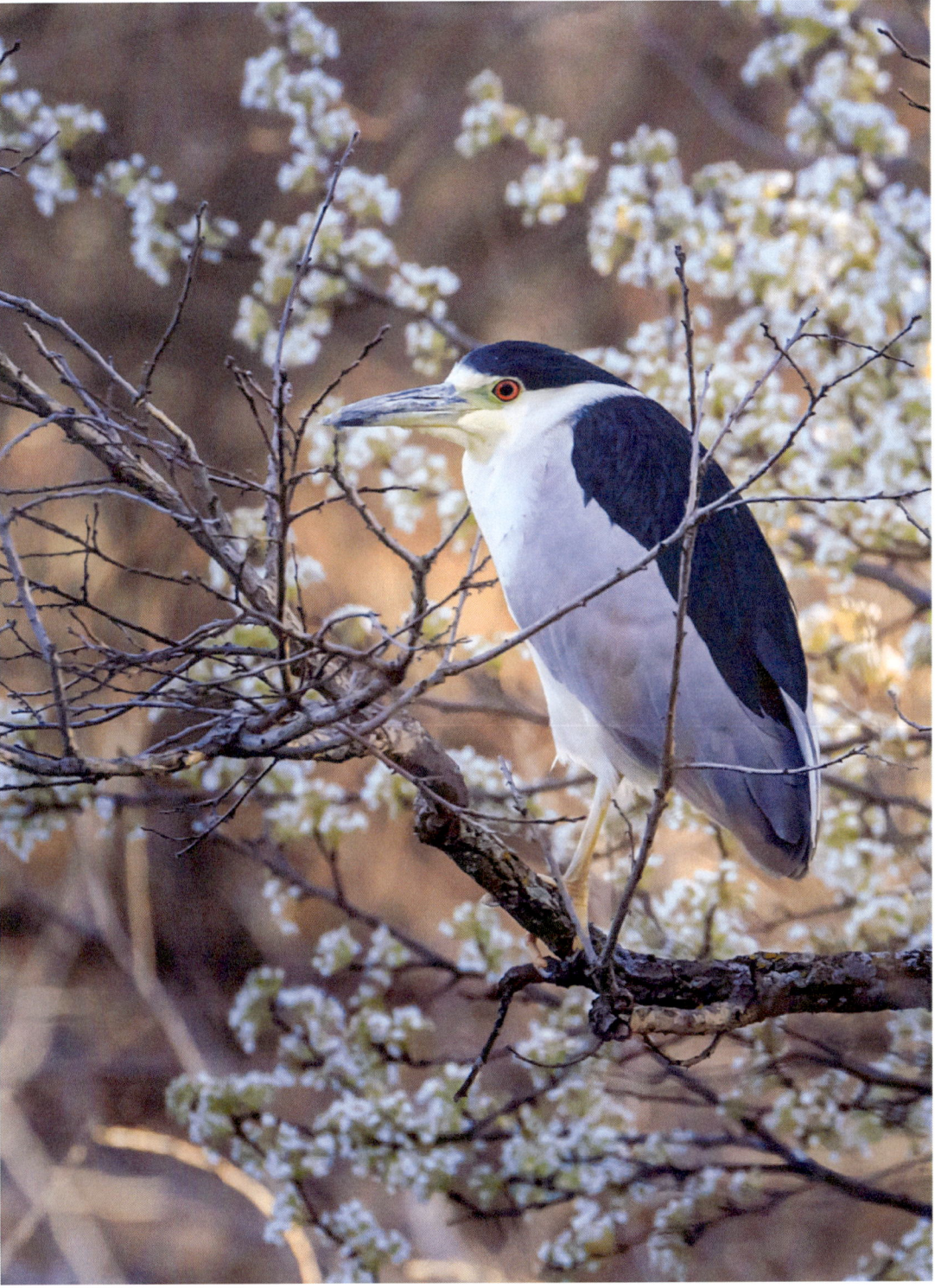

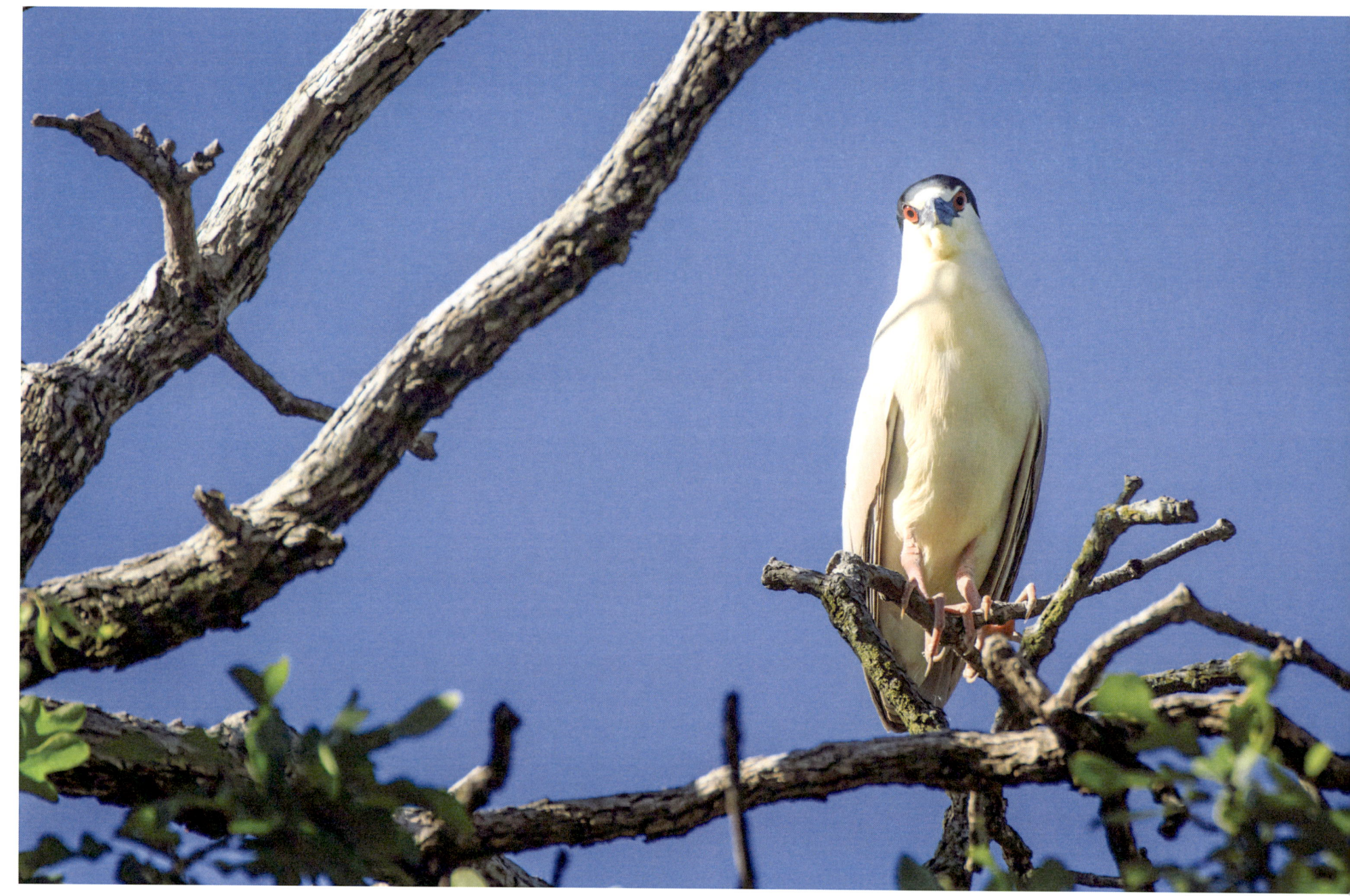

Black-crowned Night Heron Stare Down

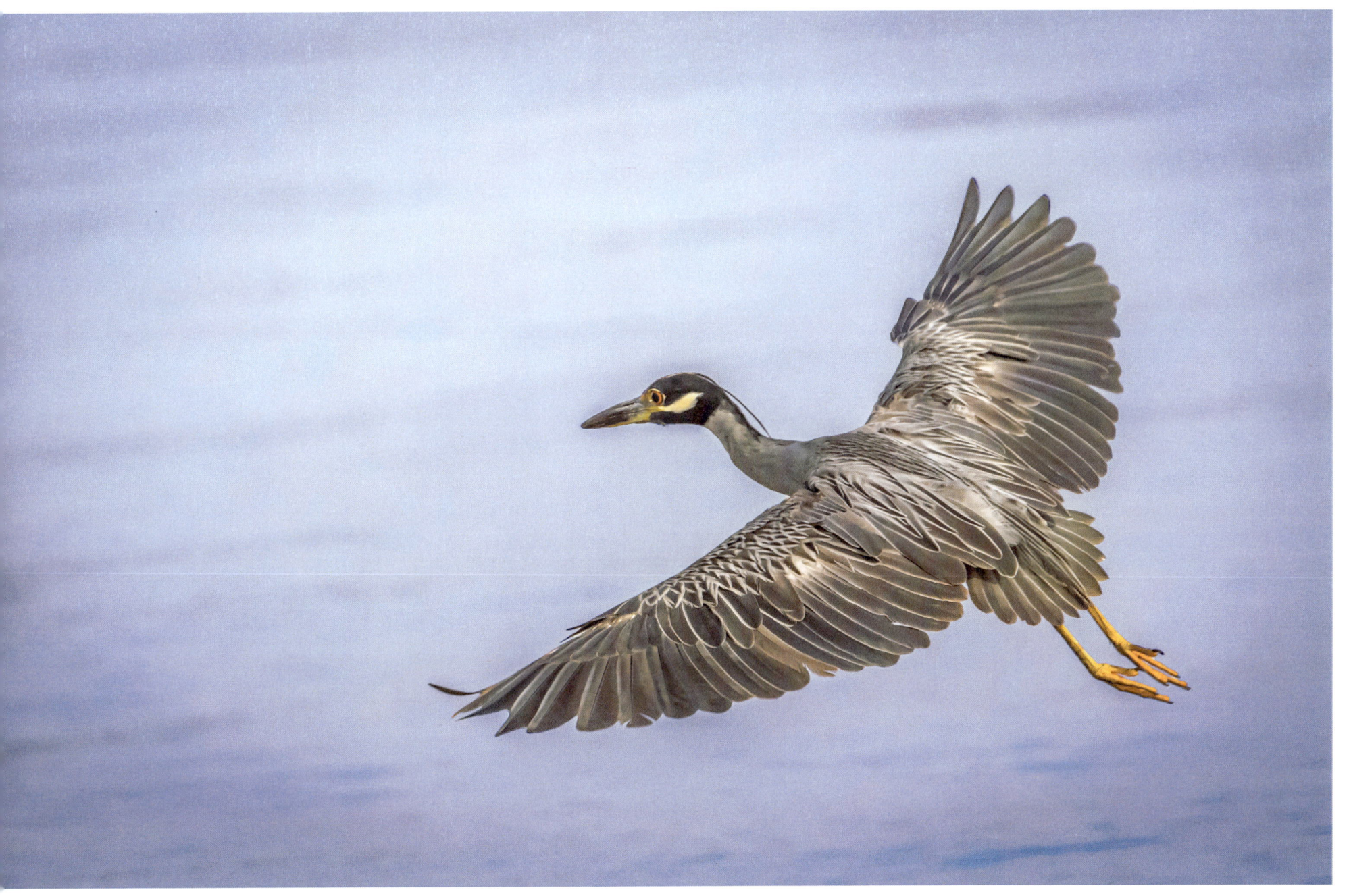
Yellow-crowned Night Heron in Flight

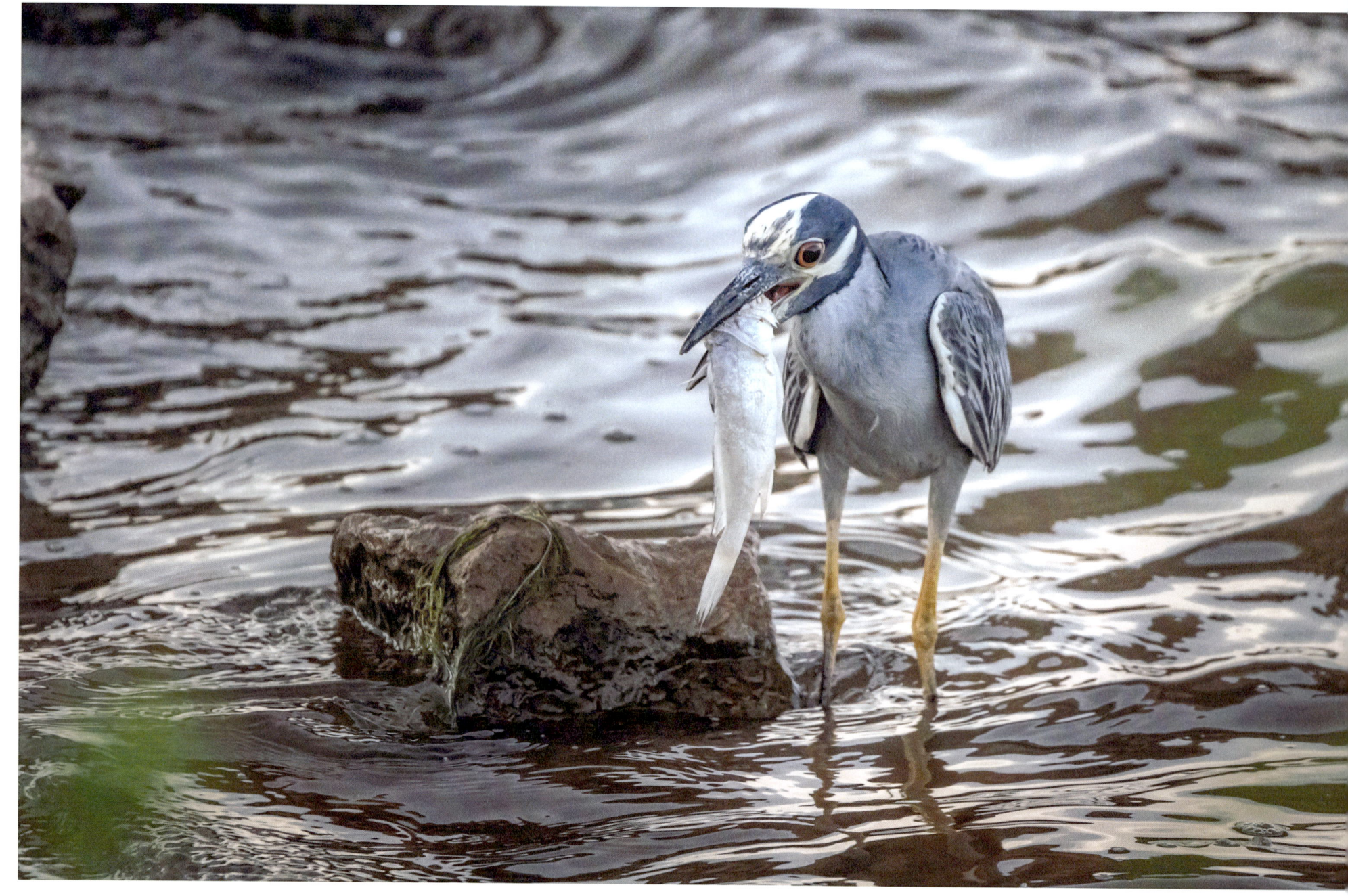

Yellow-crowned NIght Heron with a Big Fish

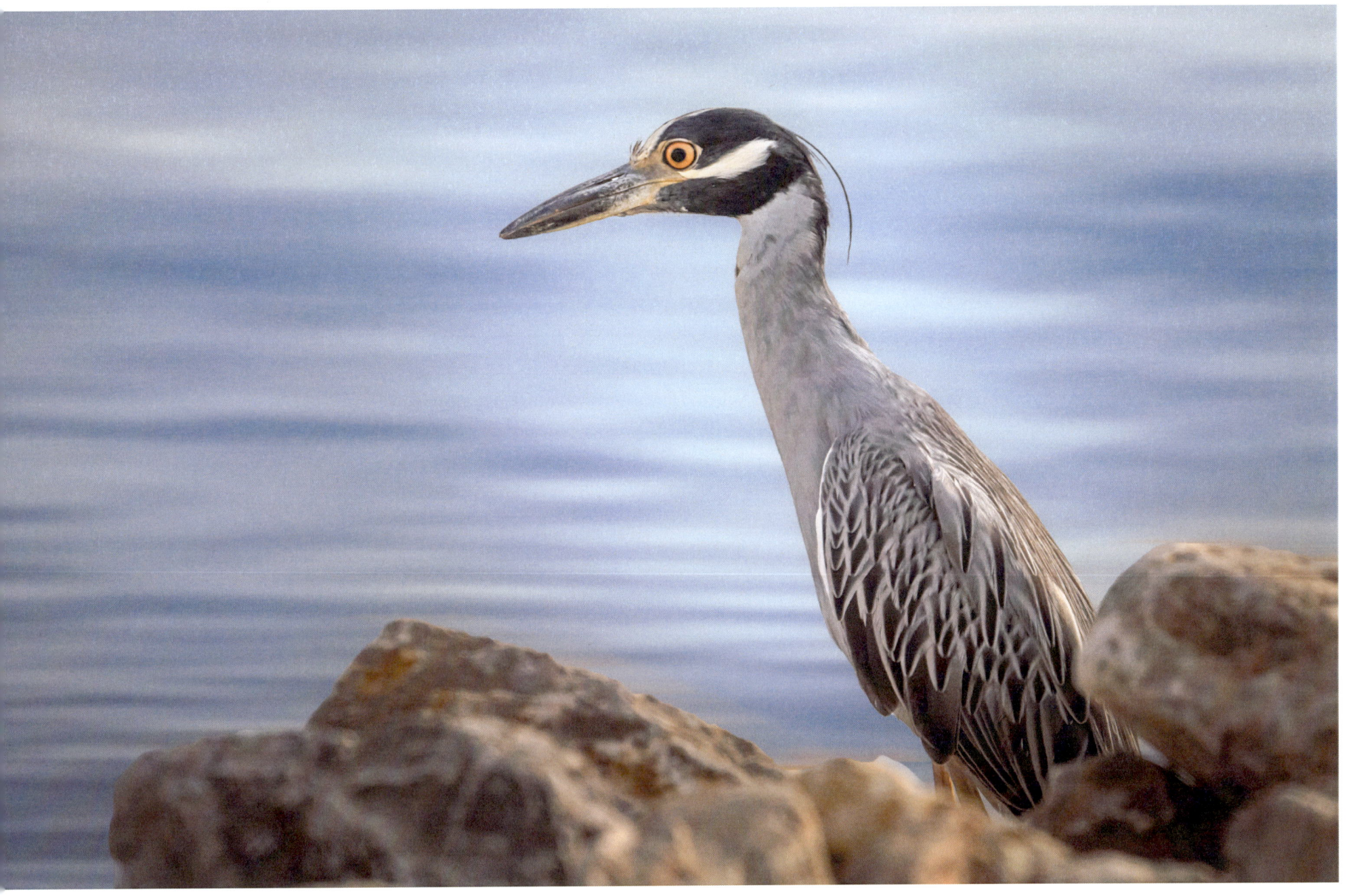

Yellow-crowned Night Heron Standing in Rocks on a Lakeshore

A Sequence
"Green Heron Fishing"

The green heron is small and (usually) secretive, but this juvenile was not at all timid. I sat on the shore and photographed him fishing only ten feet away. First he is seen peering into the water, then the dismount followed by the stalk down that narrow rail, and finally, success.

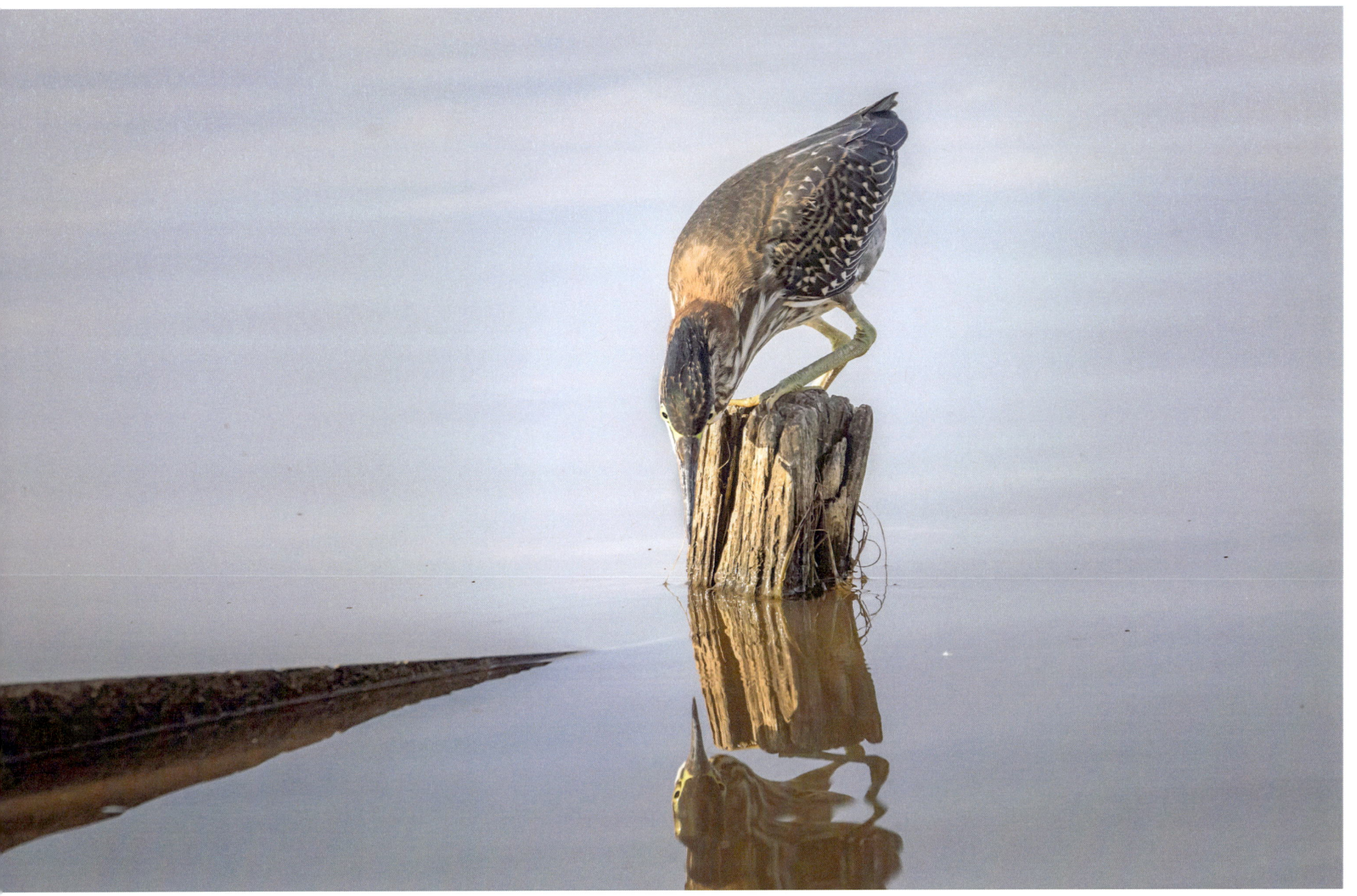

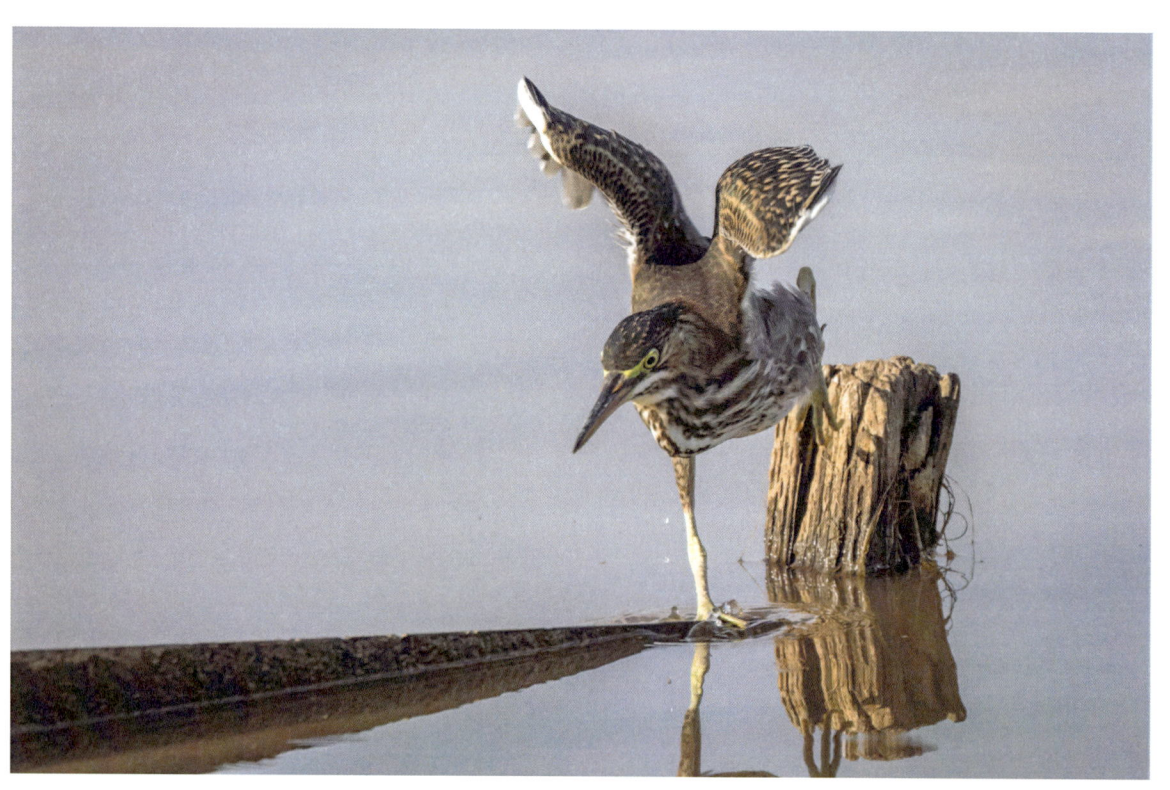
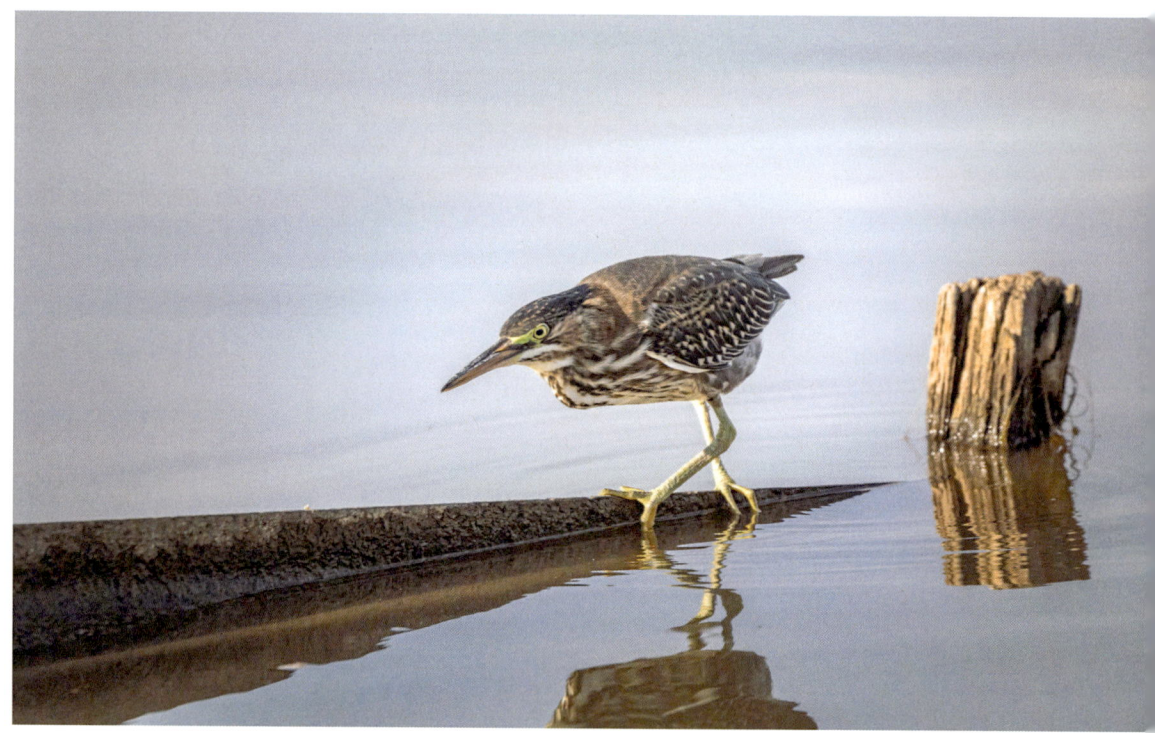

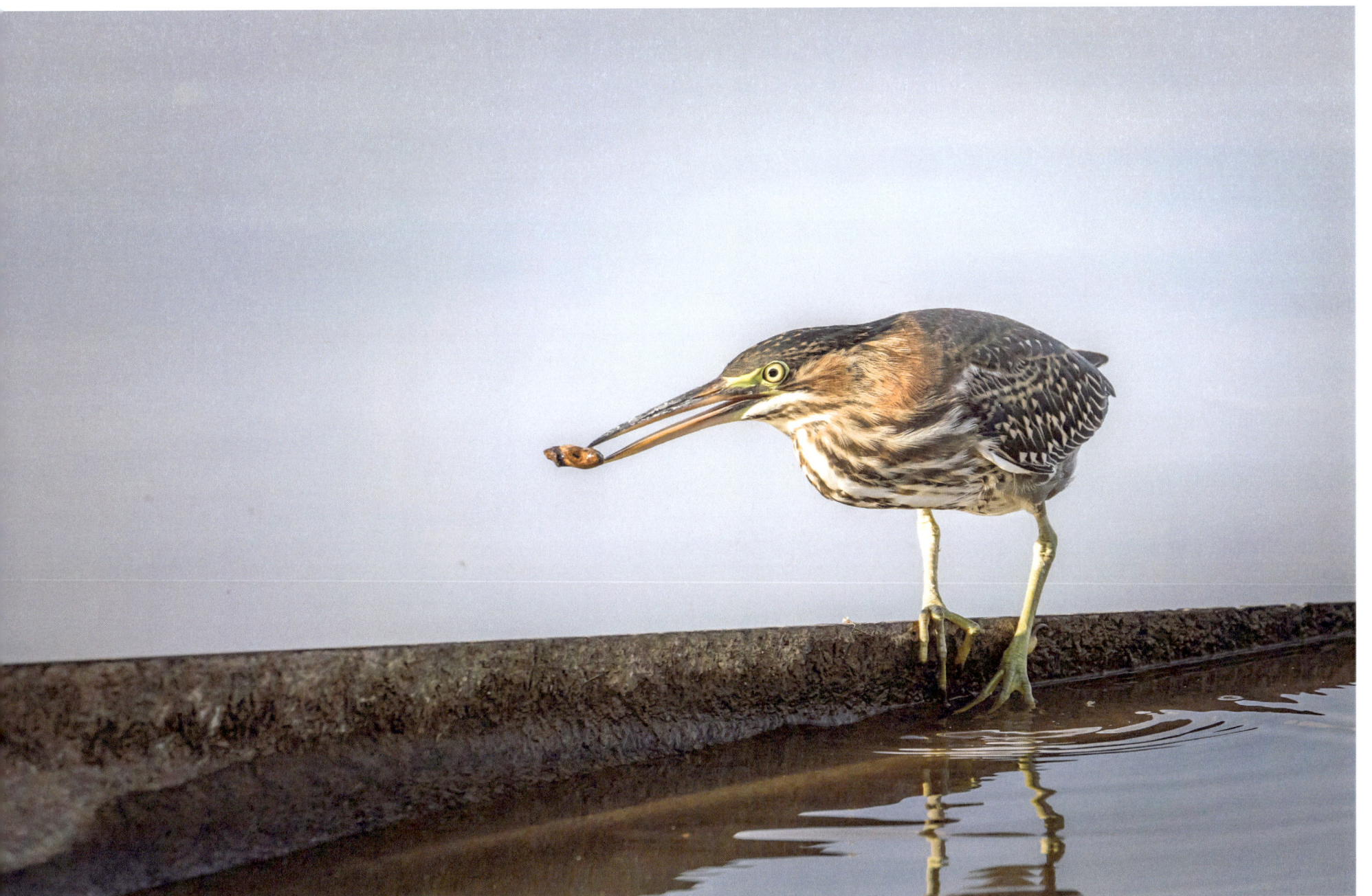

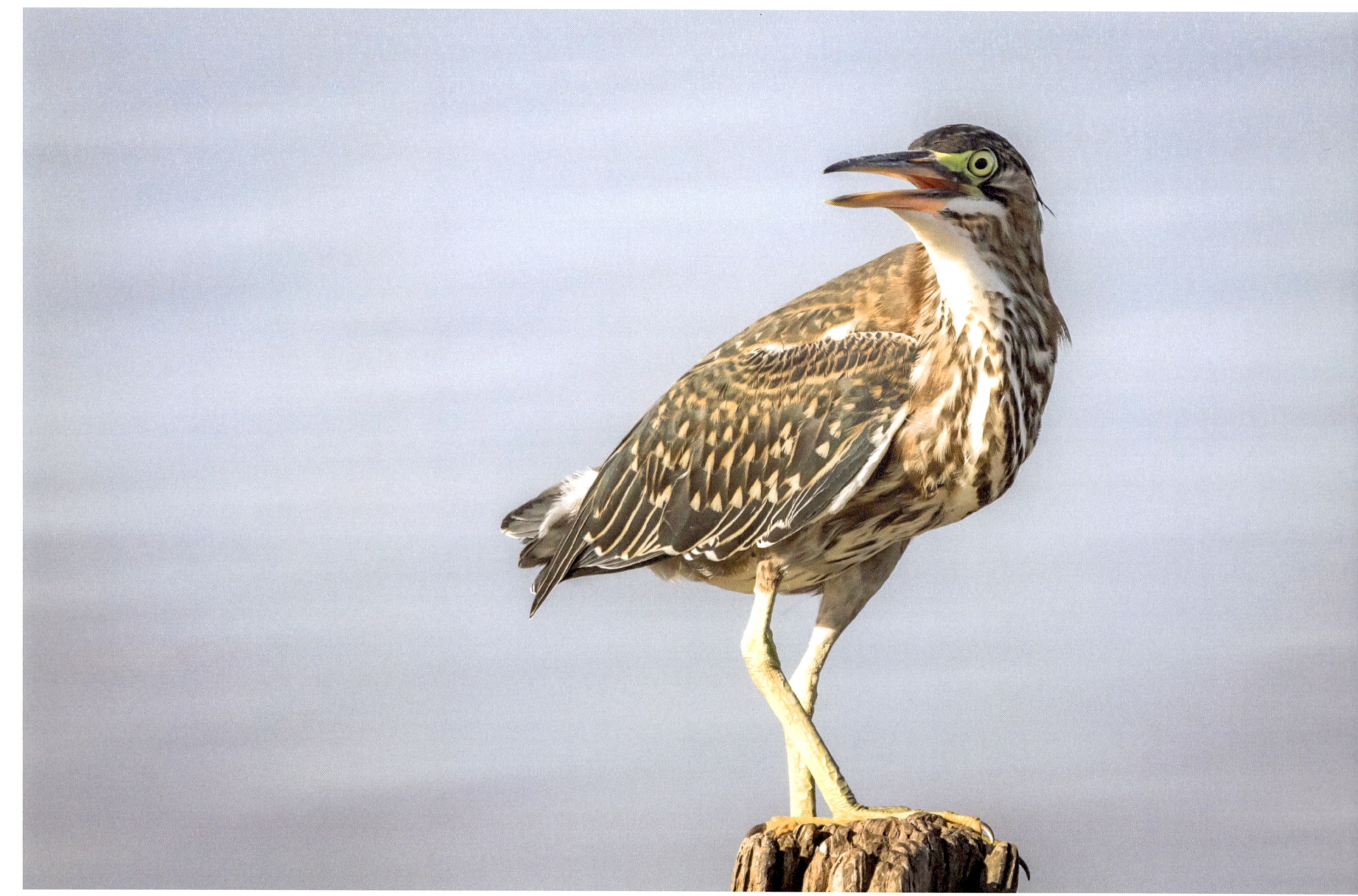

Juvenile Green Heron

Shorebirds

Long legs for wading and long bills for spearing prey near the shore, not all shorebirds fit this description, but many do. While gulls travel in large flocks and are often loud and aggressive, many other shorebirds are quiet little birds. The killdeer squeaks and runs away. The solitary sandpiper bobs its rear end up and down almost continuously. The yellowlegs stand quietly in shallow water while the willet looks its best when flying. The shorebirds are a fascinating lot.

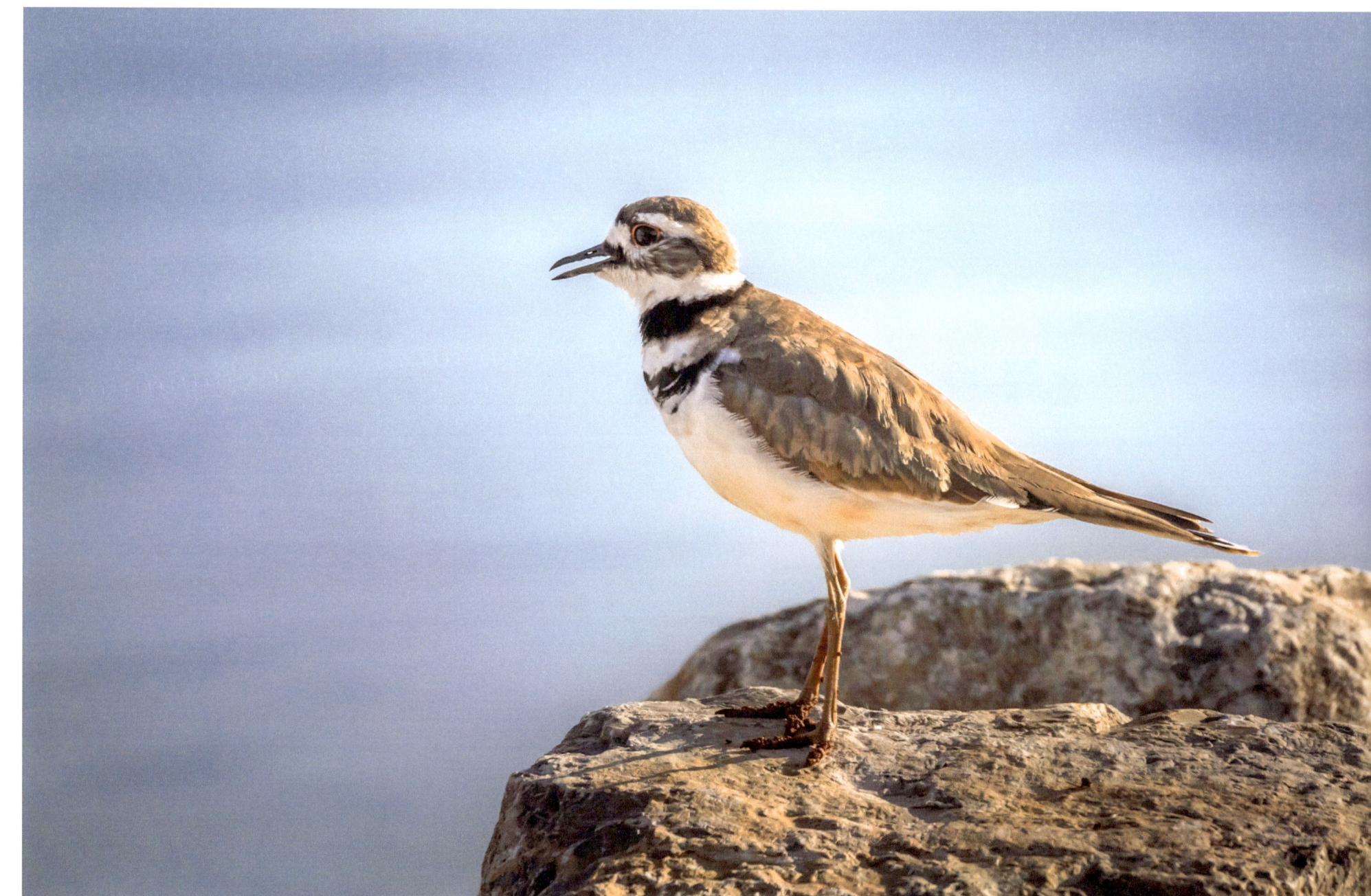

Killdeer on the Shore

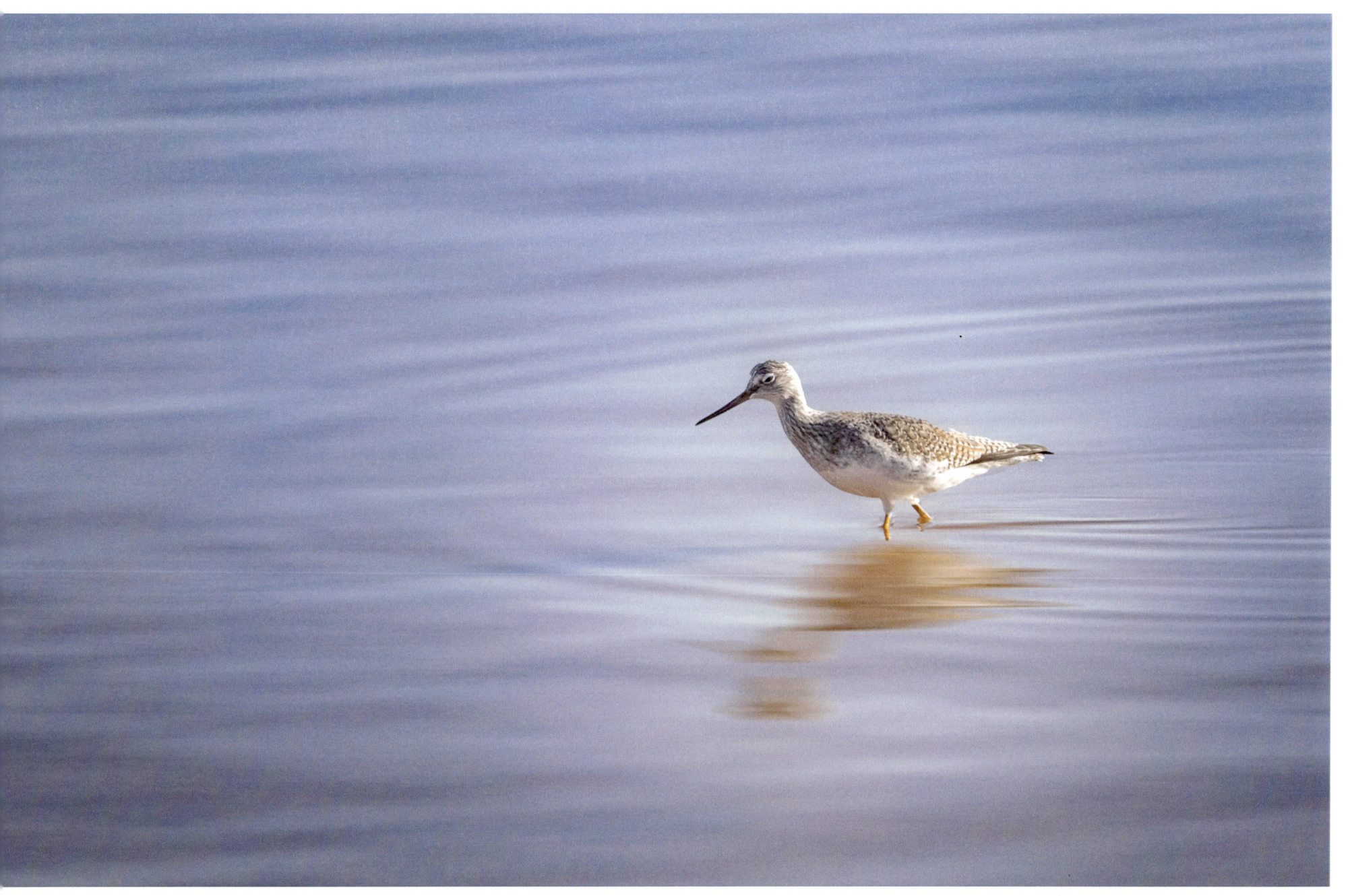

Greater Yellowlegs Wading in a Lake

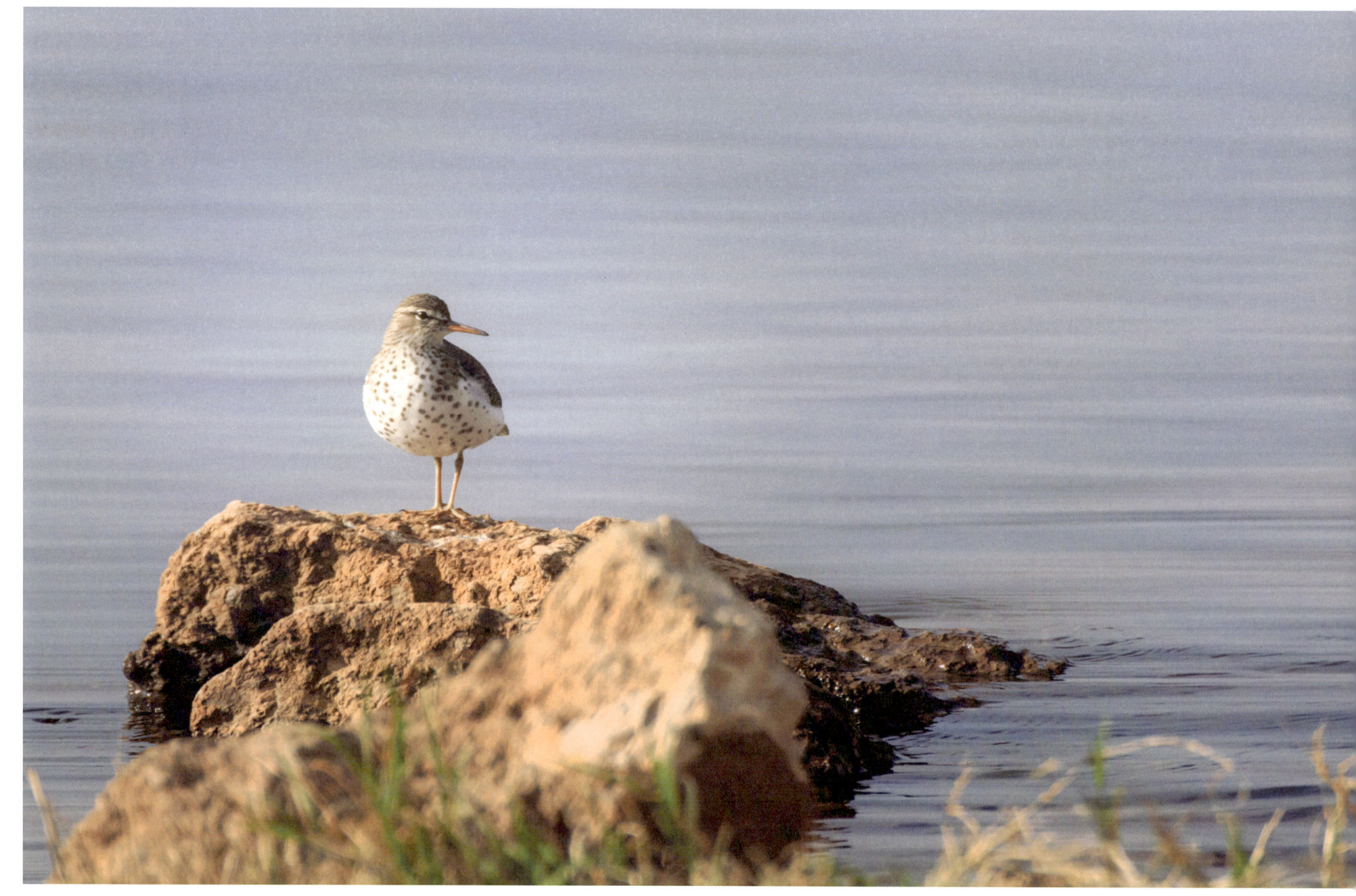

Spotted Sandpiper

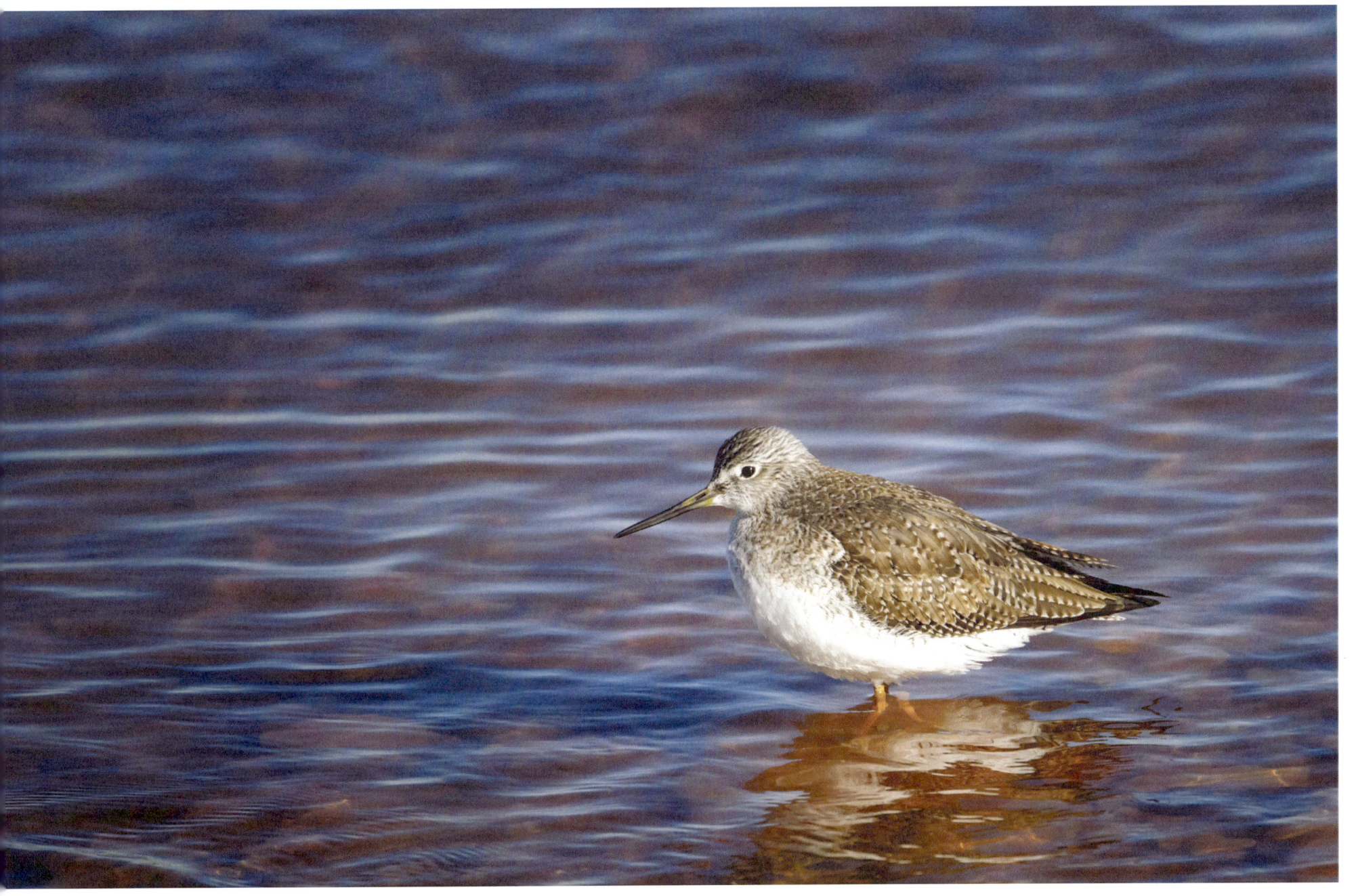

Solitary Sandpiper

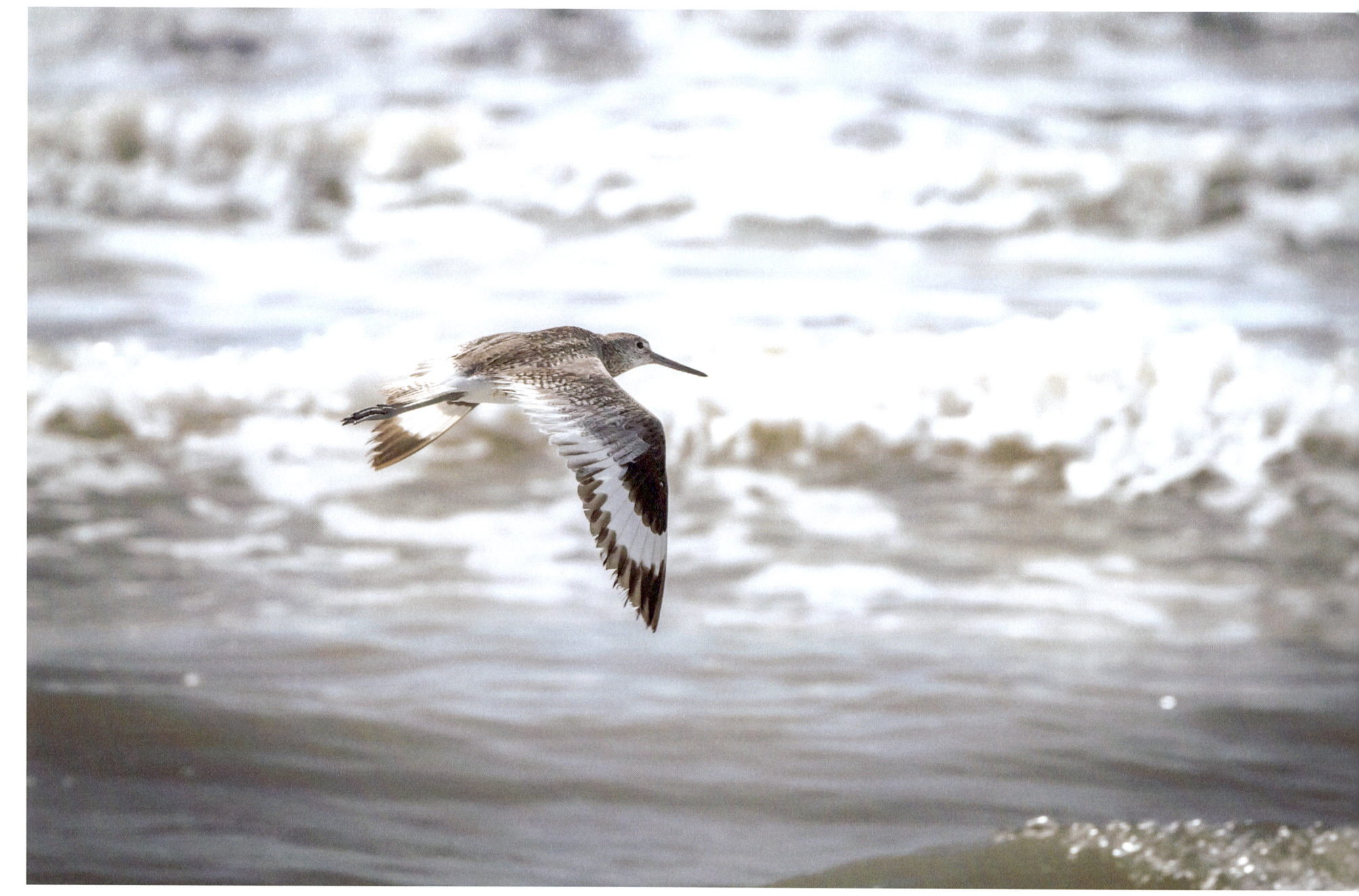

Willet in Flight Over the Ocean

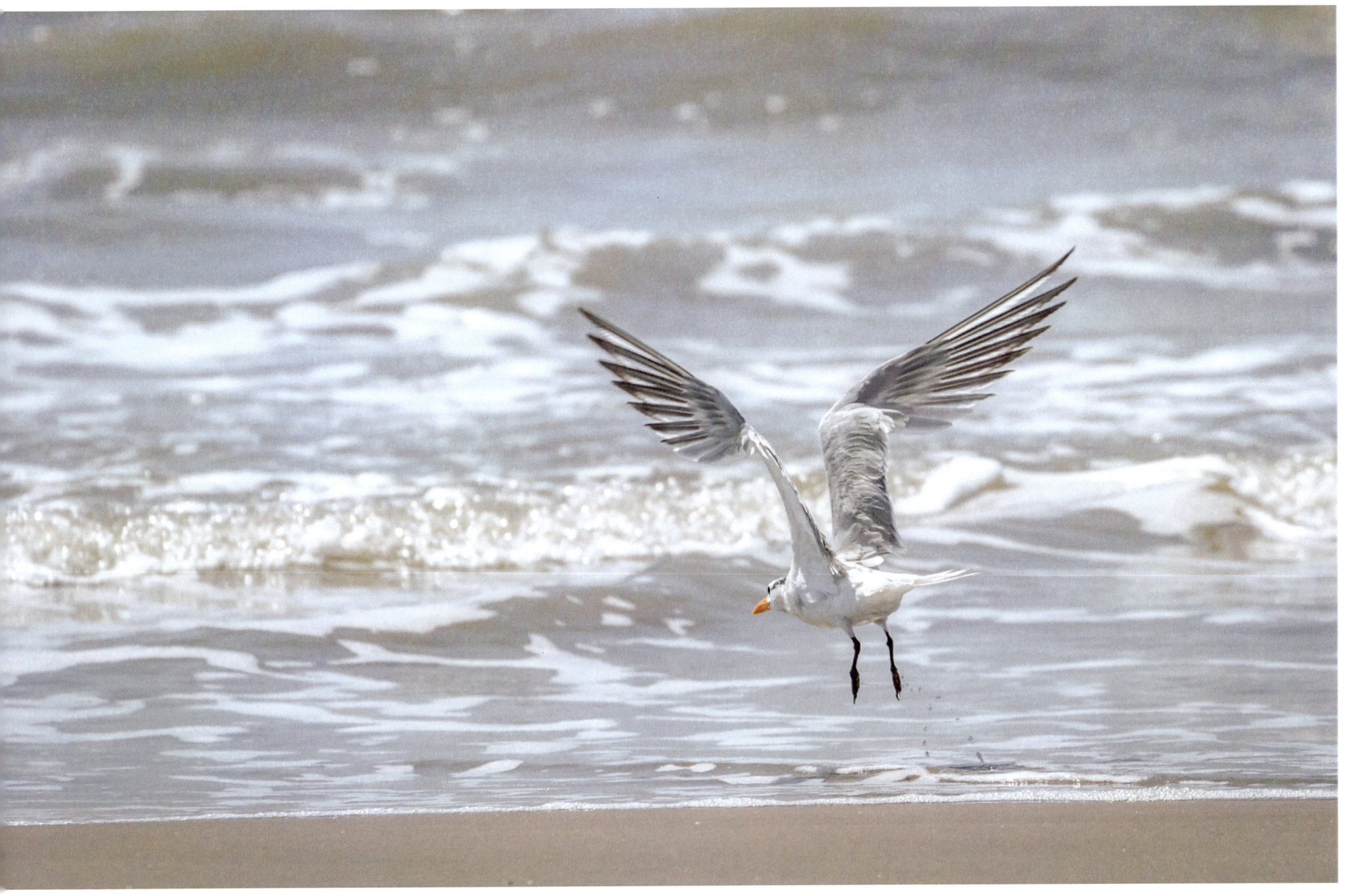

A Royal Tern Taking Off from the Beach

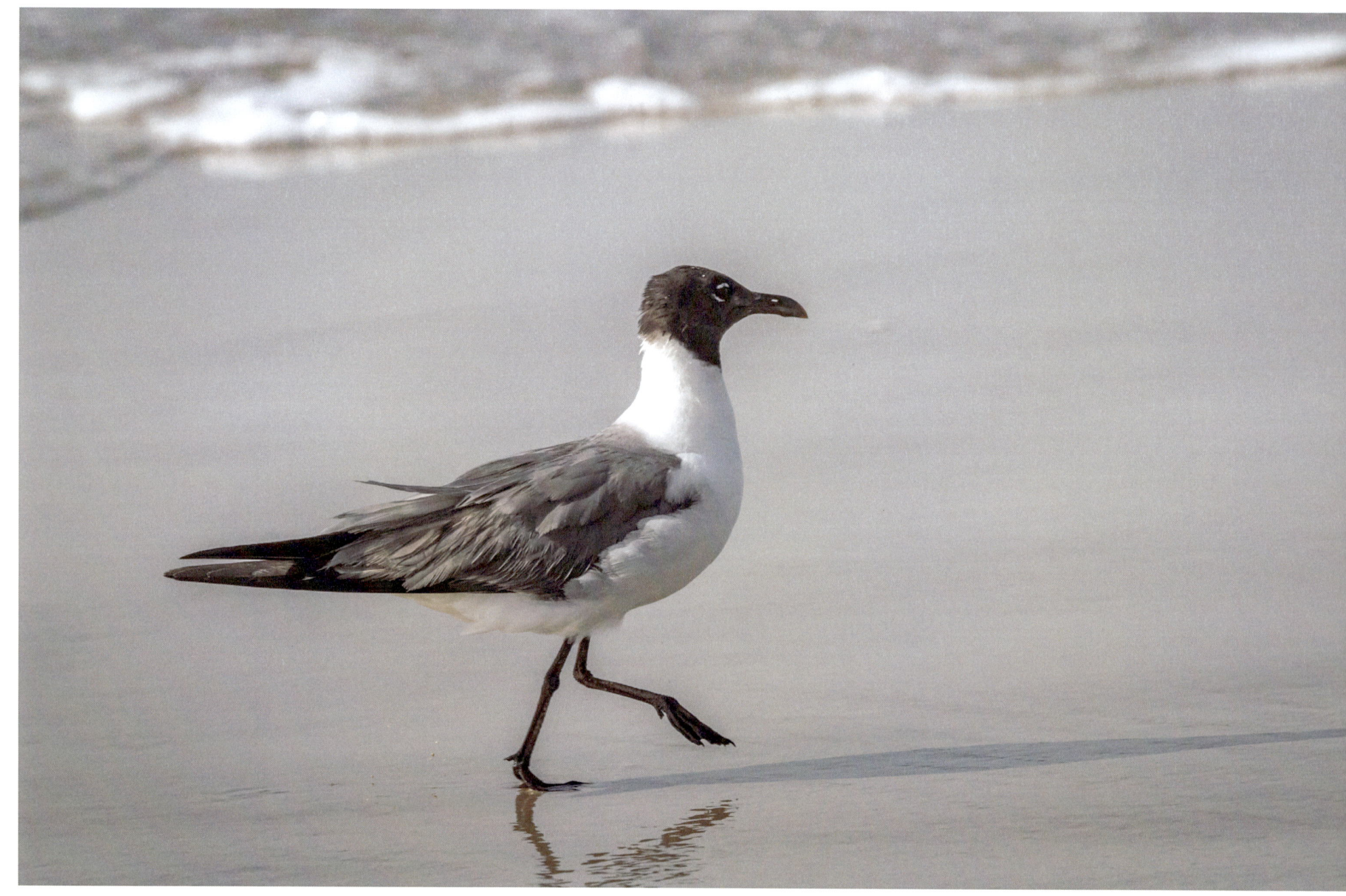

Laughing Gull Strolling on the Beach

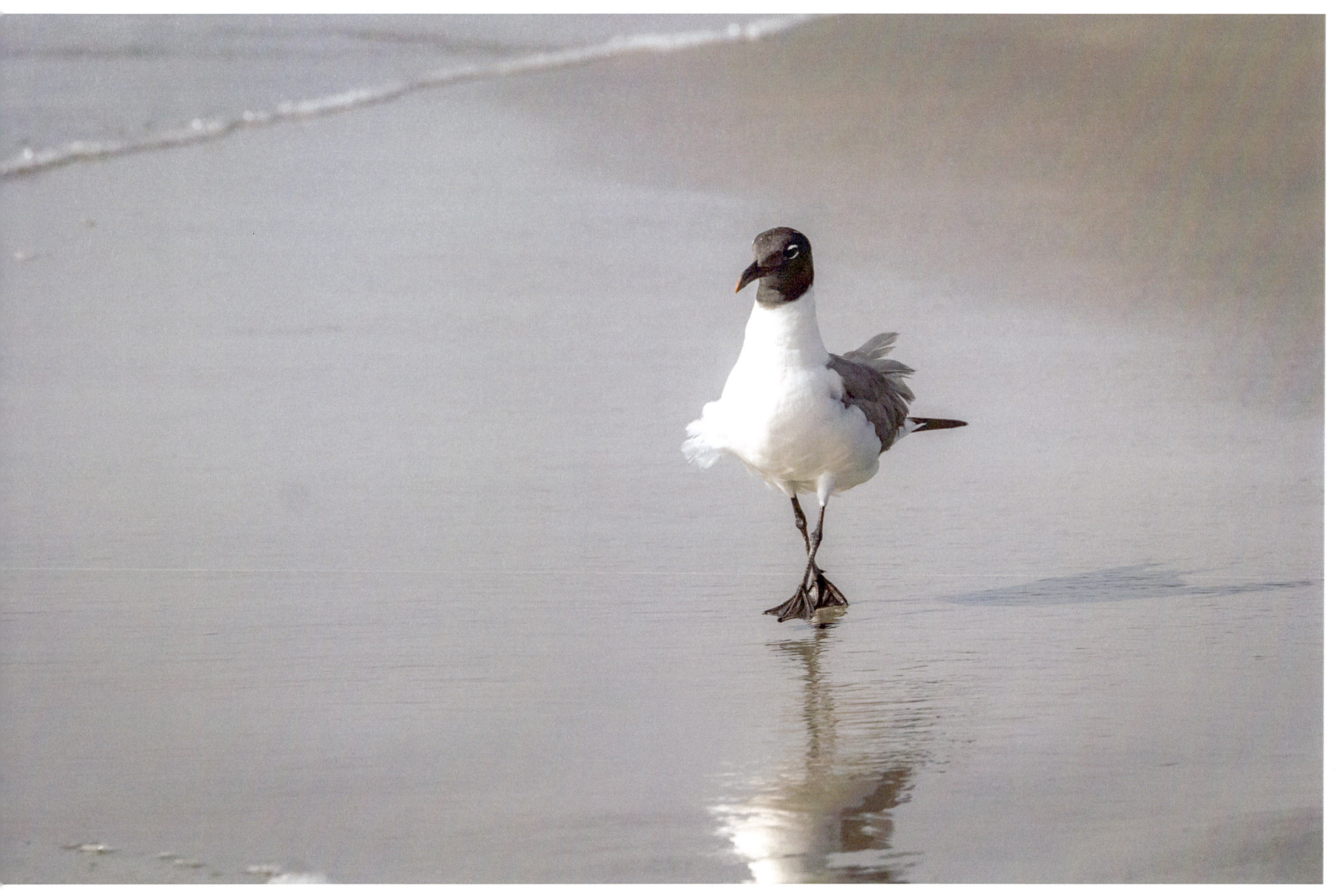

Laughing Gull Struttin' on the Beach

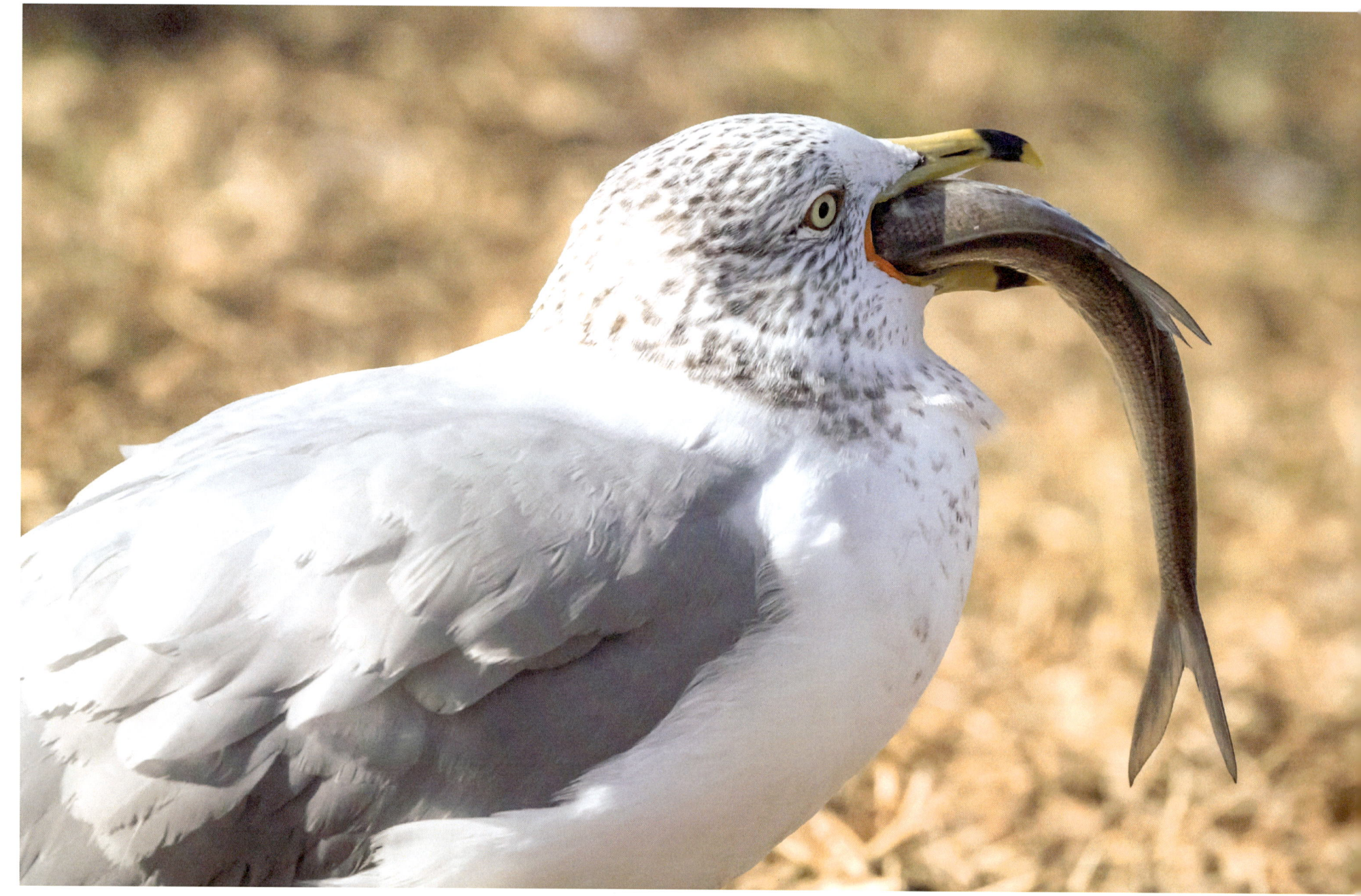

Ring-billed Gull with Dinner

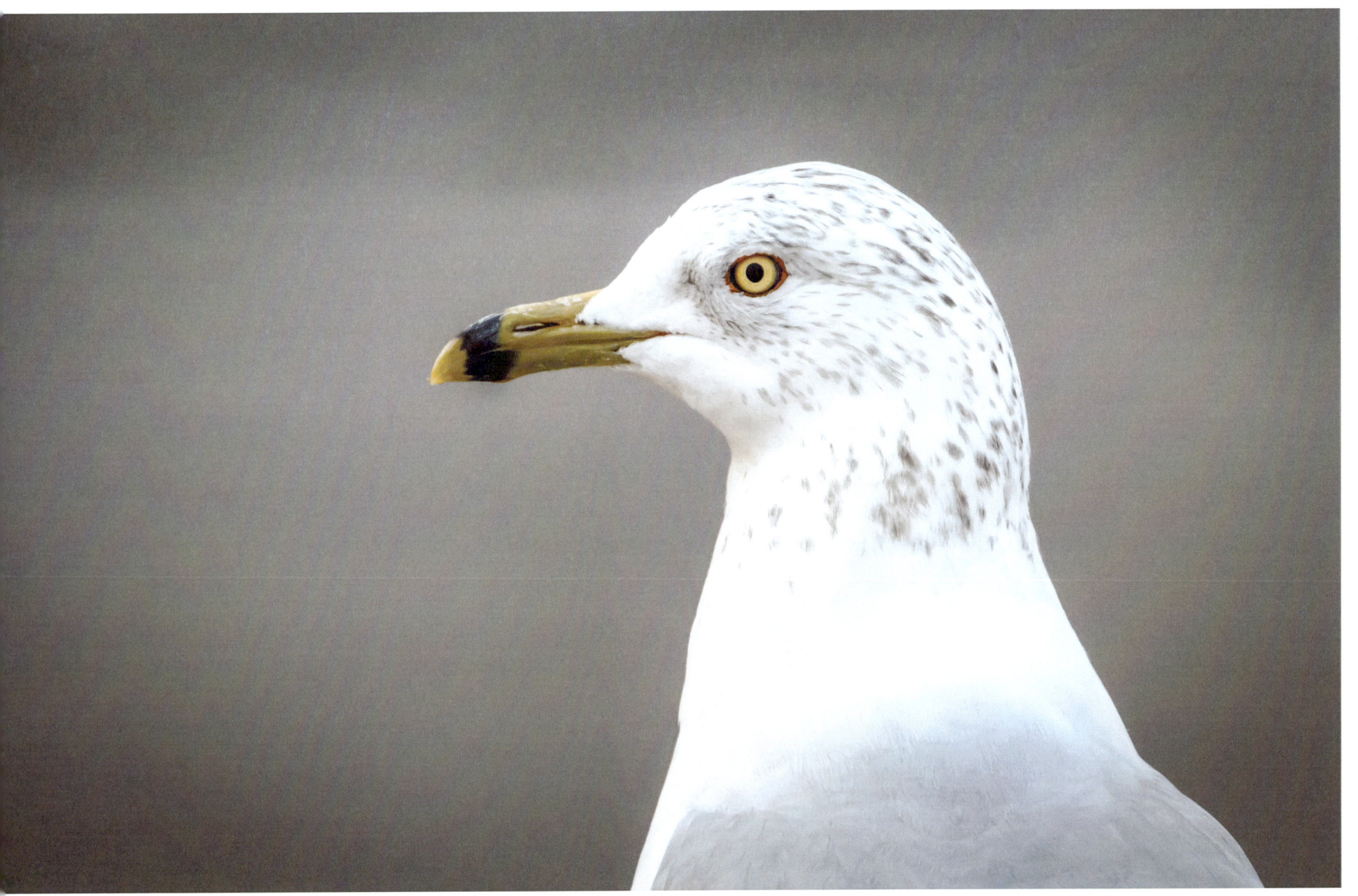

Ring-billed Gull

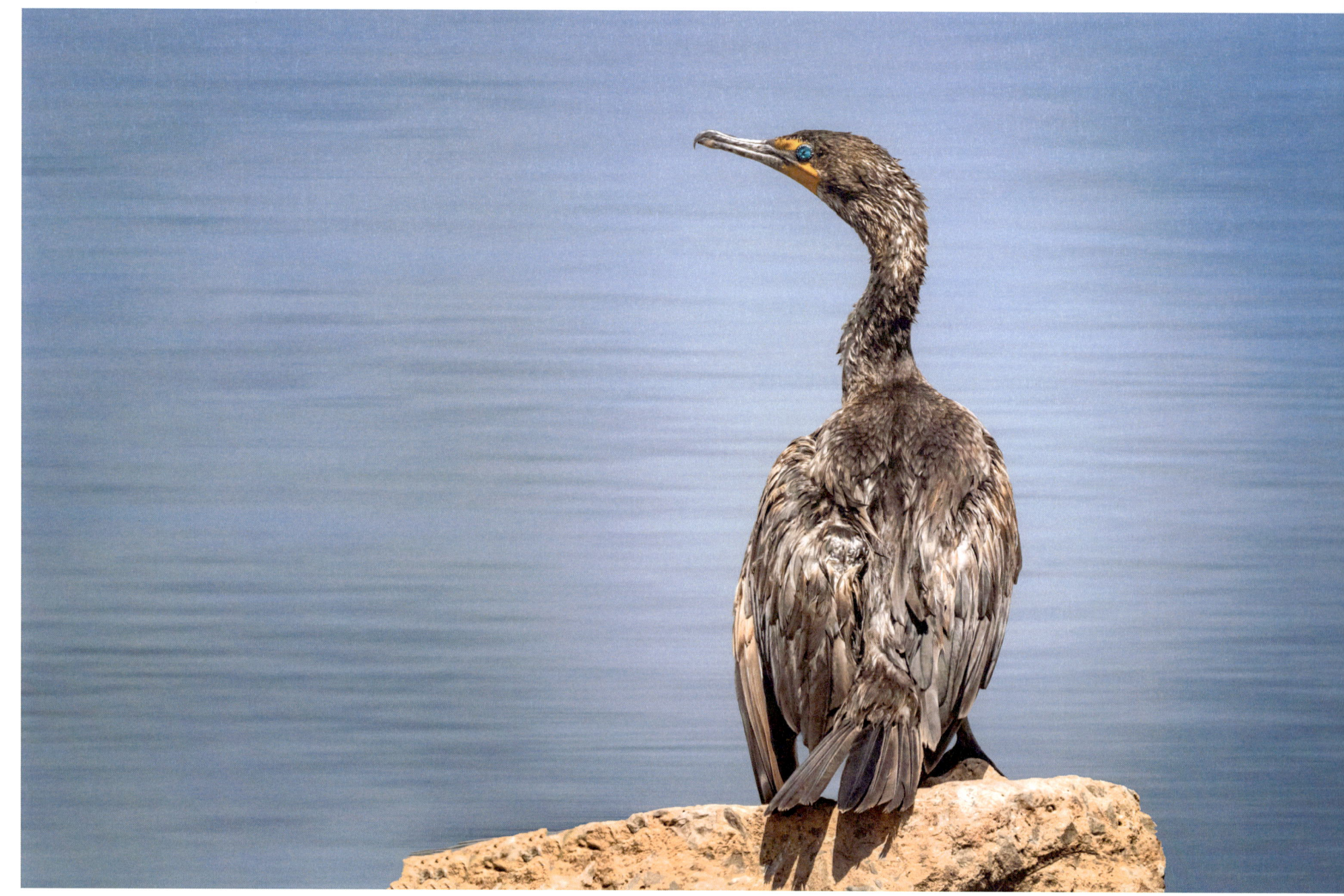

Juvenile Double-crested Cormorant

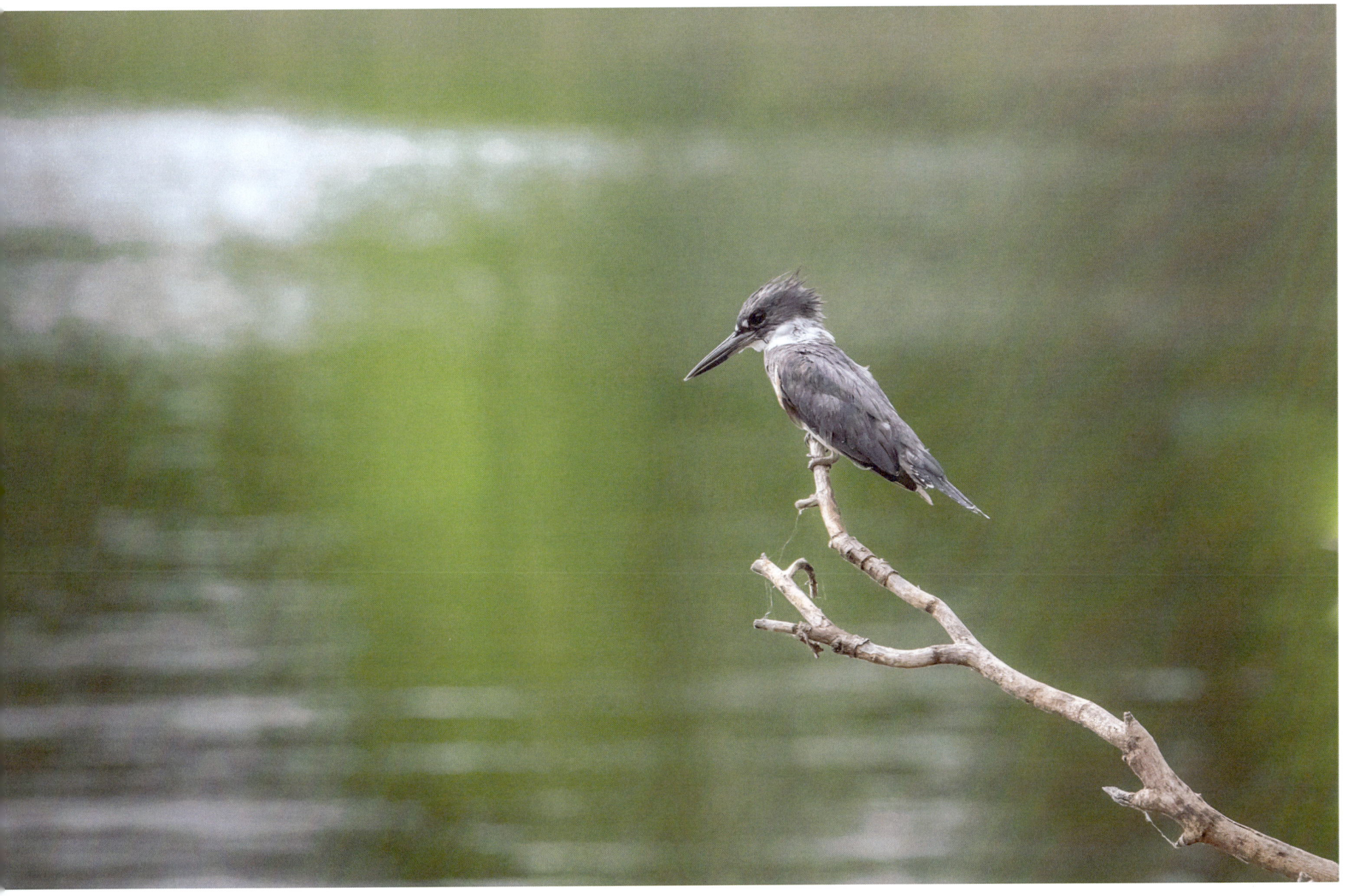

Belted Kingfisher Fishing

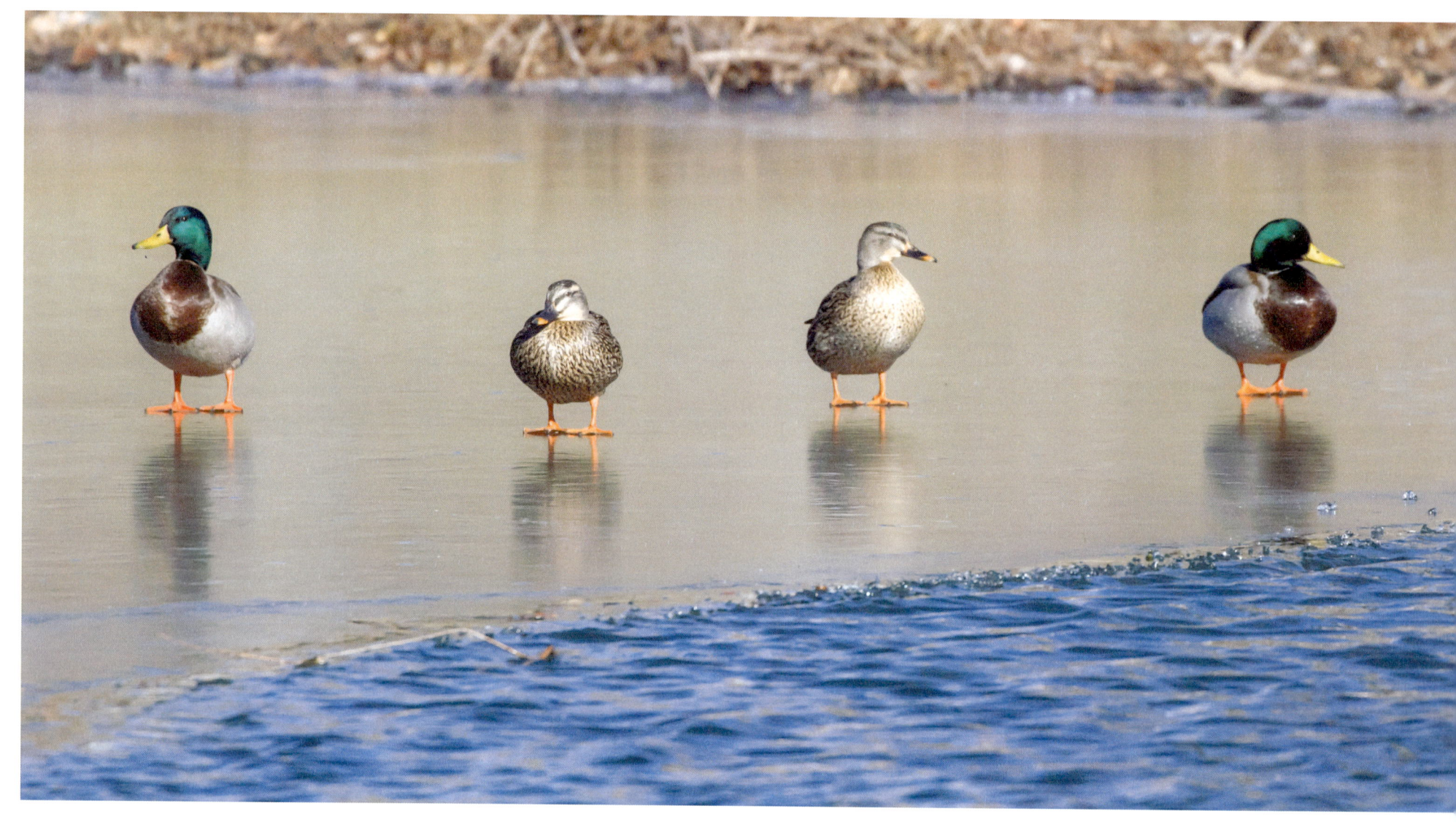

"On Frozen Pond"
Mallards Out for a Stroll on a Cold Morning

Birds of Prey

Strong, fierce, powerful, majestic. How many other such adjectives are used to describe these birds? Think of the terrifyingly beautiful osprey's golden eyes. Consider how many warplanes are named for birds of prey. To most of us, hawks, eagles, and falcons represent the very essence of power and nobility.

Other birds are efficient hunters, but when was a new fighter jet last named the "Egret"? Raptors' regal bearing and stern look serves them well. Even though some of them have some less than noble habits, we remain convinced that they represent the best aspects of human character.

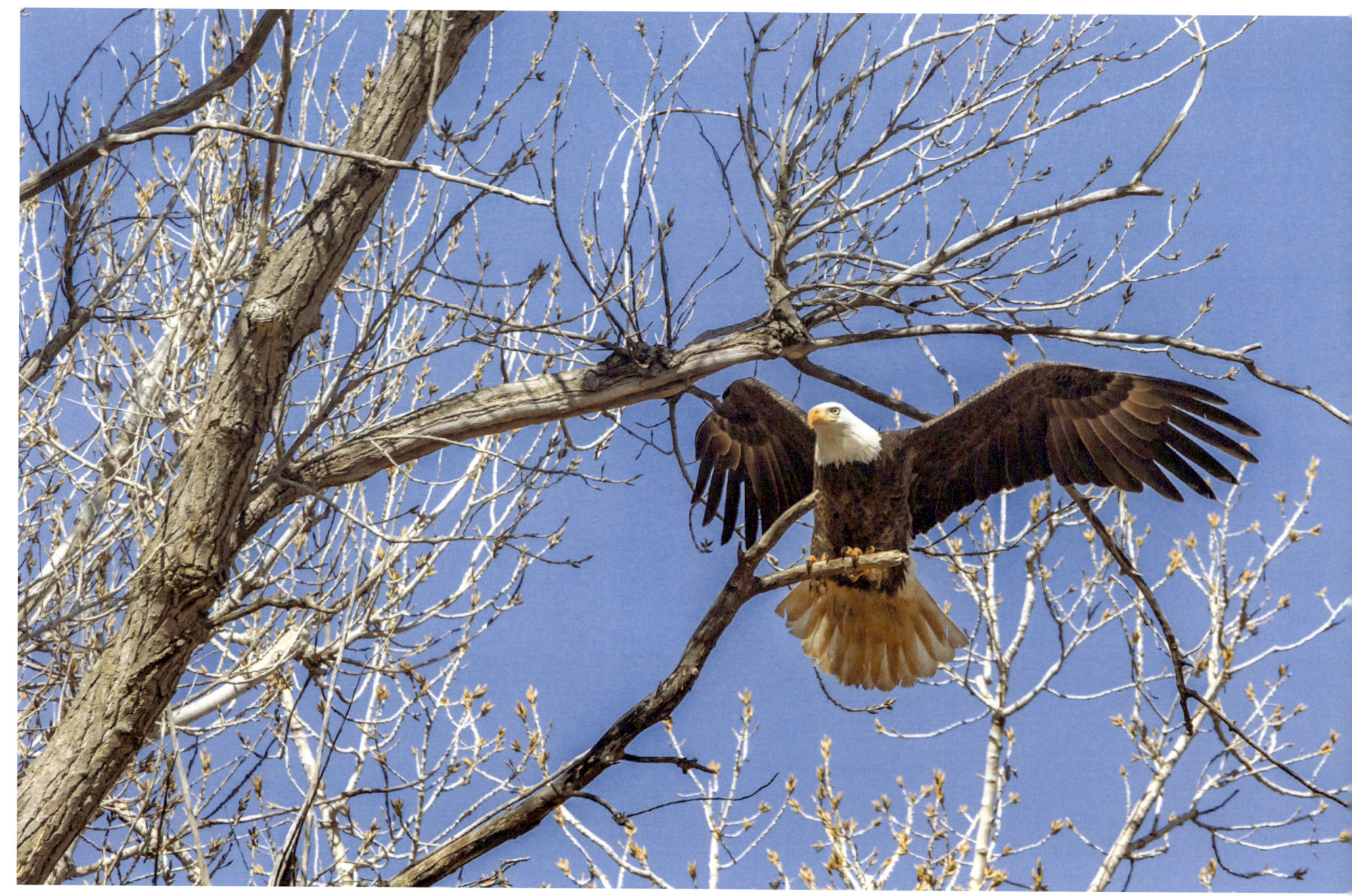

"The Eagle Has Landed"
Bald Eagle Returning to the Nest

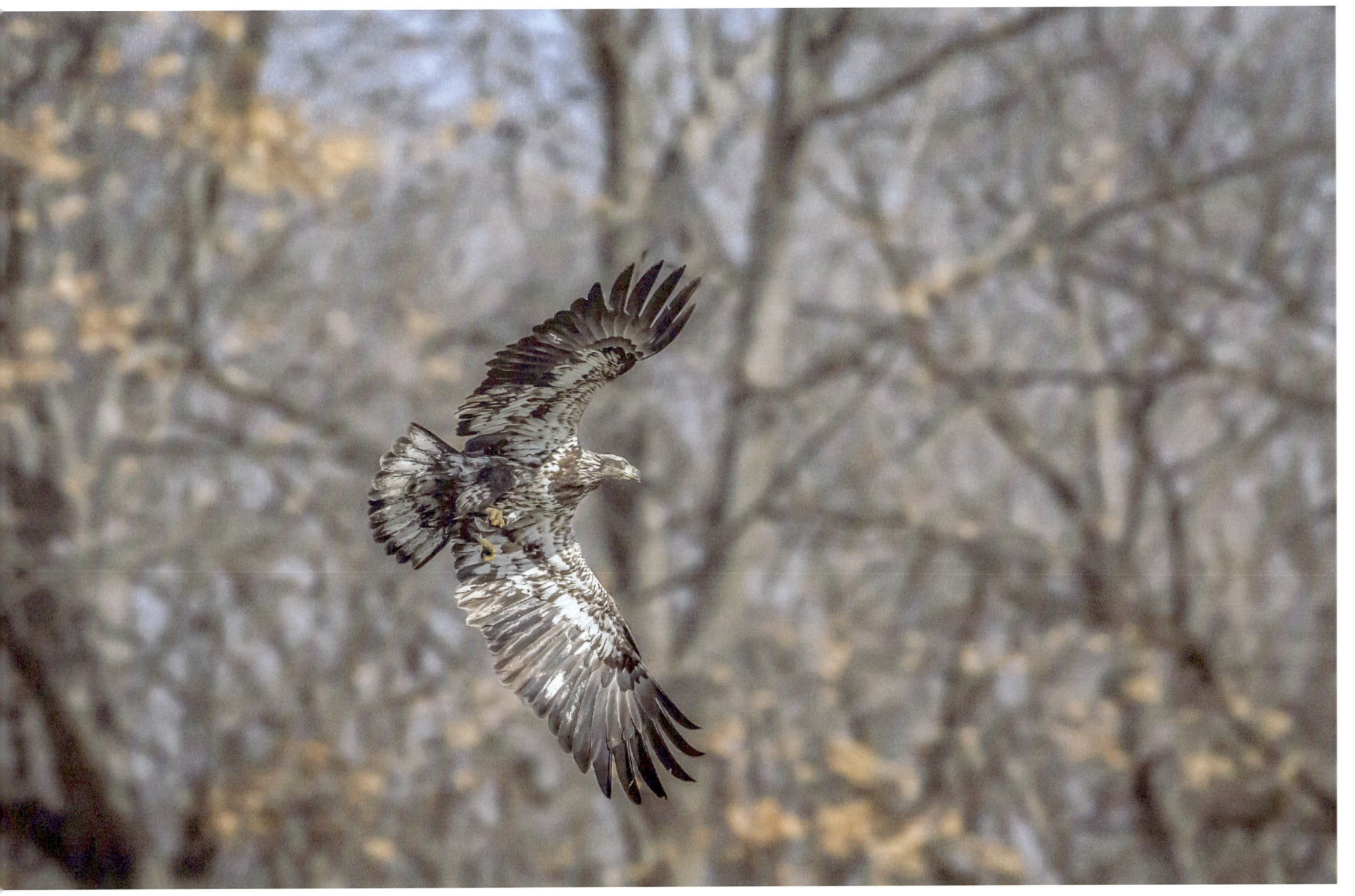

Juvenile Bald Eagle Fishing over the Neosho River

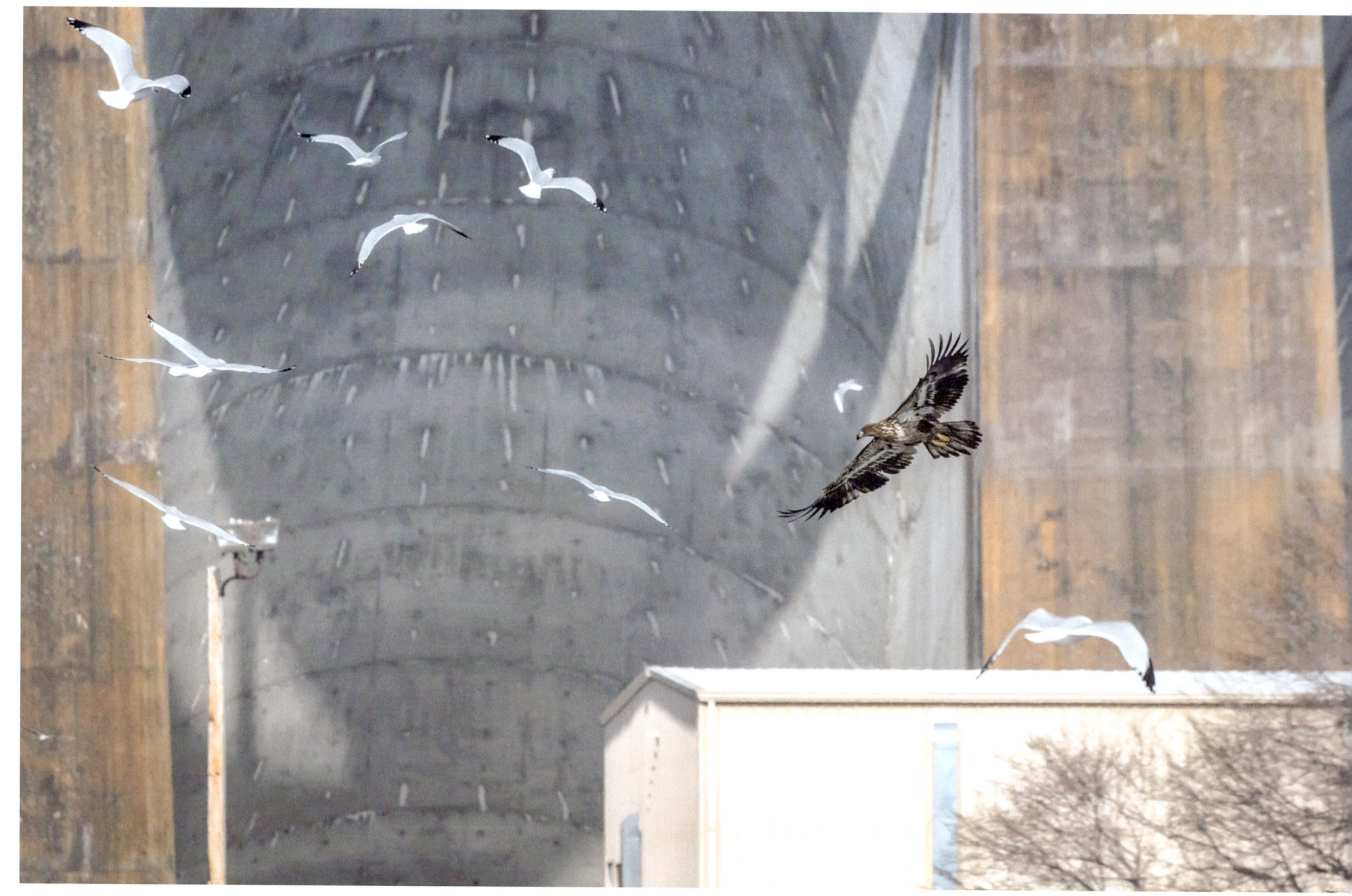

Immature Eagle Flying with Gulls Under the Pensacola Dam

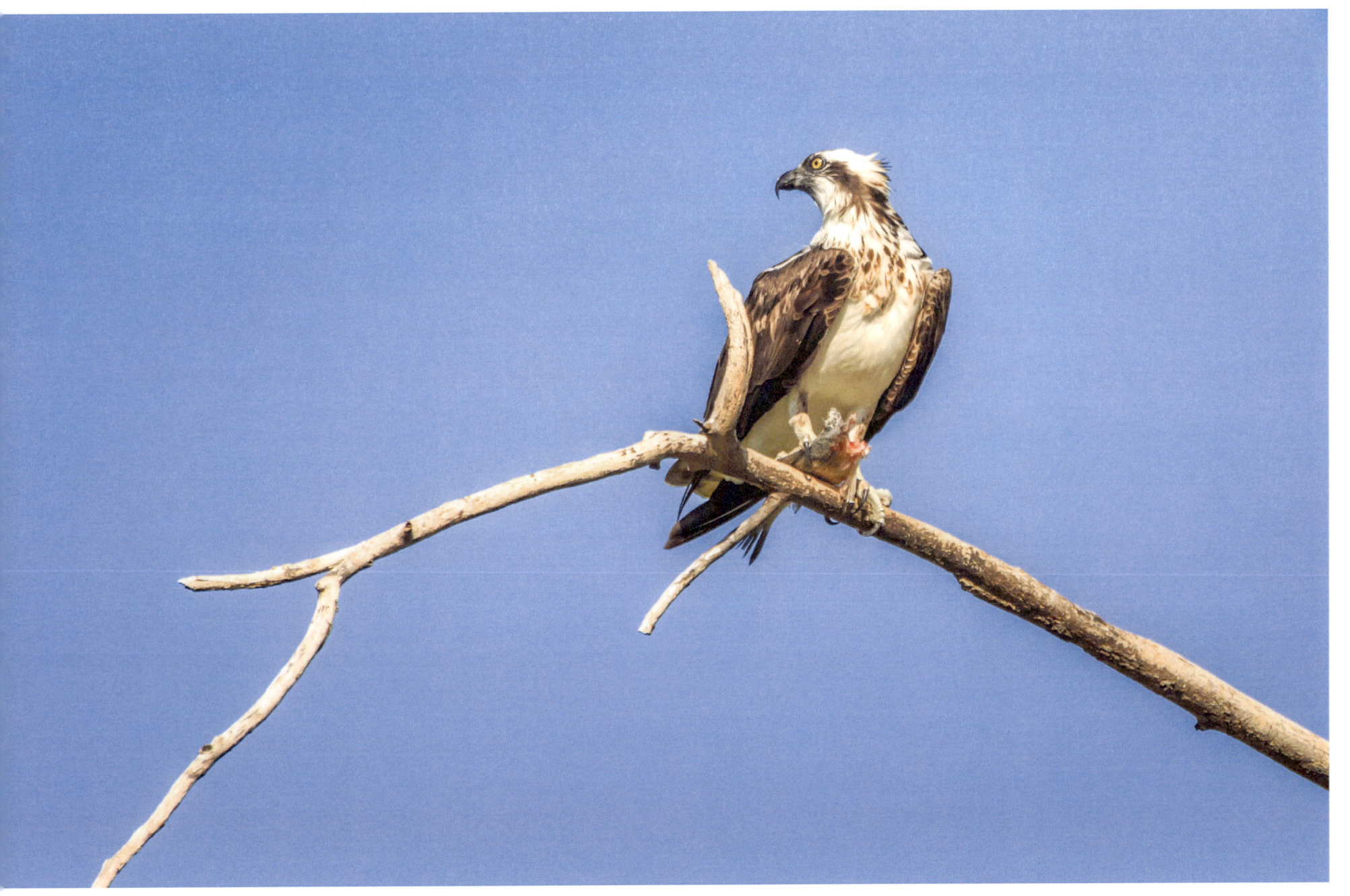

Osprey on a Branch with Its Catch

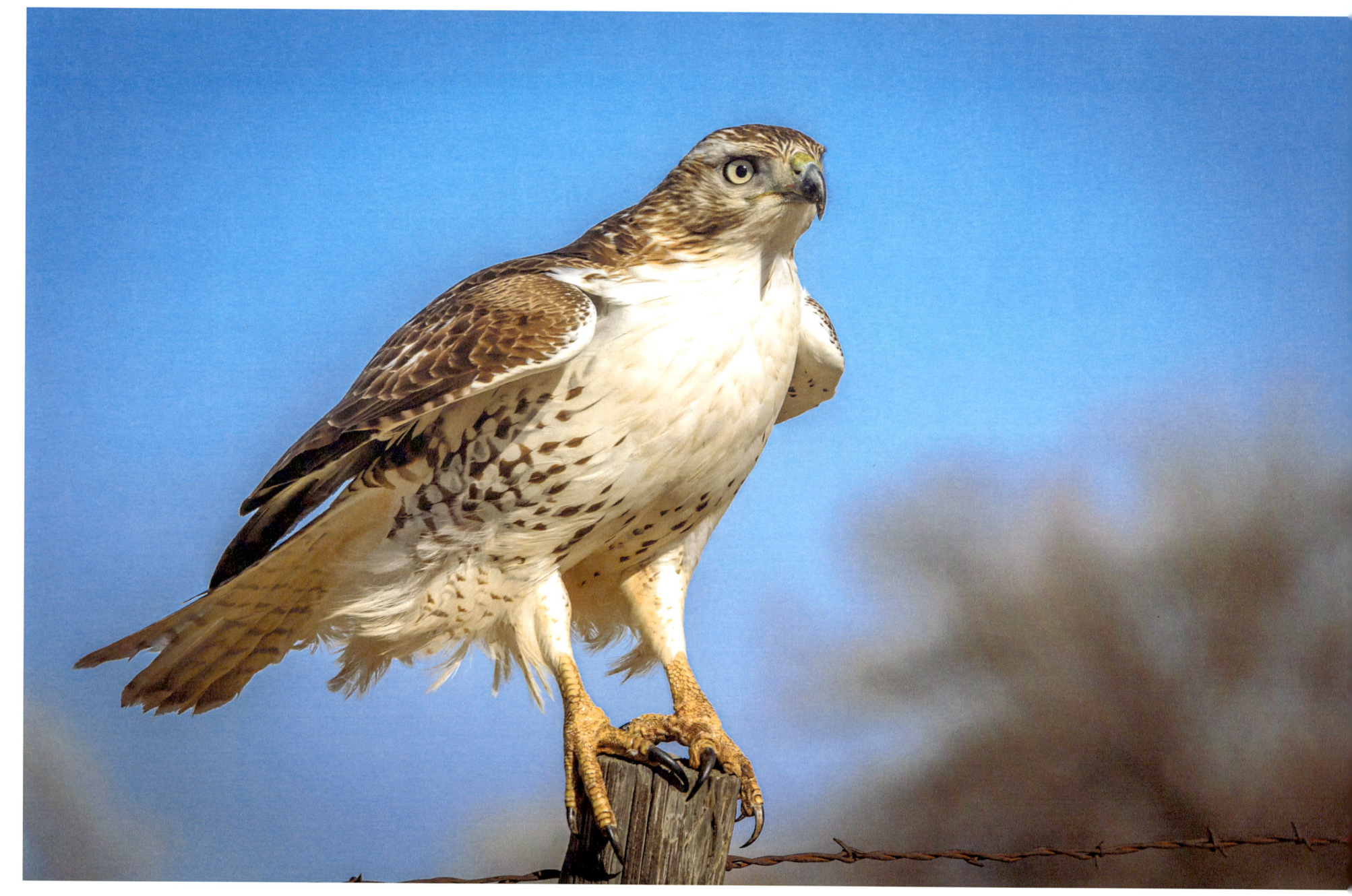

Red-tailed Hawk

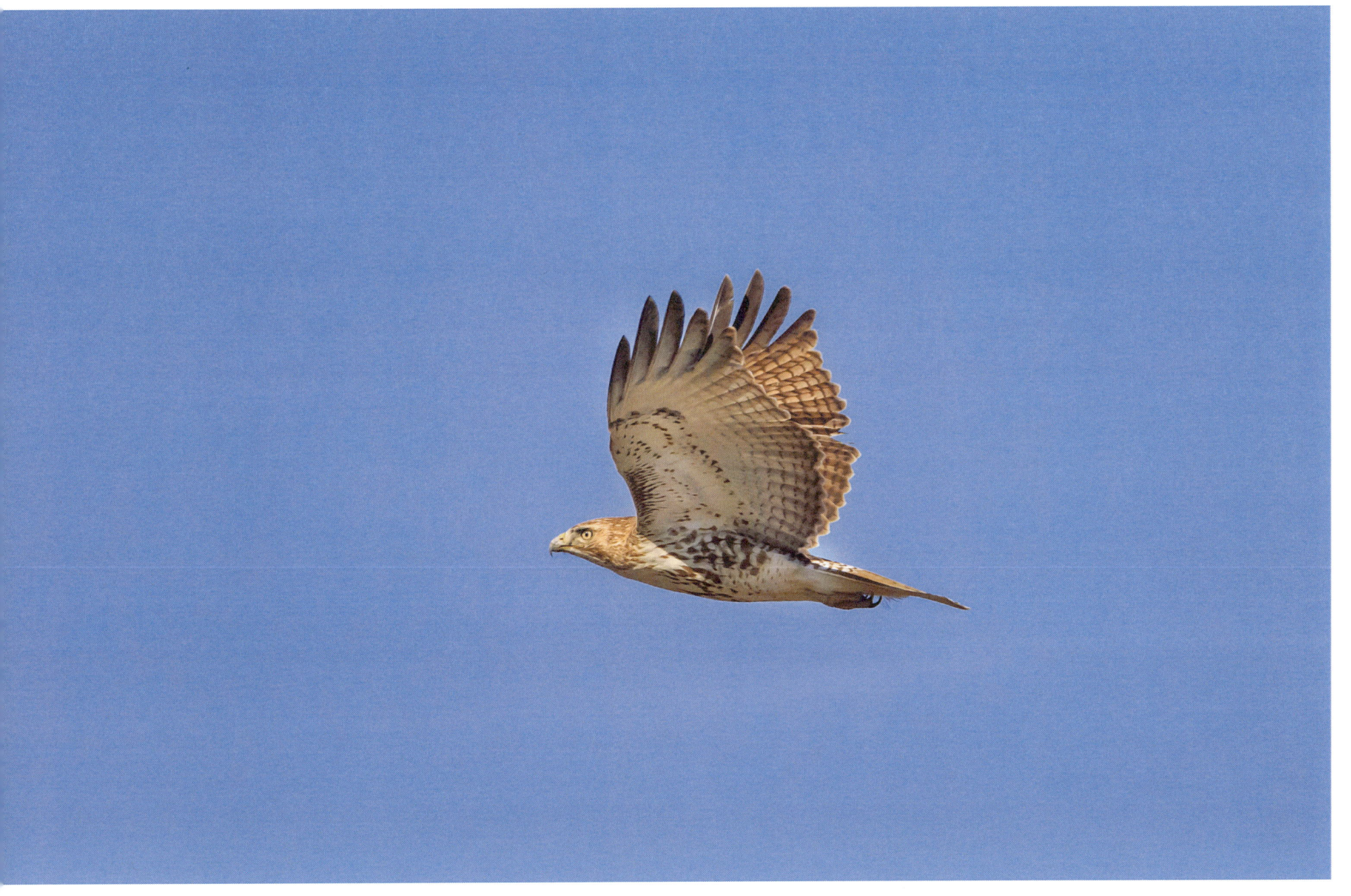

Red-tailed Hawk in Flight

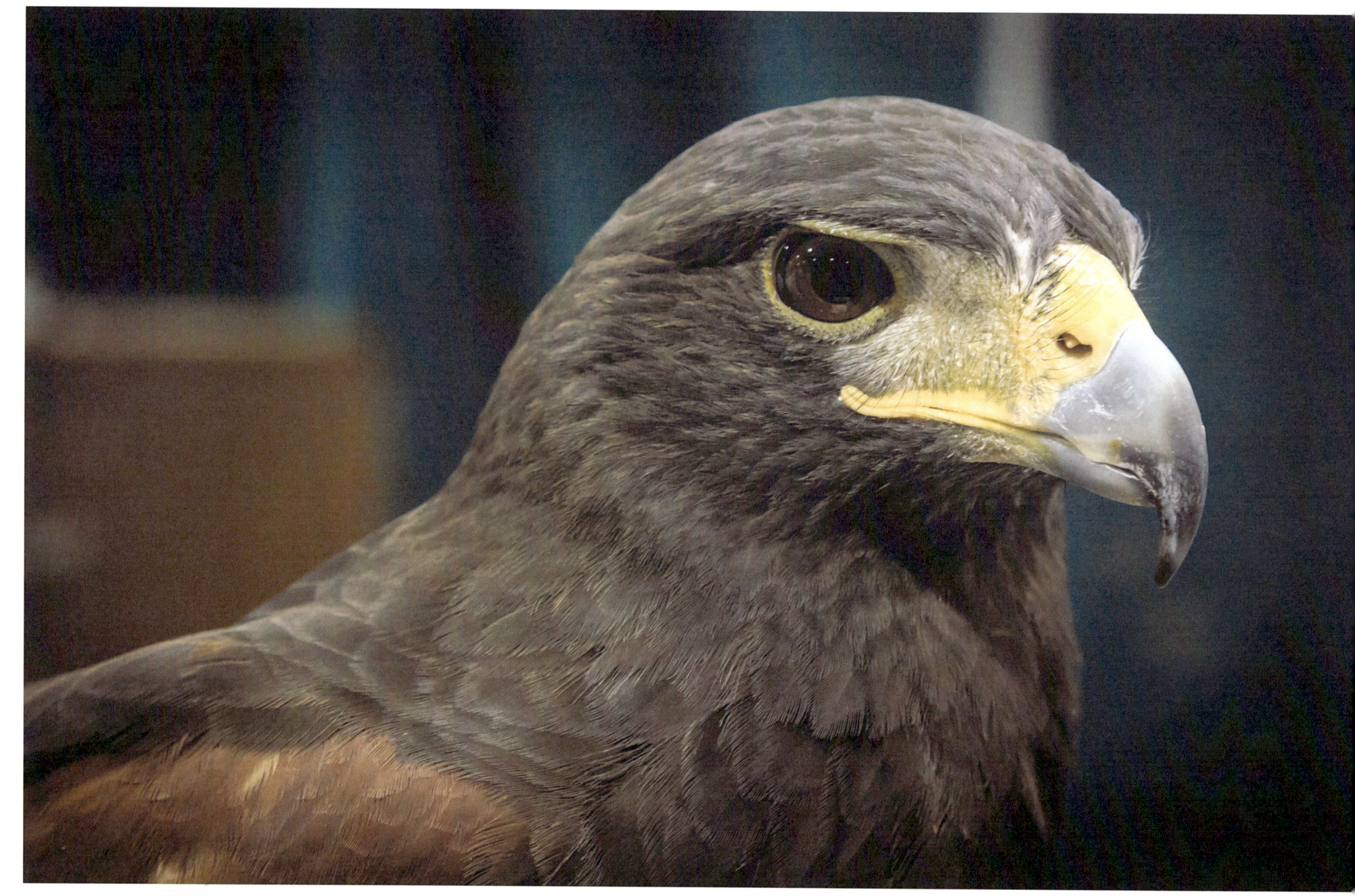

Harris's Hawk

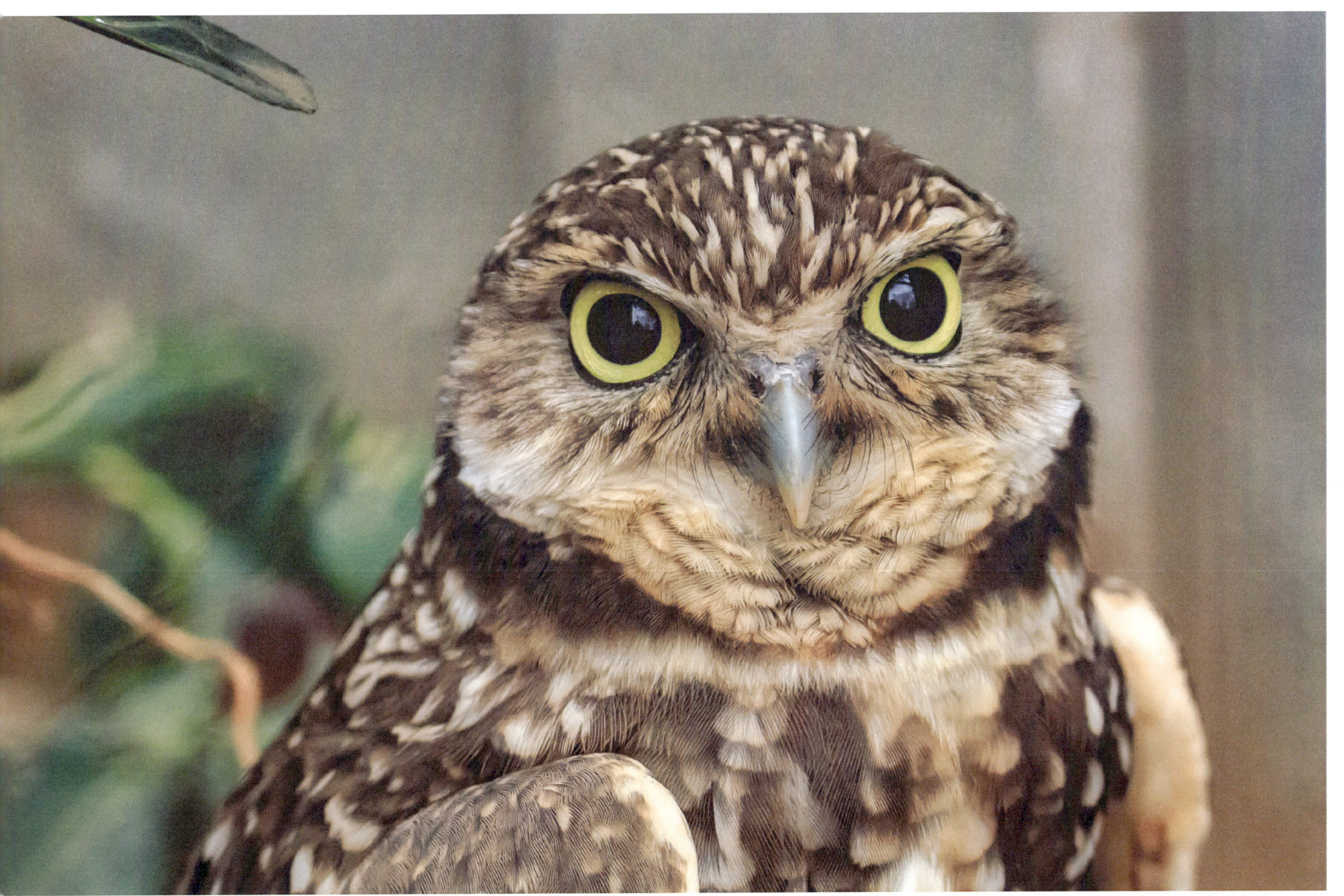
Burrowing Owl Up Close

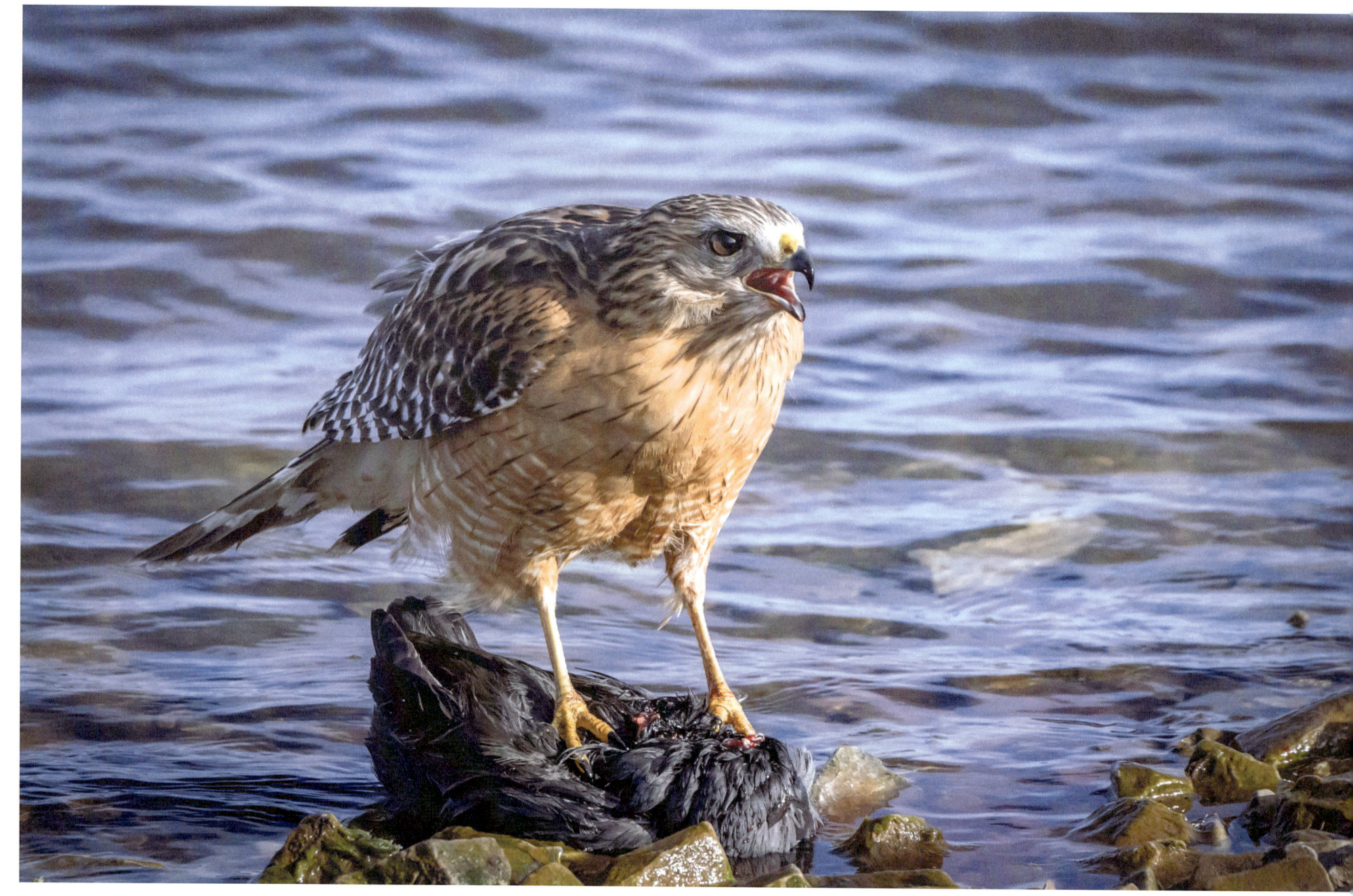

Red-shouldered Hawk Protecting His Kill

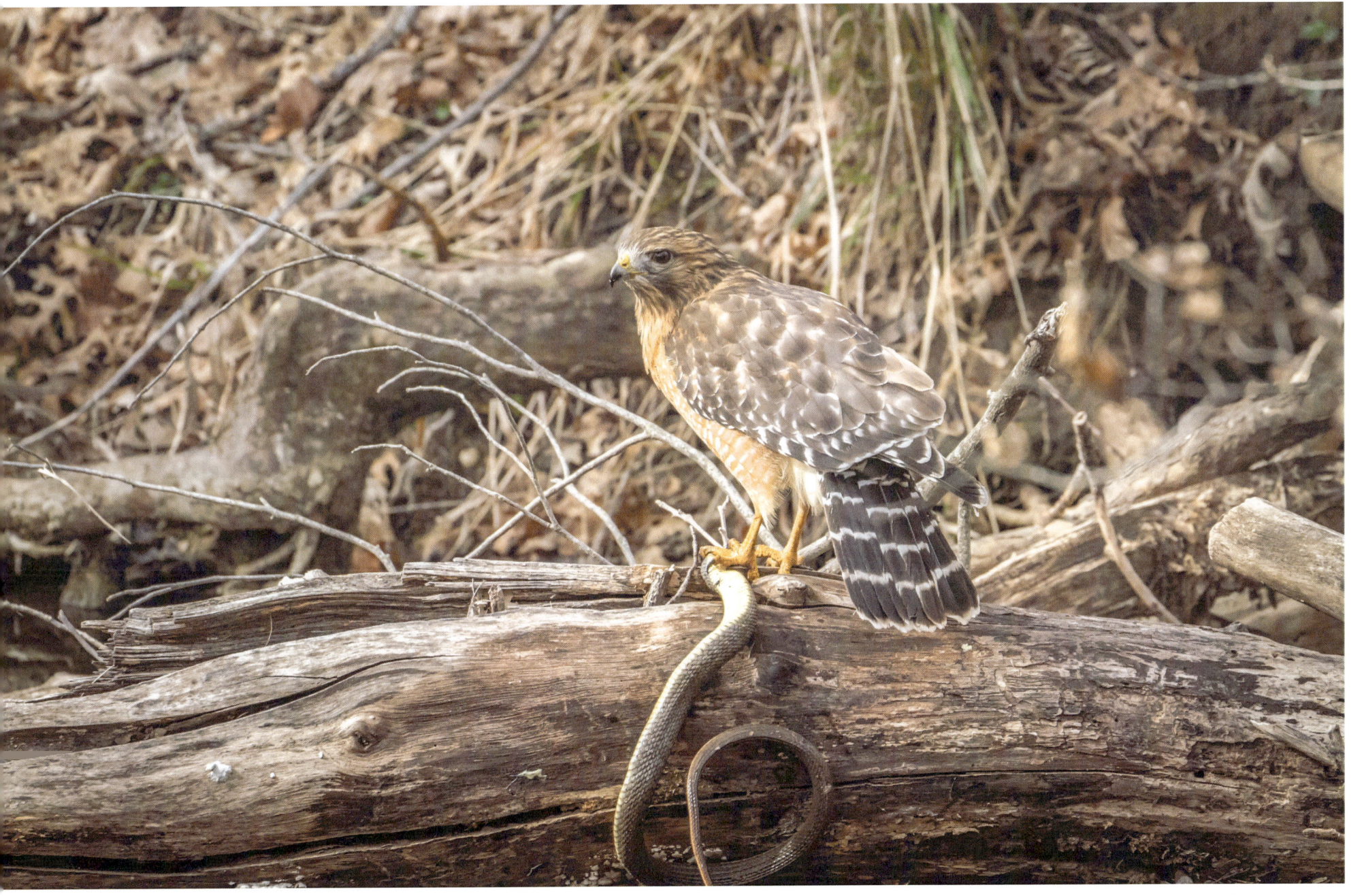

Red-shouldered Hawk Enjoying a Snake for Dinner

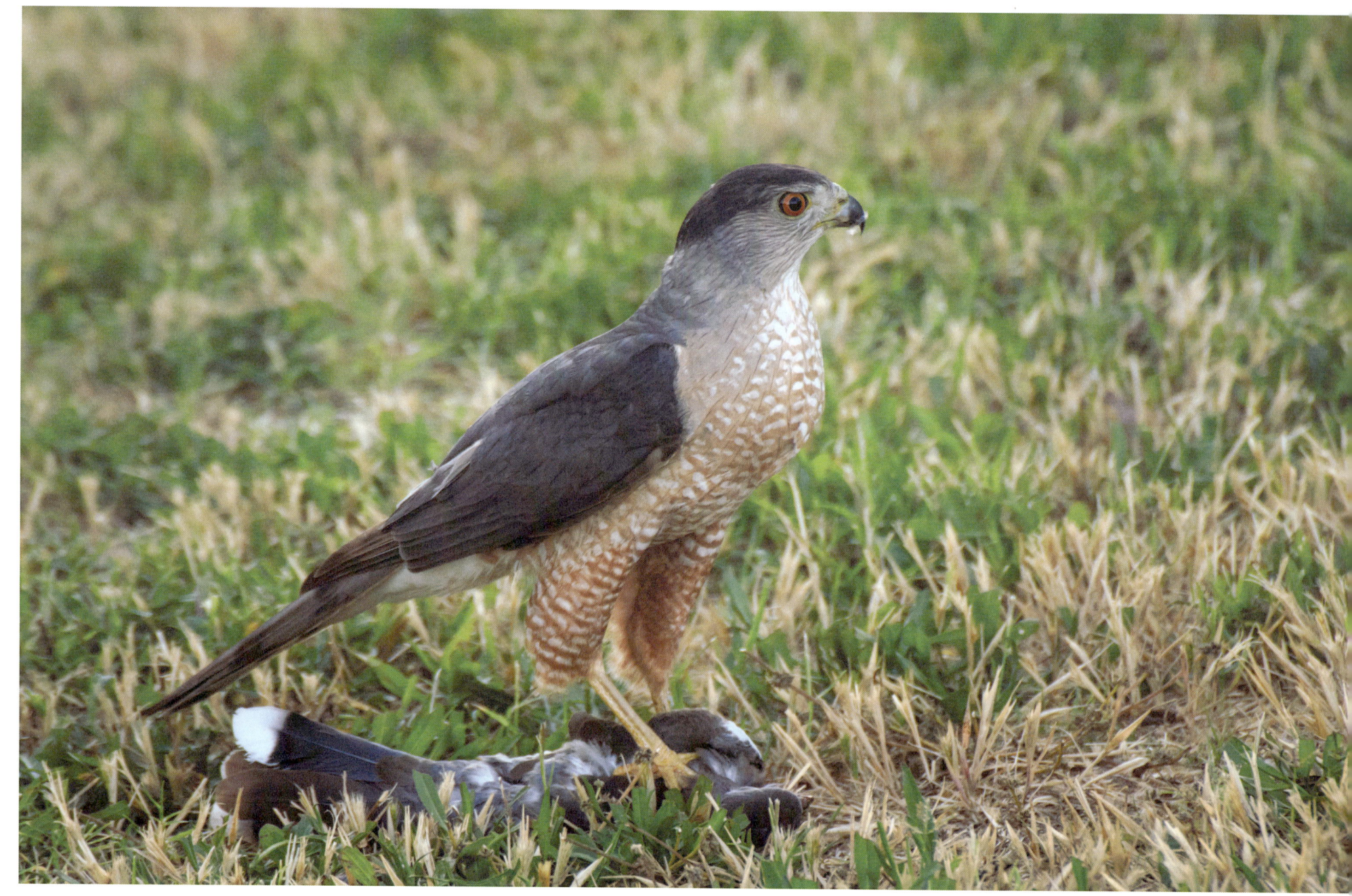

Cooper's Hawk with a Blue Jay Kill

Mississippi Kite

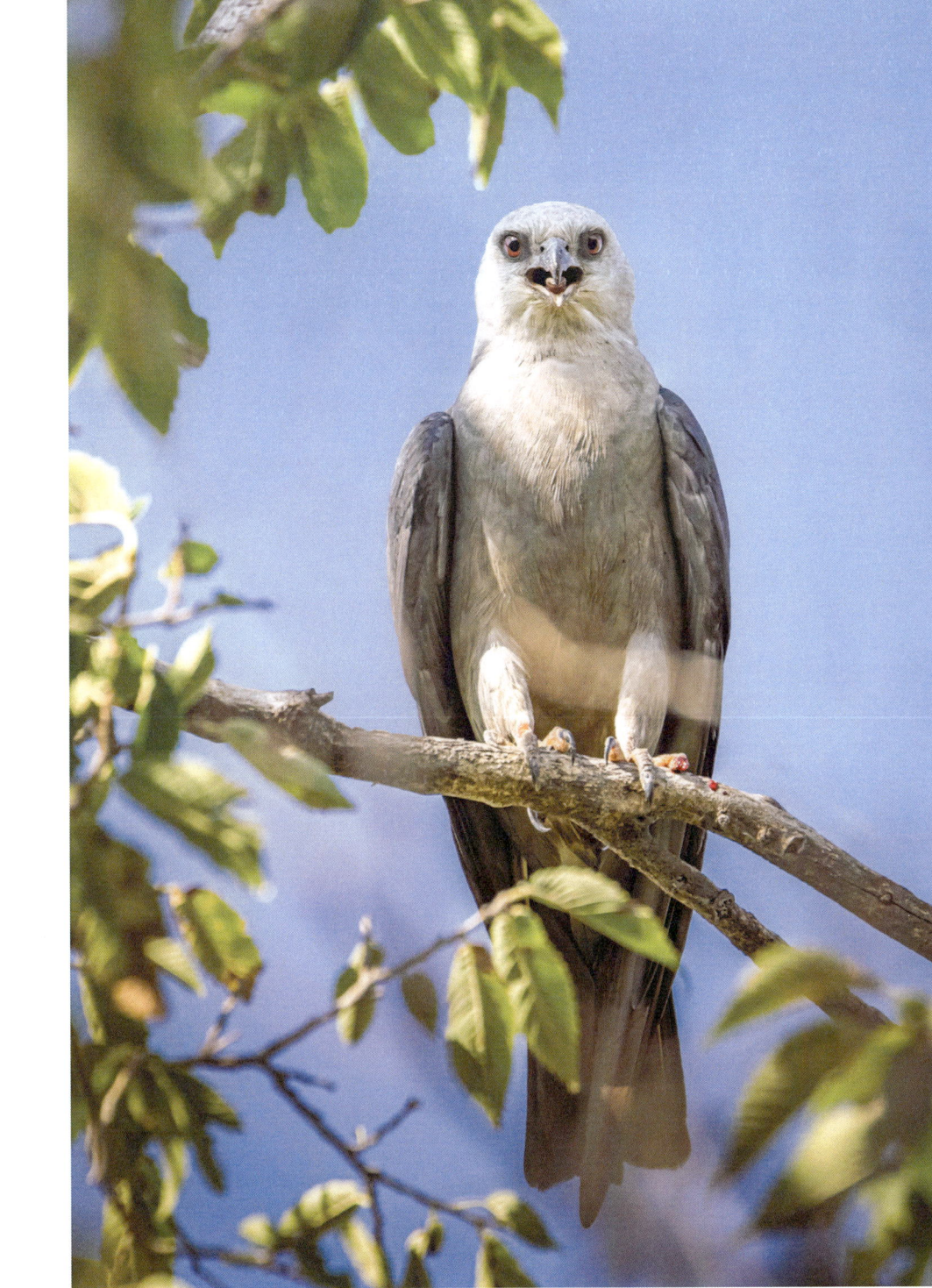

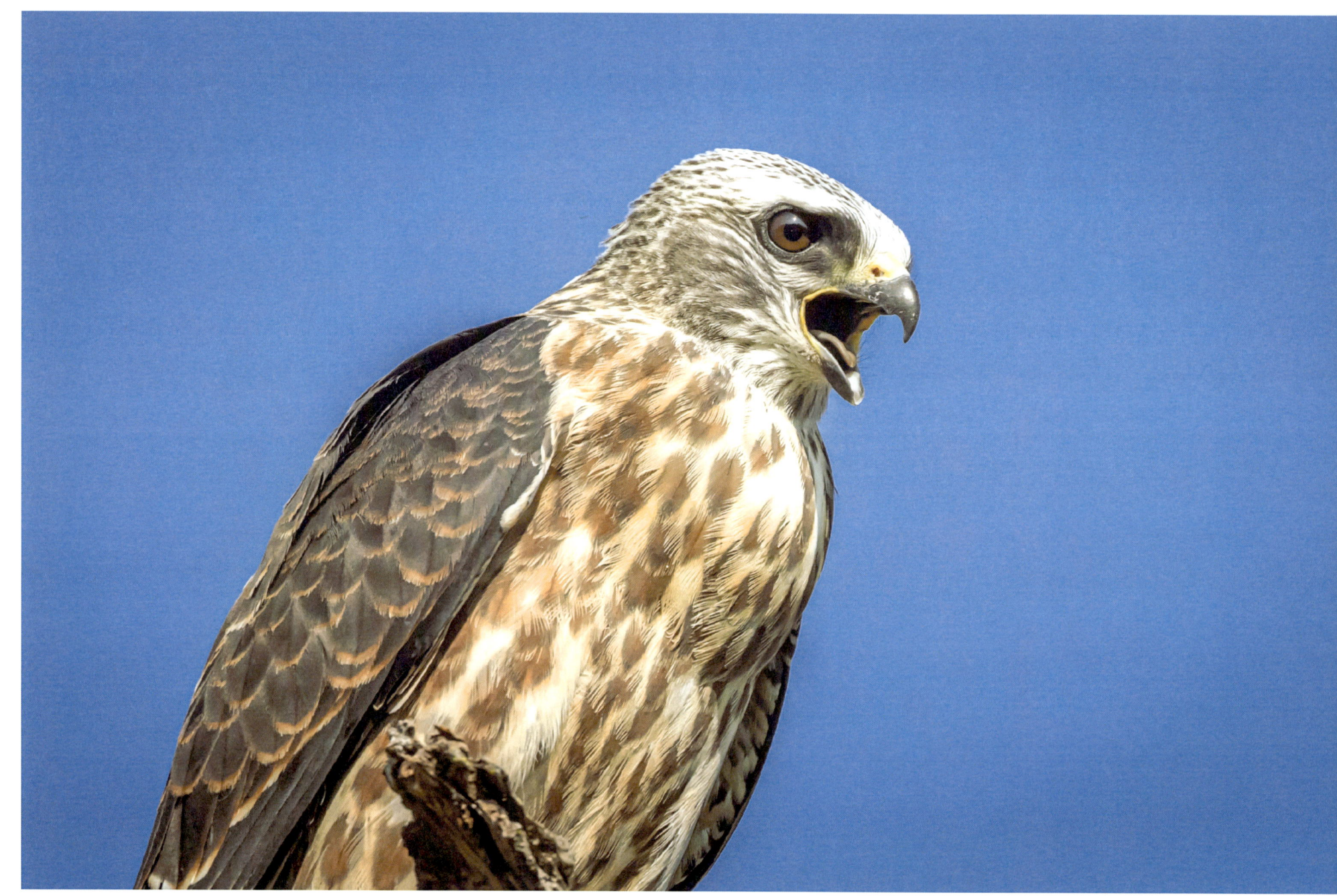
Unhappy Juvenile Mississippi Kite

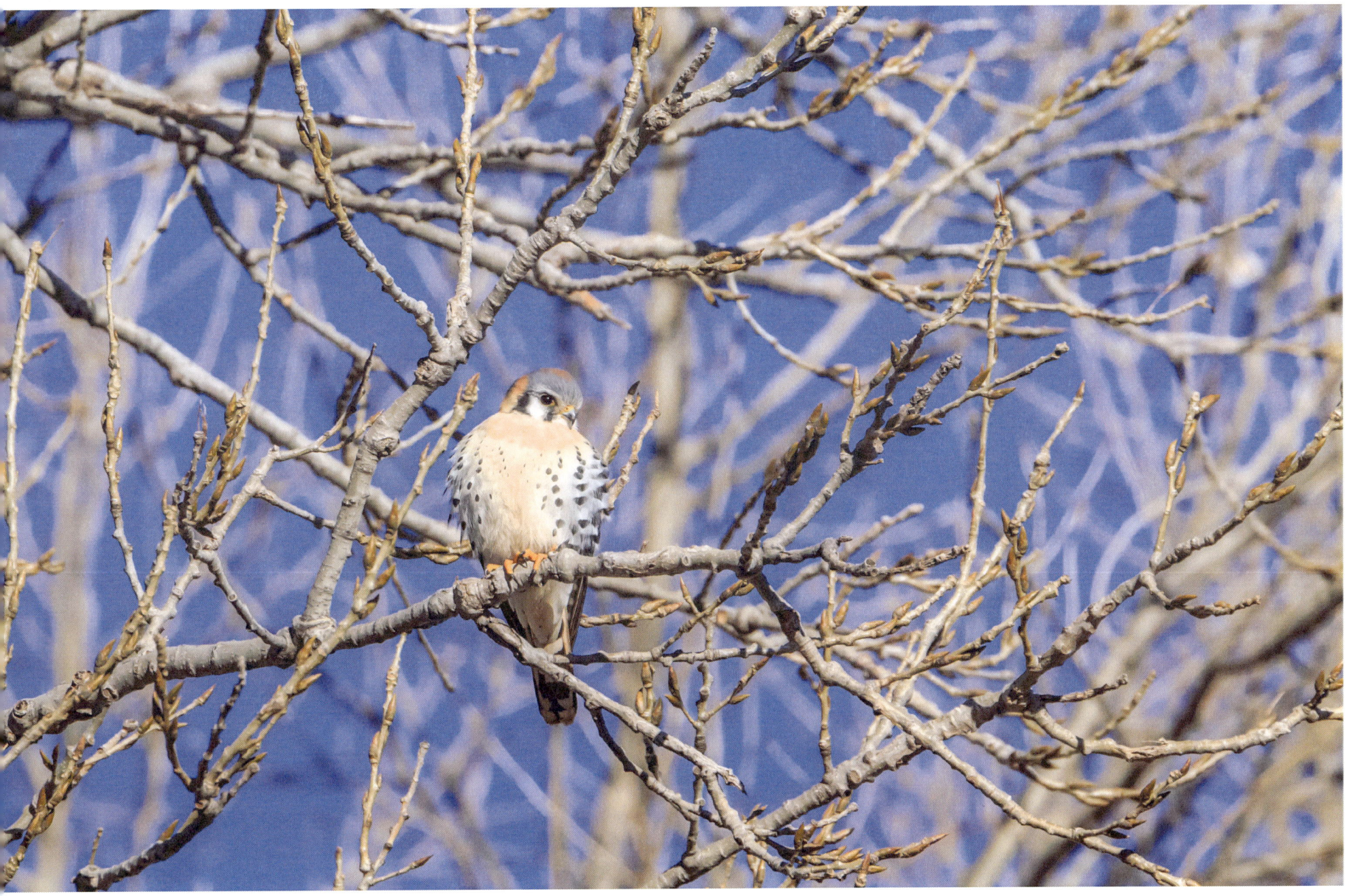

American Kestrel

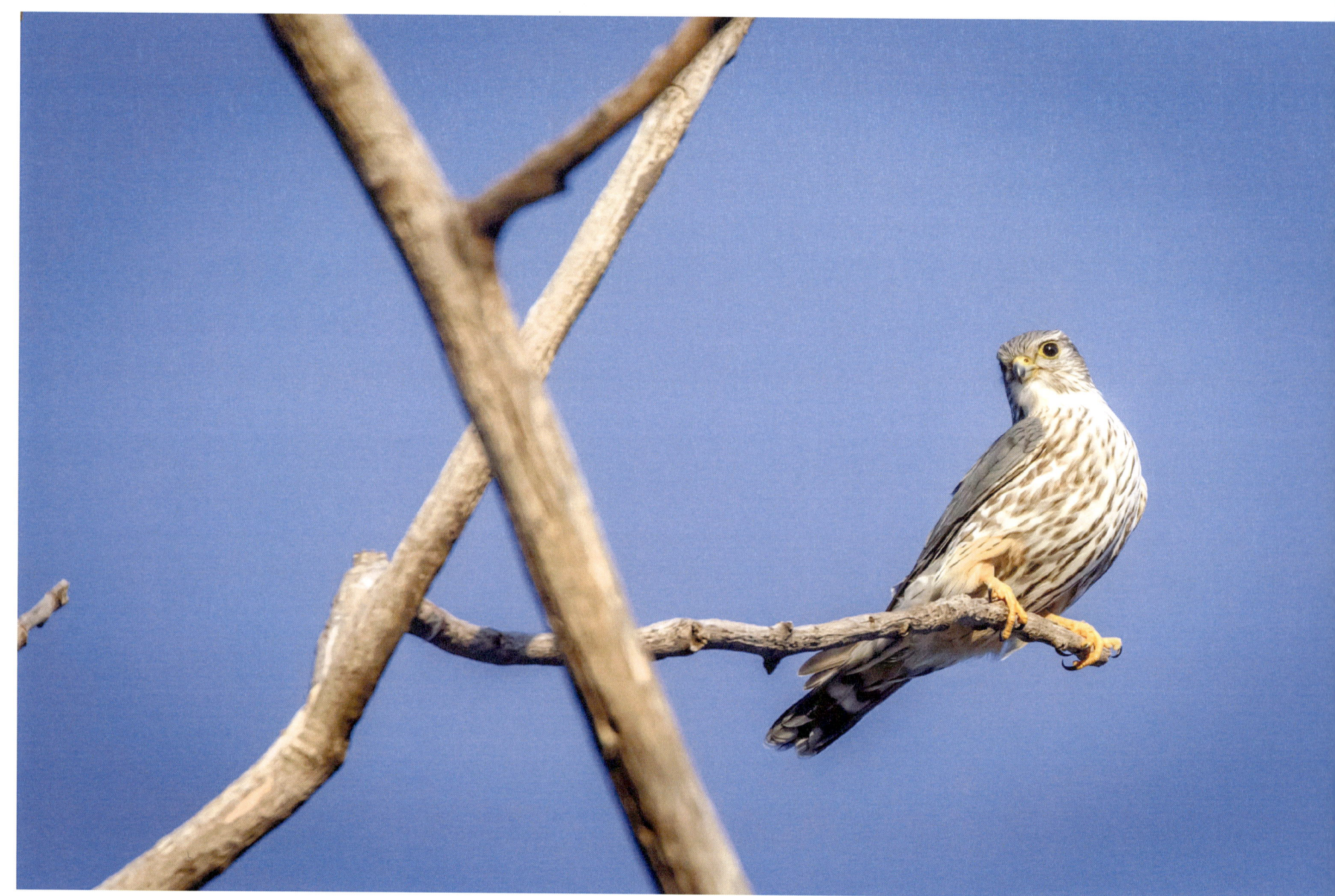

Merlin on a Dead Tree

Small Birds

Bug-catchers and songbirds, along with all the other little birds from hummingbirds to the odd looking (and hard-to-see) common nighthawk, are plentiful in Oklahoma. Situated ideally on the Central Flyway migratory route, it is also more diverse in landforms and plant and animal life than any other similar-sized state. Across the state, eastern woodlands gradually give way to western prairies and desert mountains.

Here the western kingbird and its eastern cousin live in the same field. Oklahoma is the western edge of the range of many eastern species and the eastern edge of many western species. As the seasons change, many of the winged residents leave and make way for others. The population and variety of bird life in Oklahoma is astonishing!

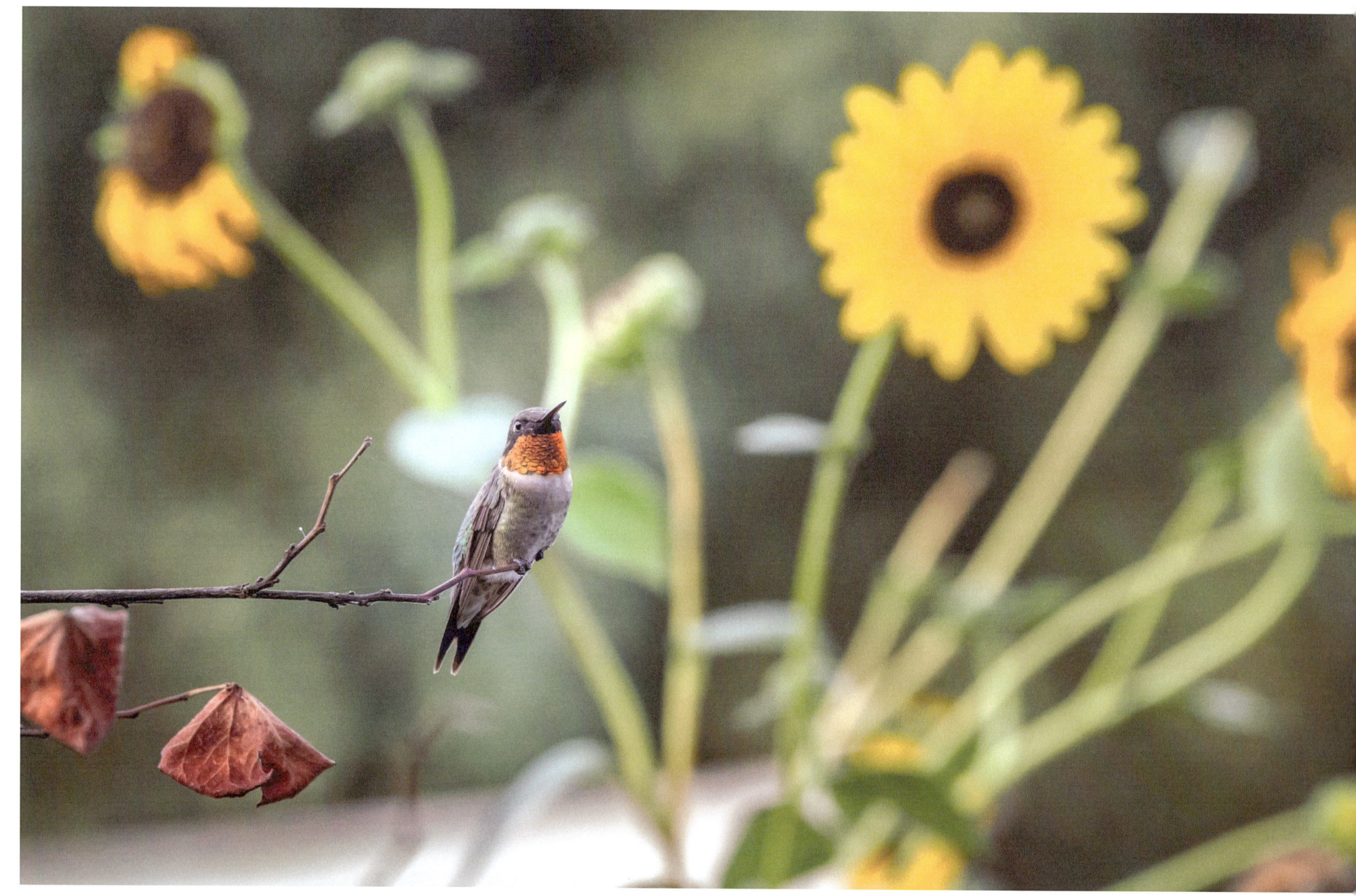

Male Ruby-throated Hummingbird in a Garden

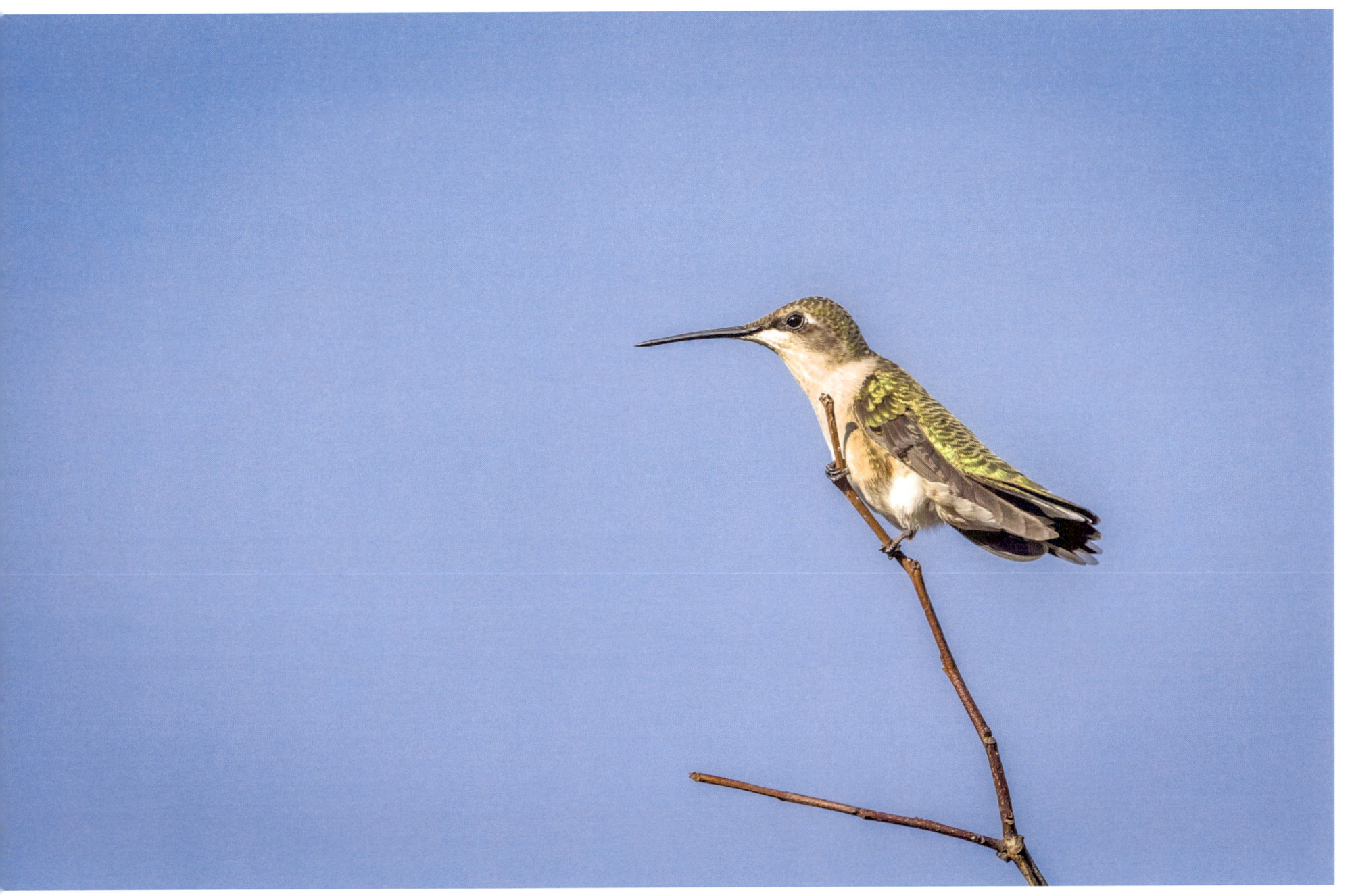

Female Ruby-throated Hummingbird

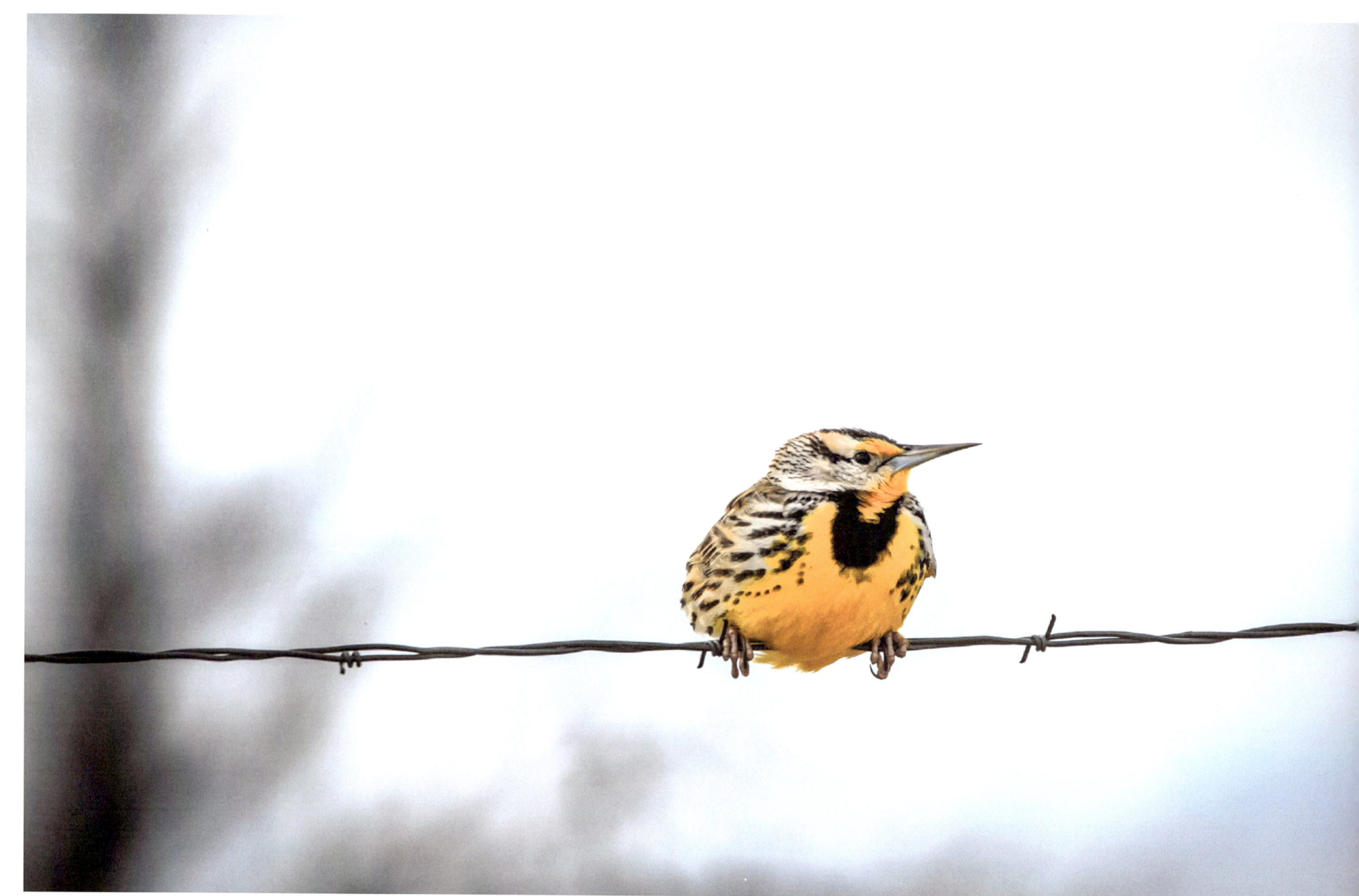

Eastern Meadowlark Perched on a Fence

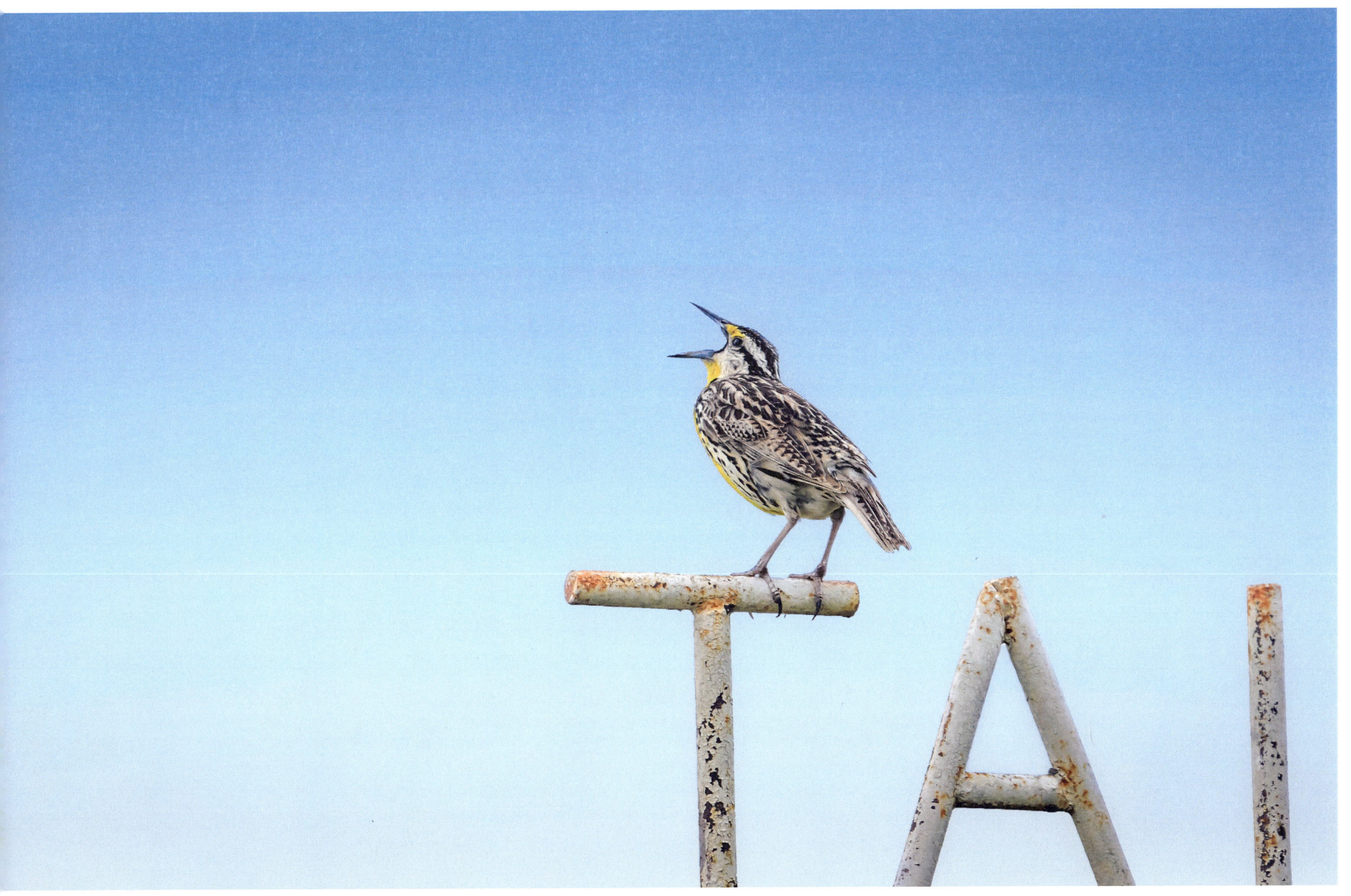

Eastern Meadowlark Perched atop the Entrance Sign at Oklahoma's Tall Grass Prairie Singing Its Welcome to Refuge Visitors

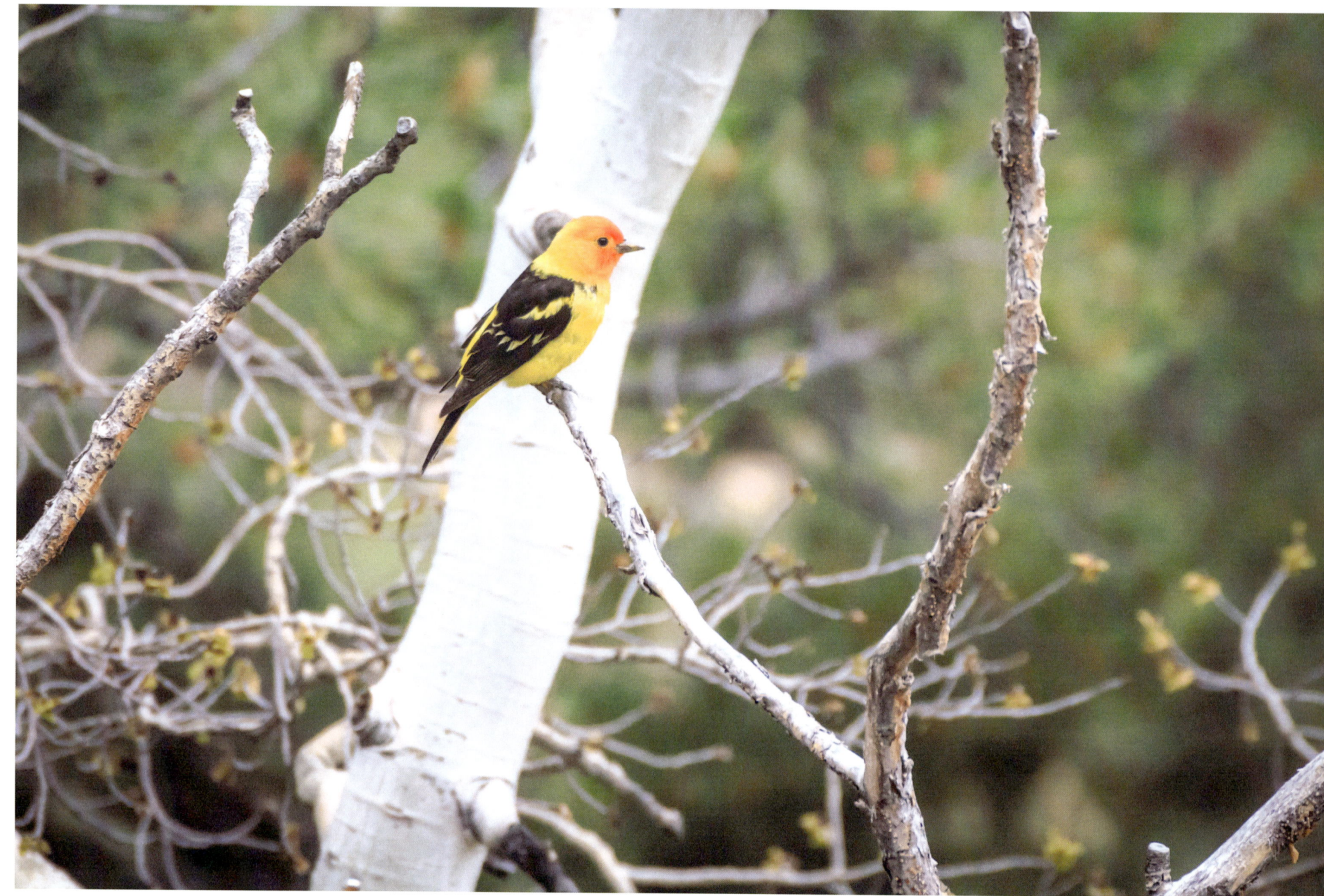

Western Tanager

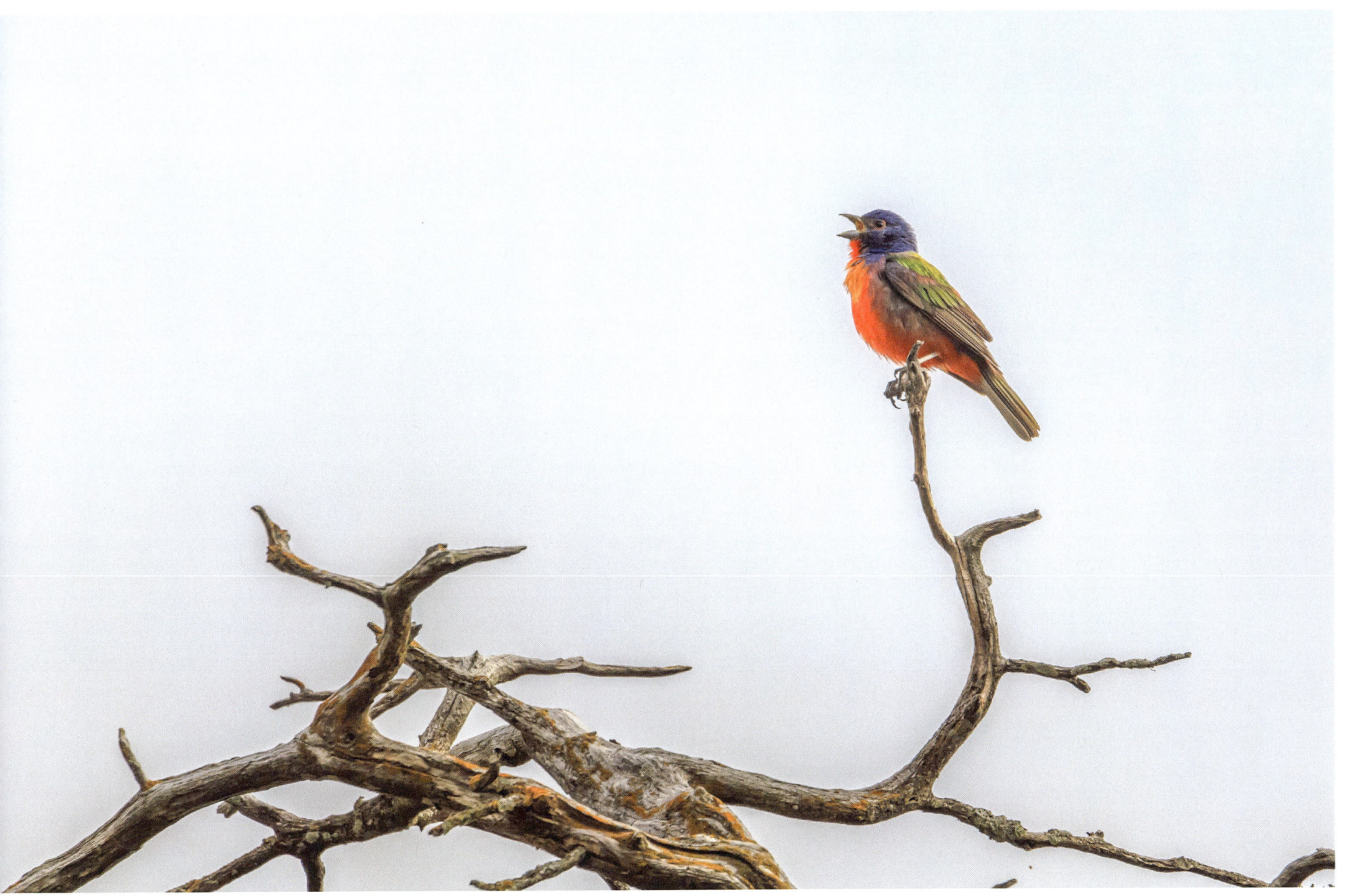

Painted Bunting in Full Song on a Dead Tree

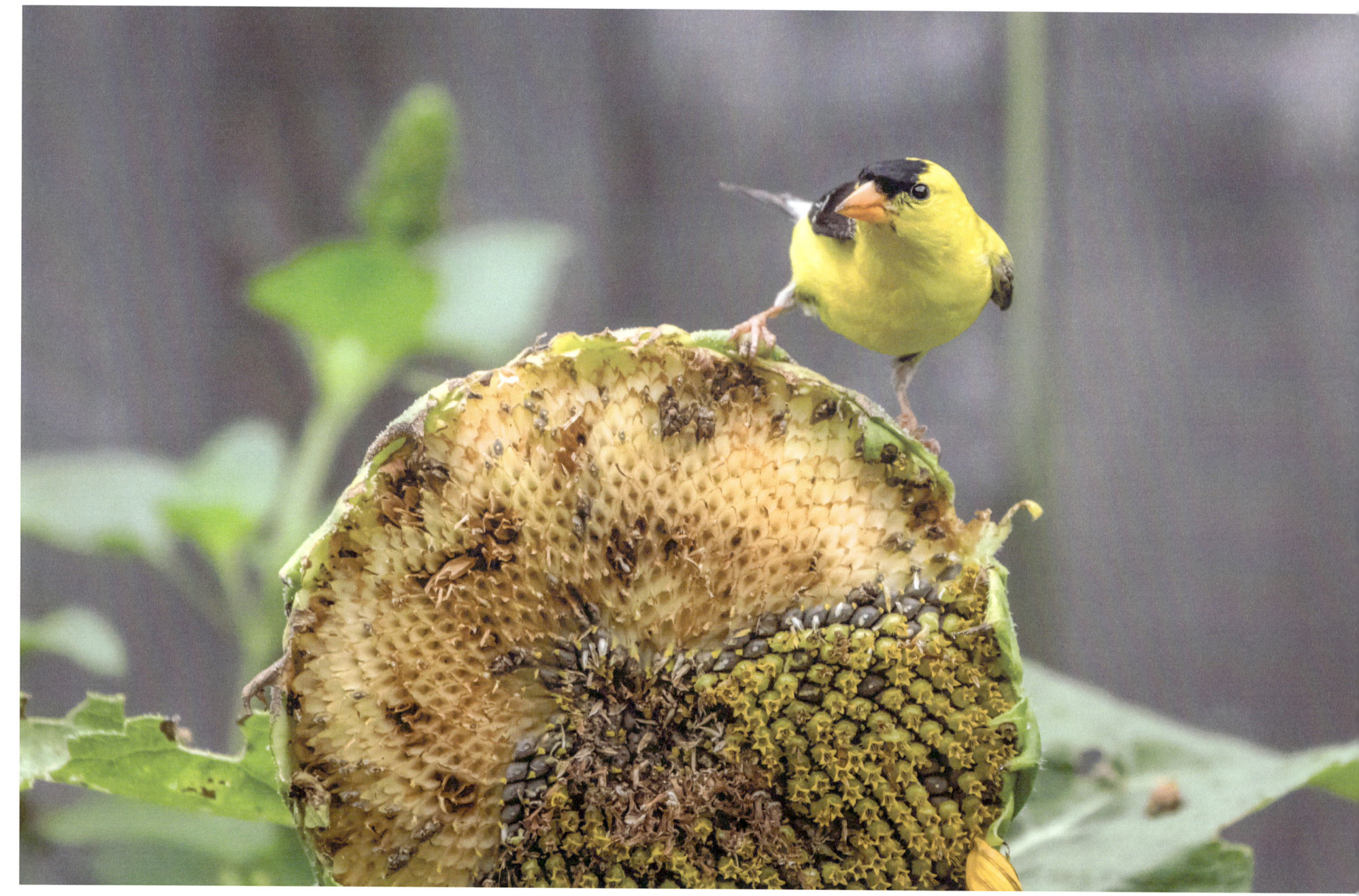

Goldfinch Enjoying Sunflower Seeds in a Garden

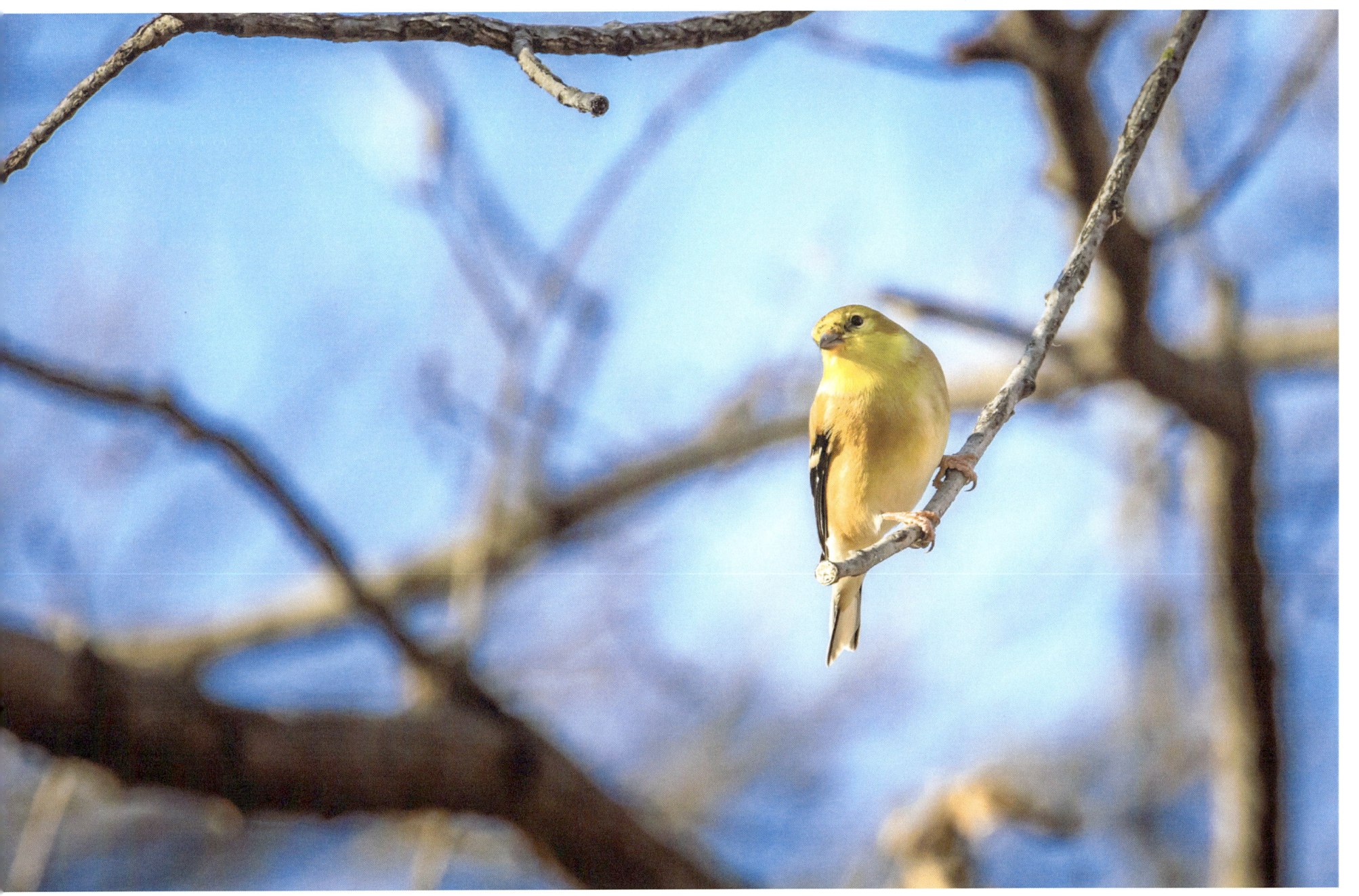

Goldfinch Perched

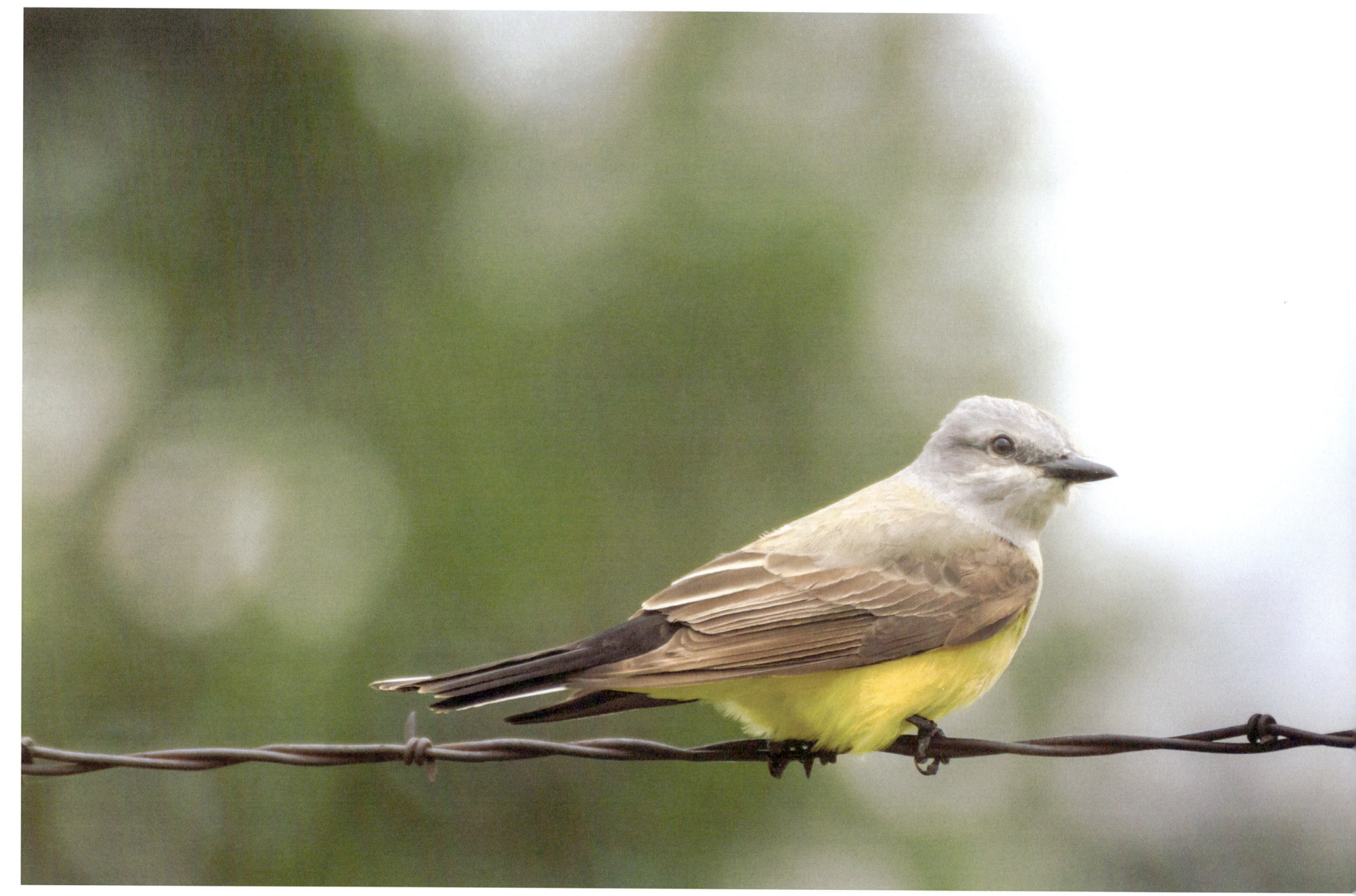

Western Kingbird

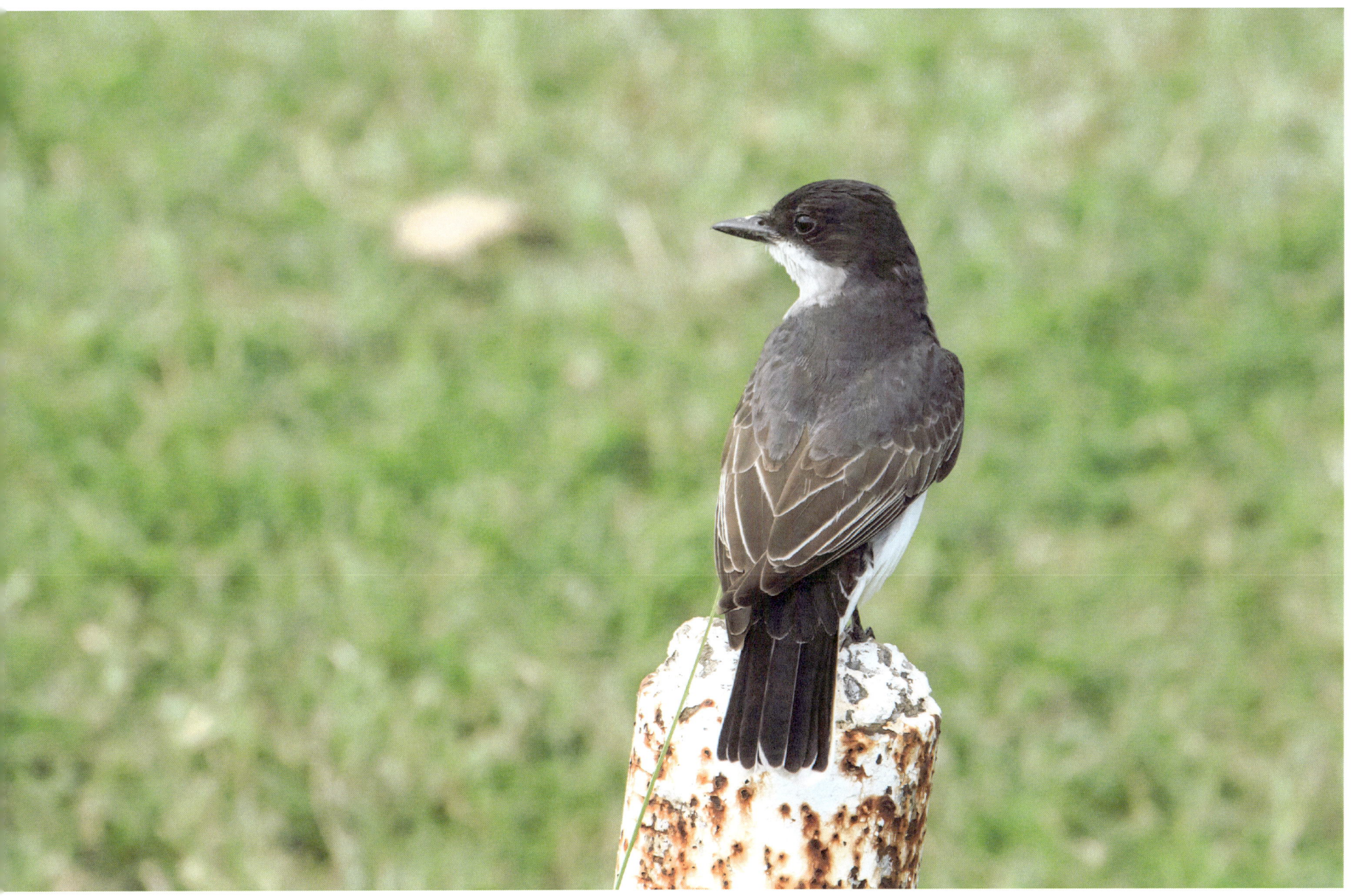

Eastern Kingbird

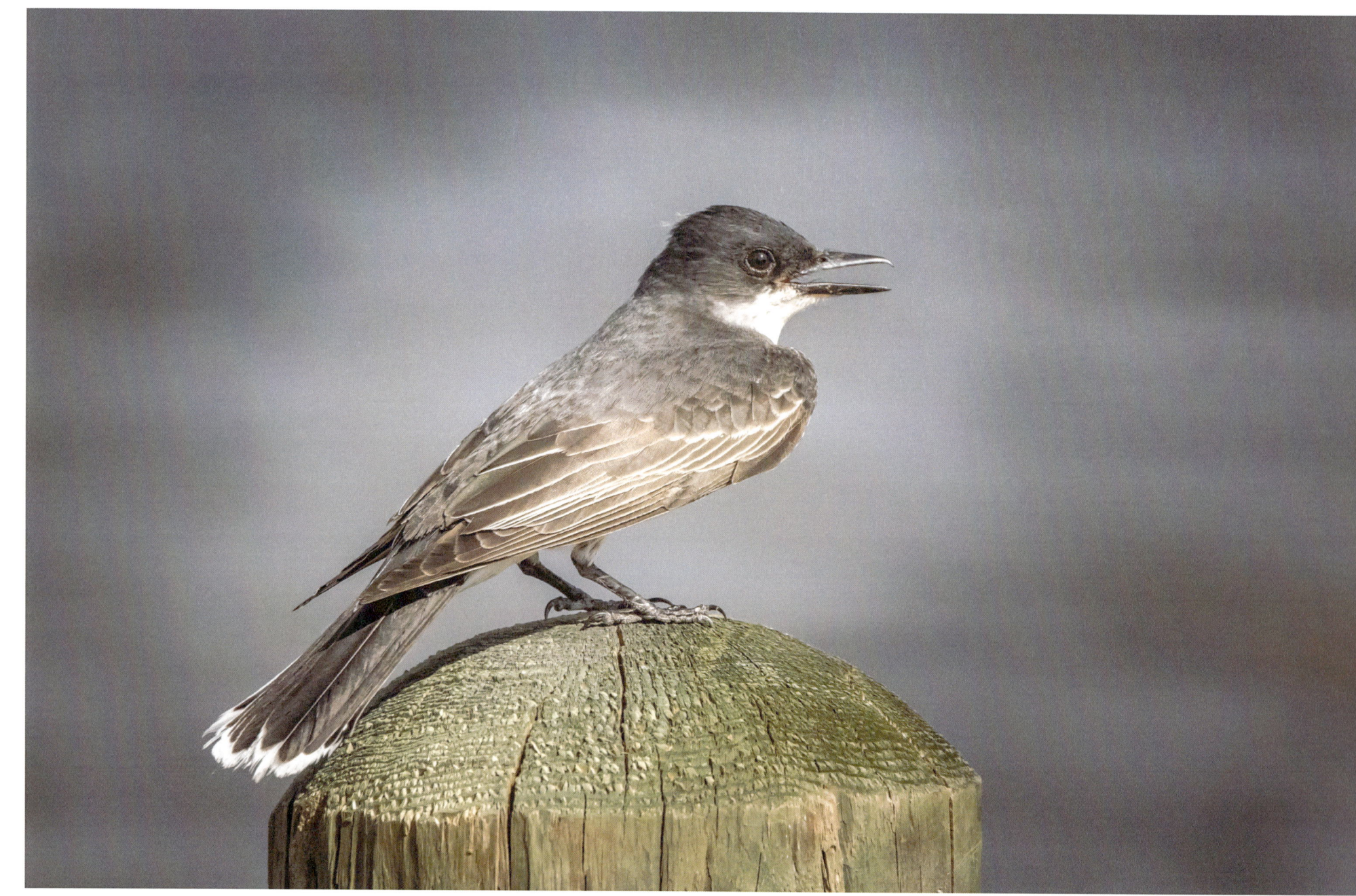

Eastern Kingbird

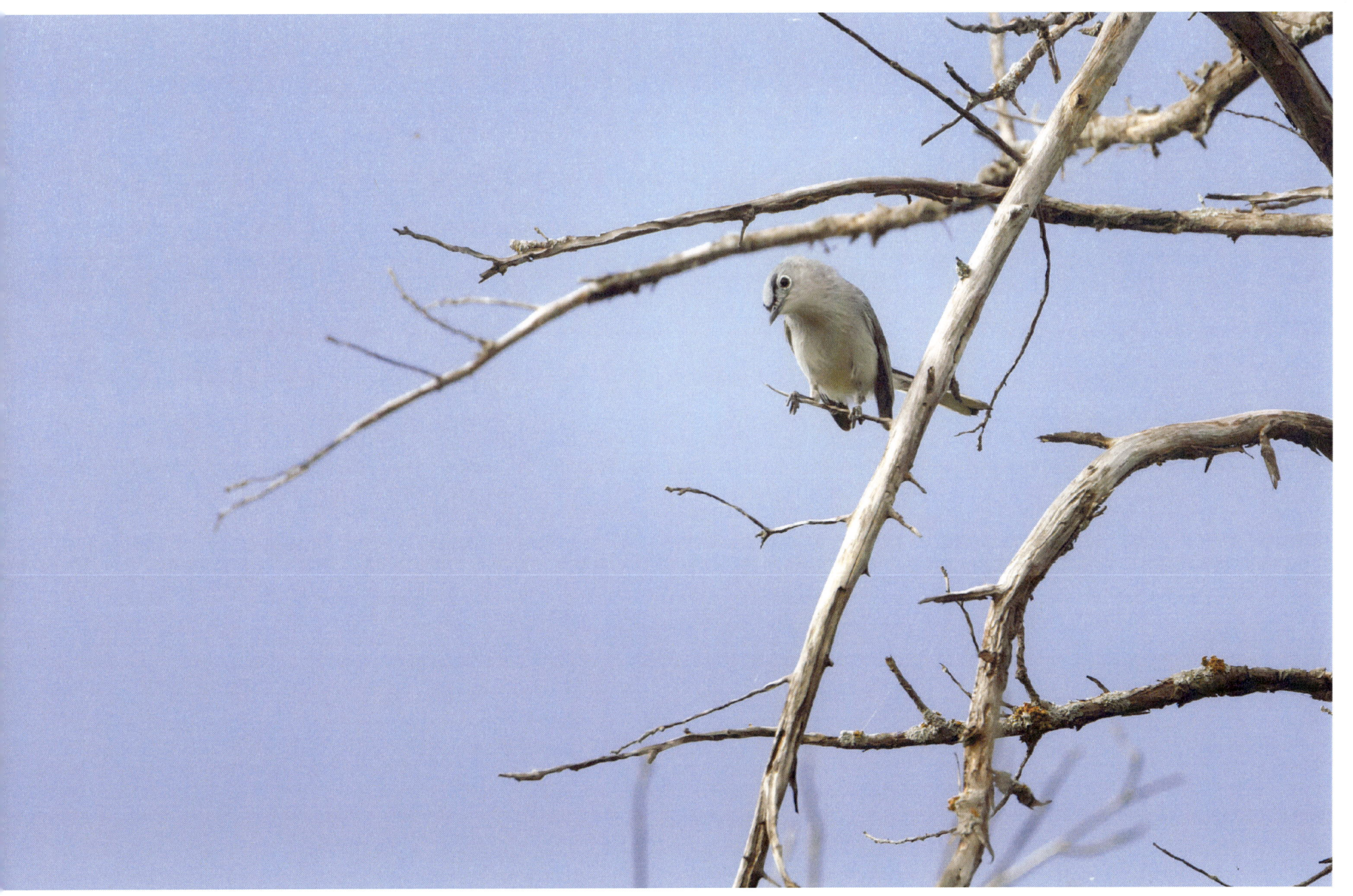

Blue Gray Gnatcatcher

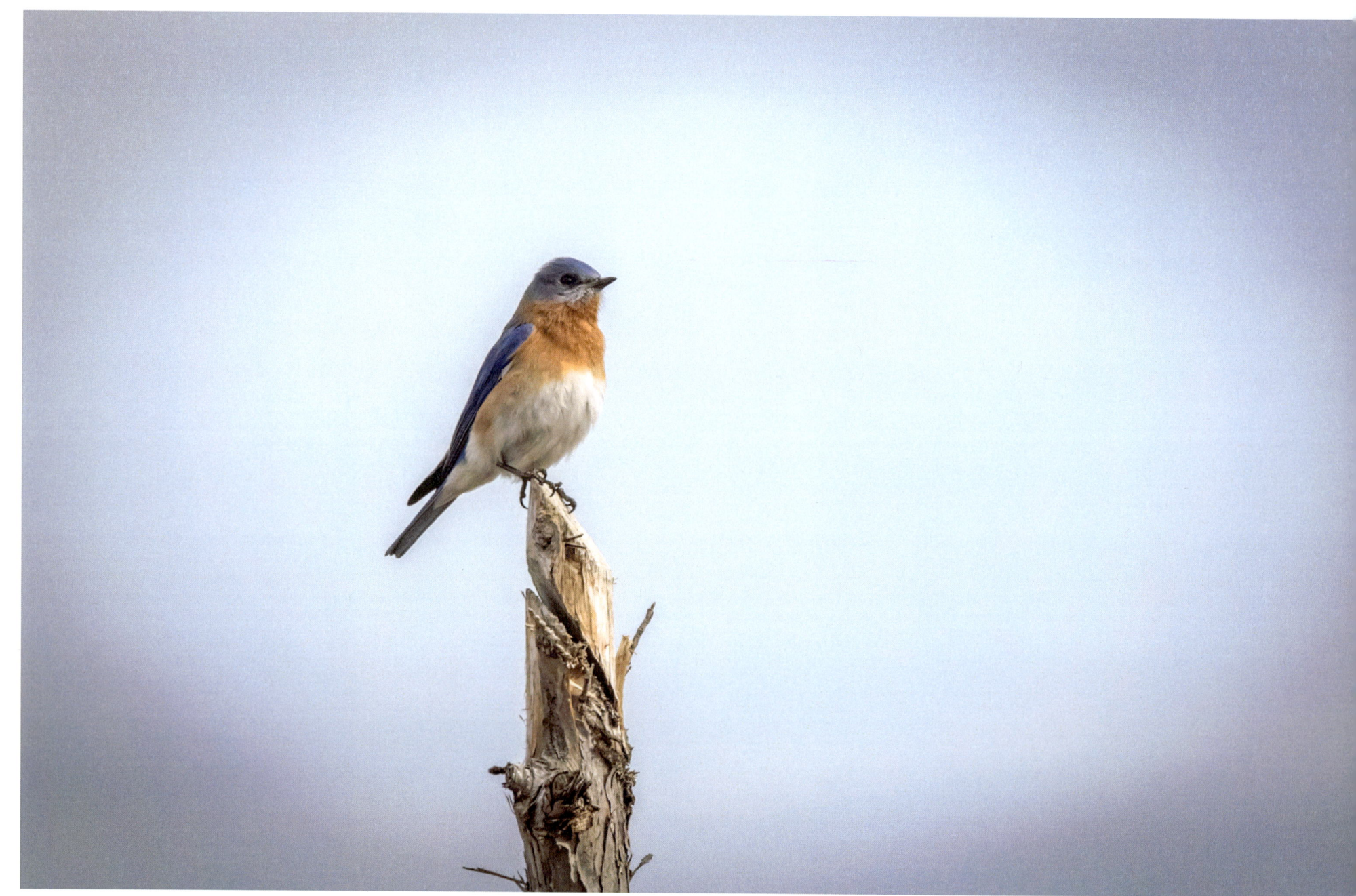

Eastern Bluebird

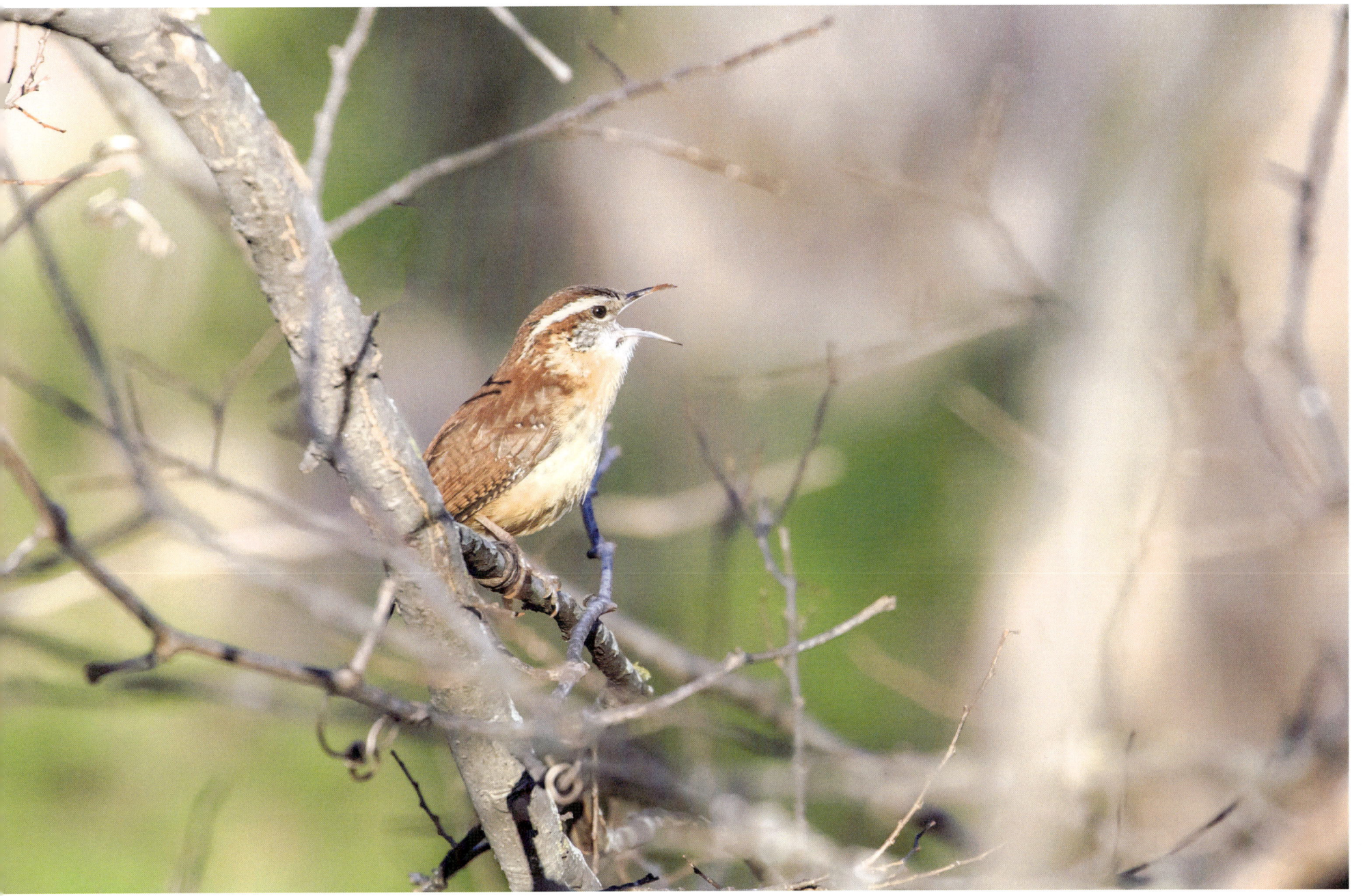

Carolina Wren in Full Song

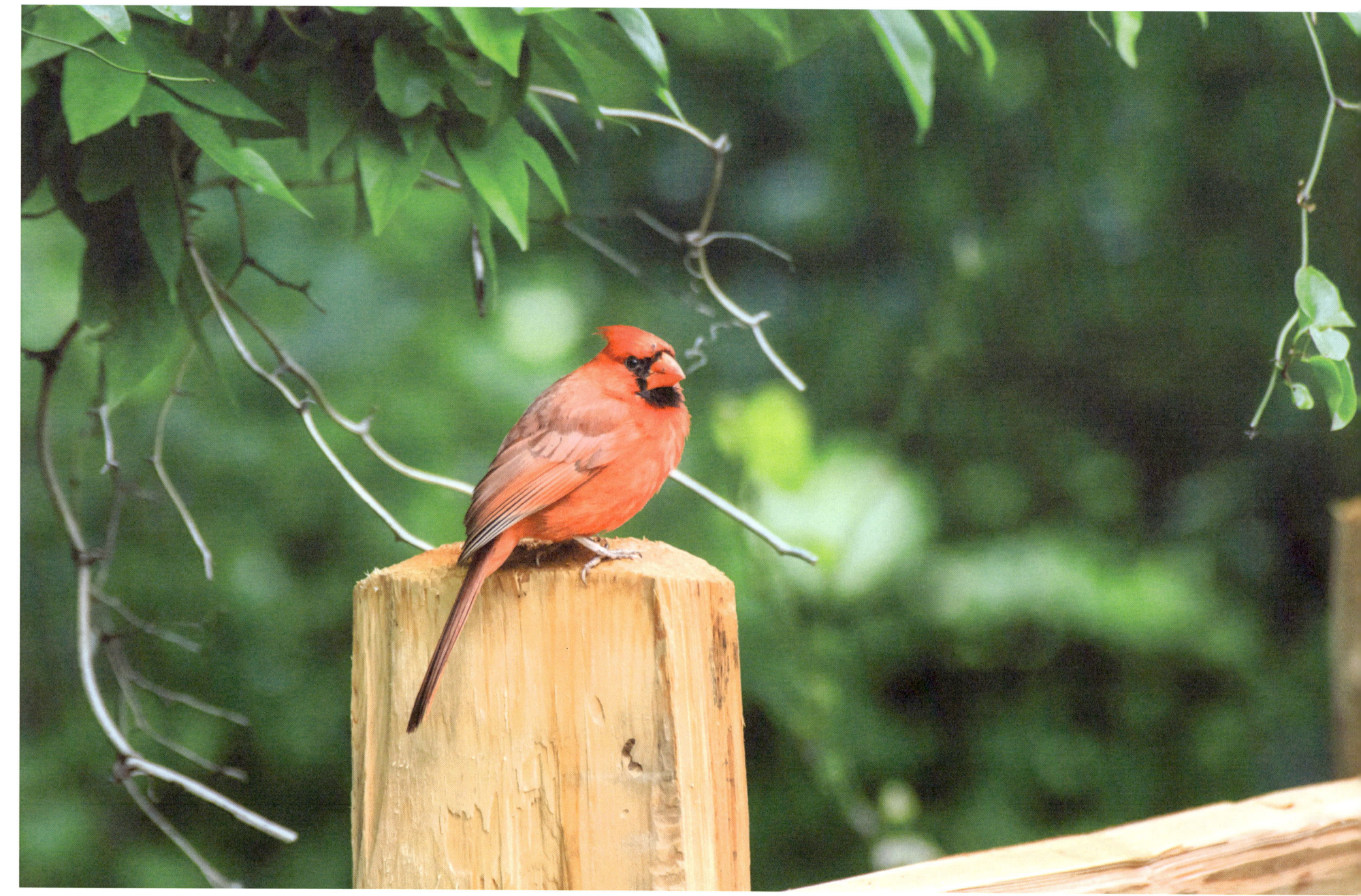

Male Cardinal

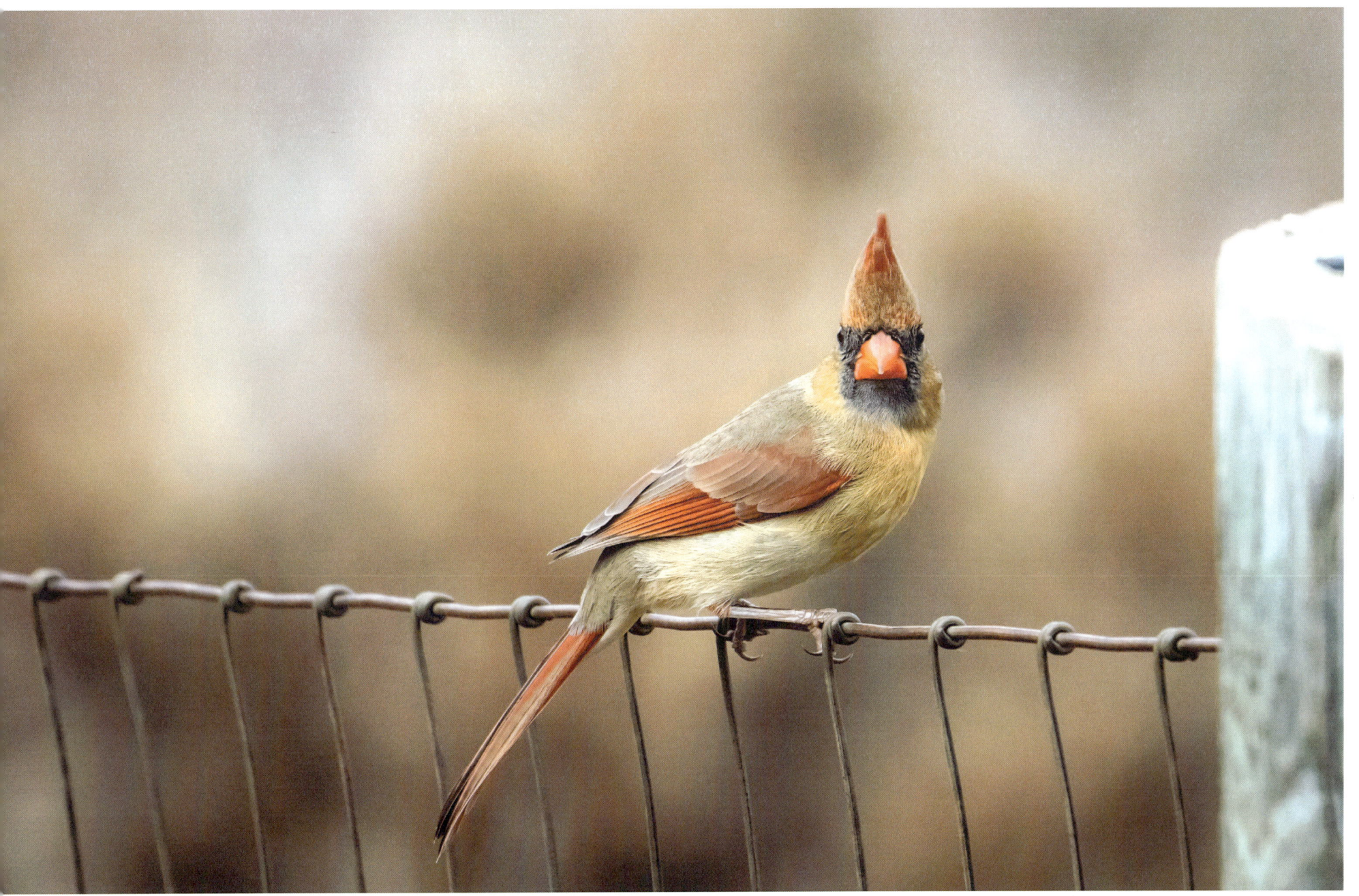

Female Cardinal Resting on a Fence

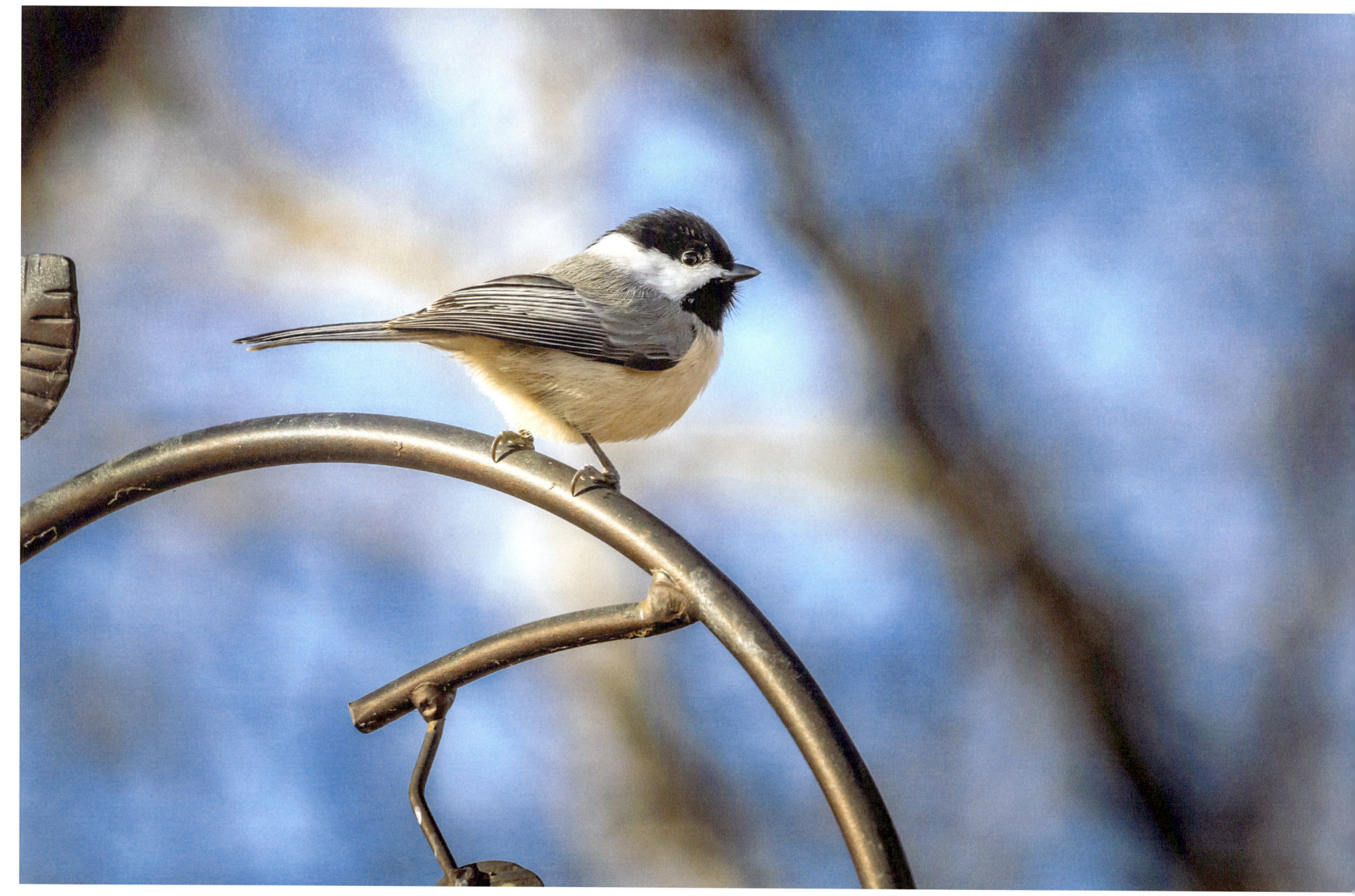

Black-capped Chickadee

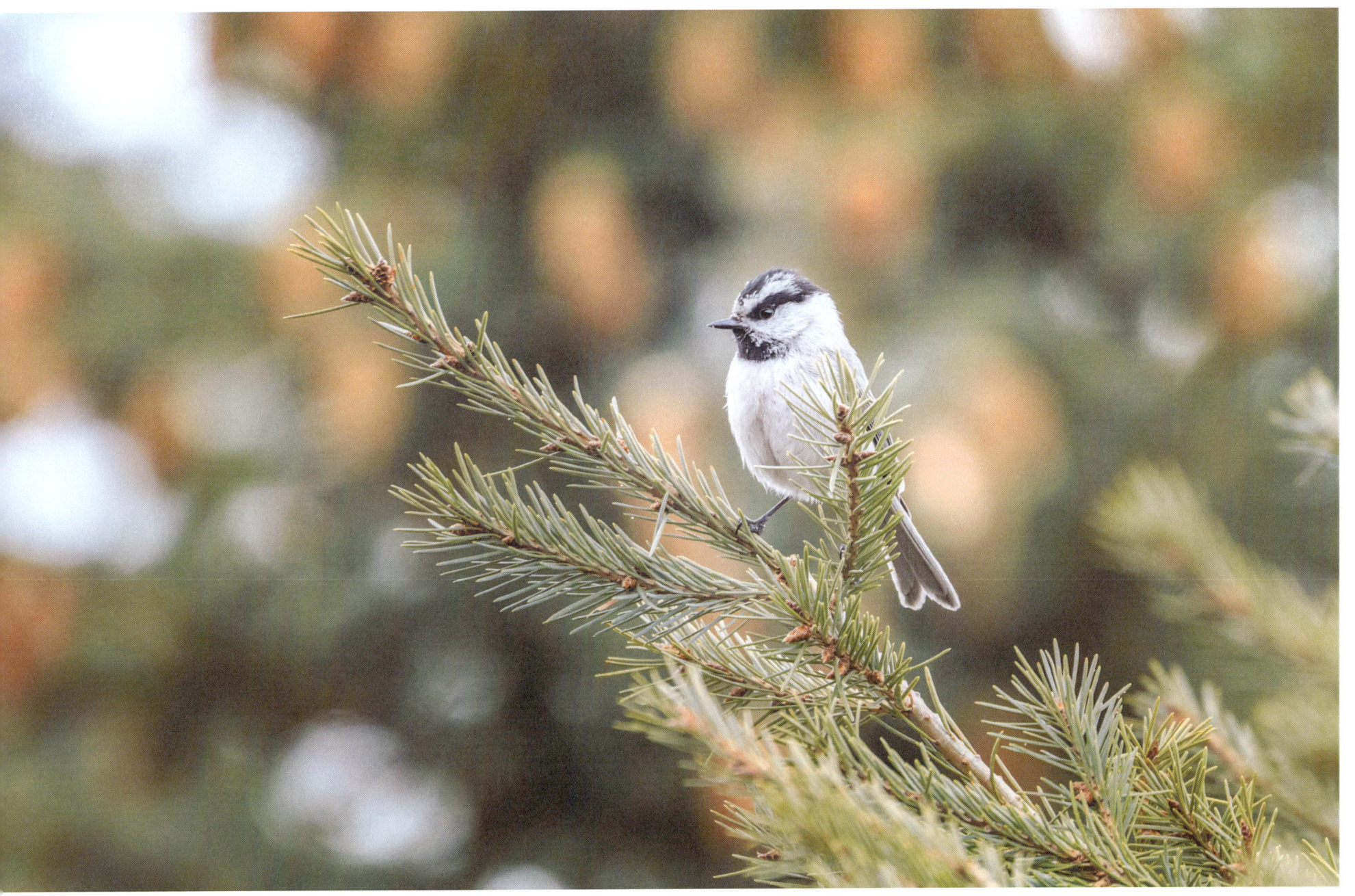

Mountain Chickadee

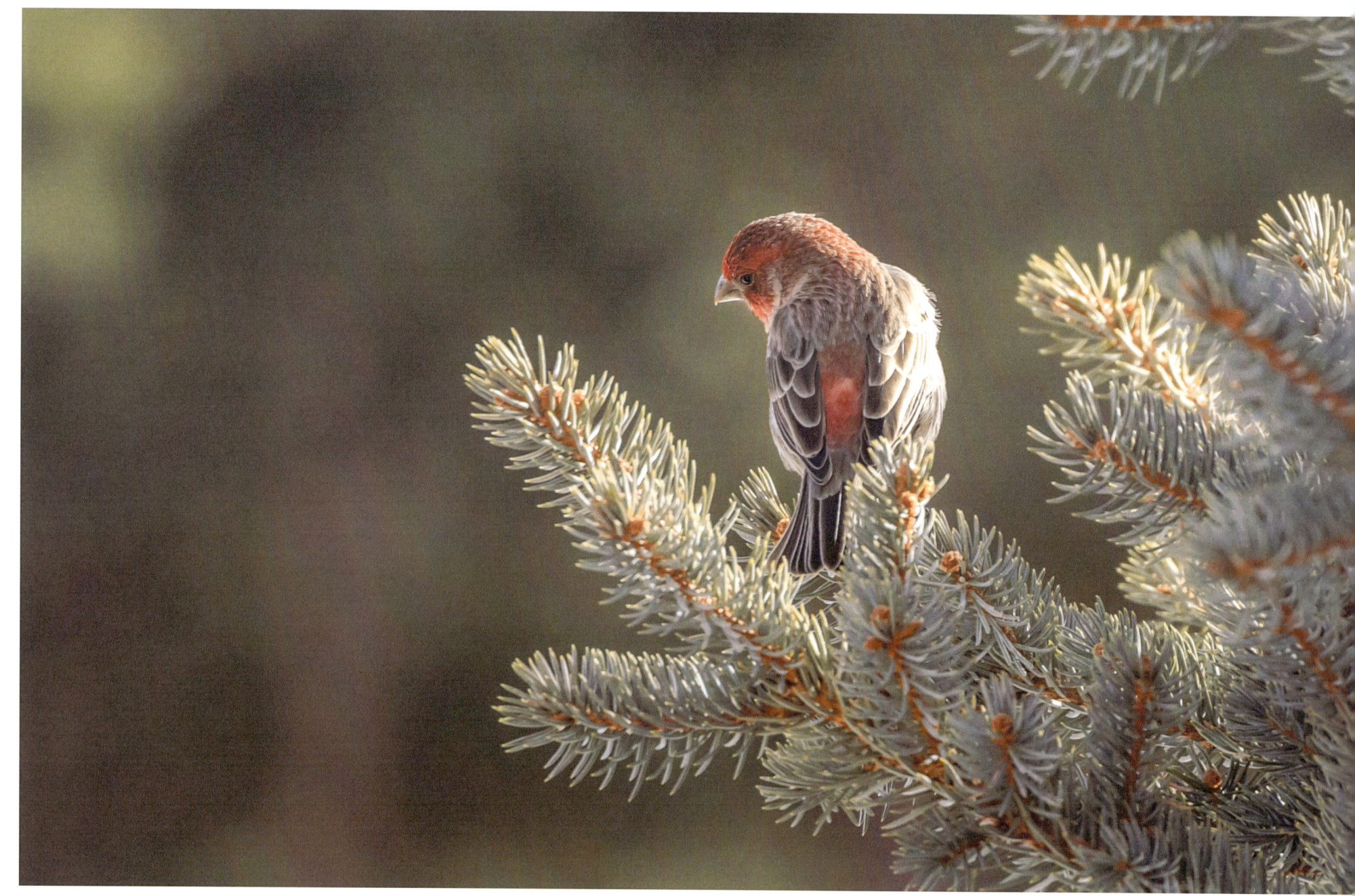

House Finch Resting in a Tree and Showing Off His Beautiful Back

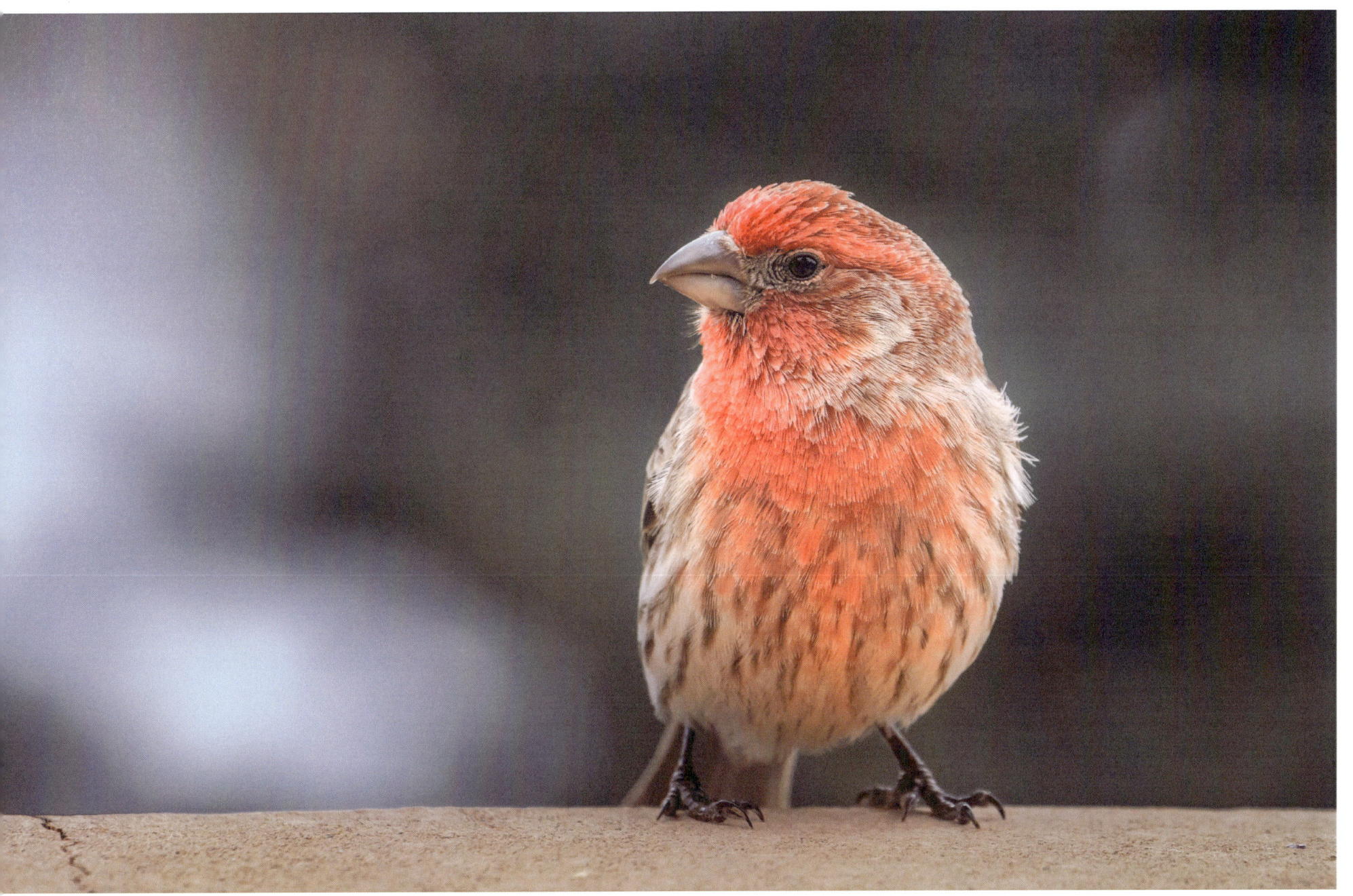

House Finch Close Up

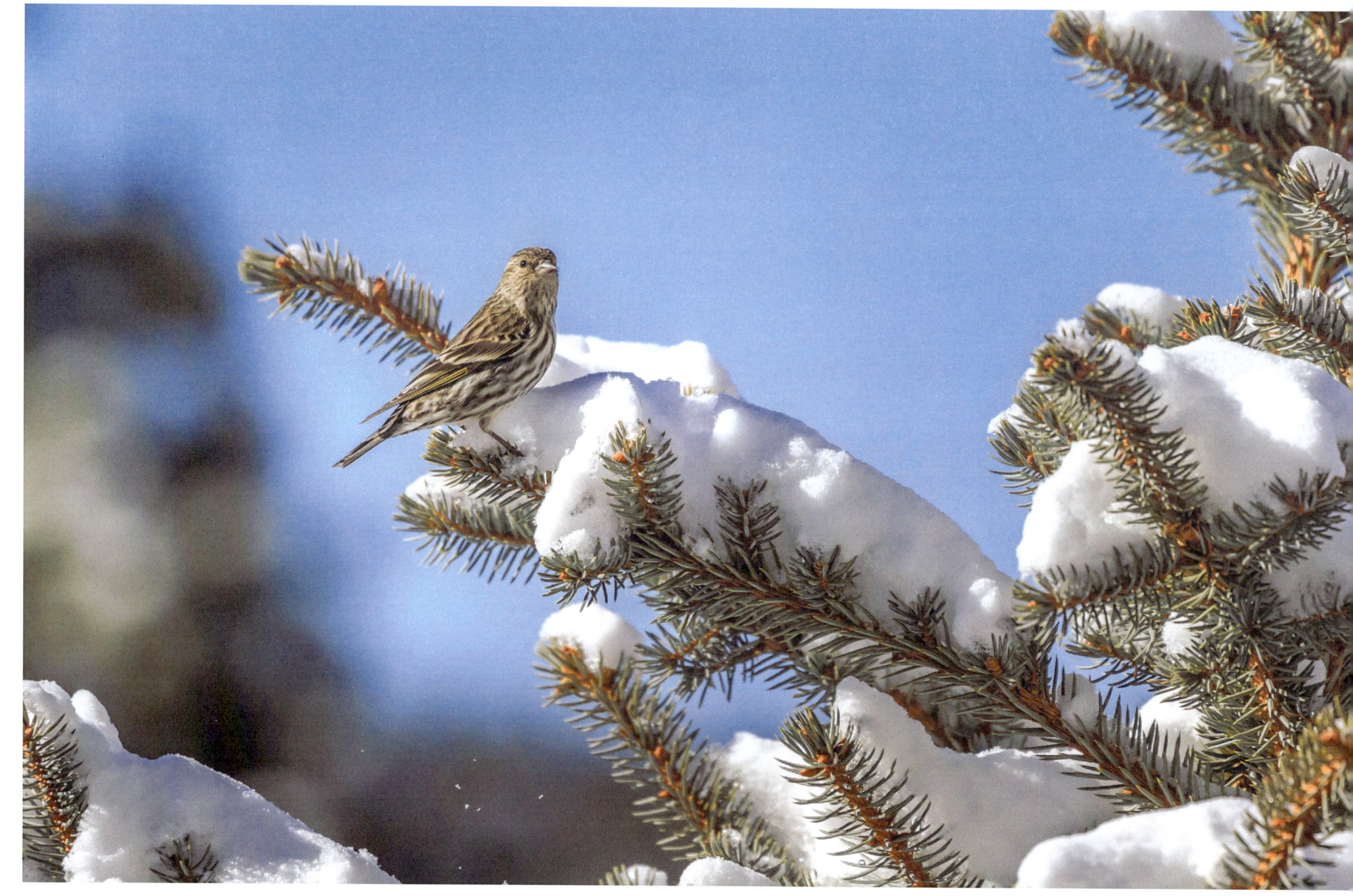

Pine Siskin in the Snow

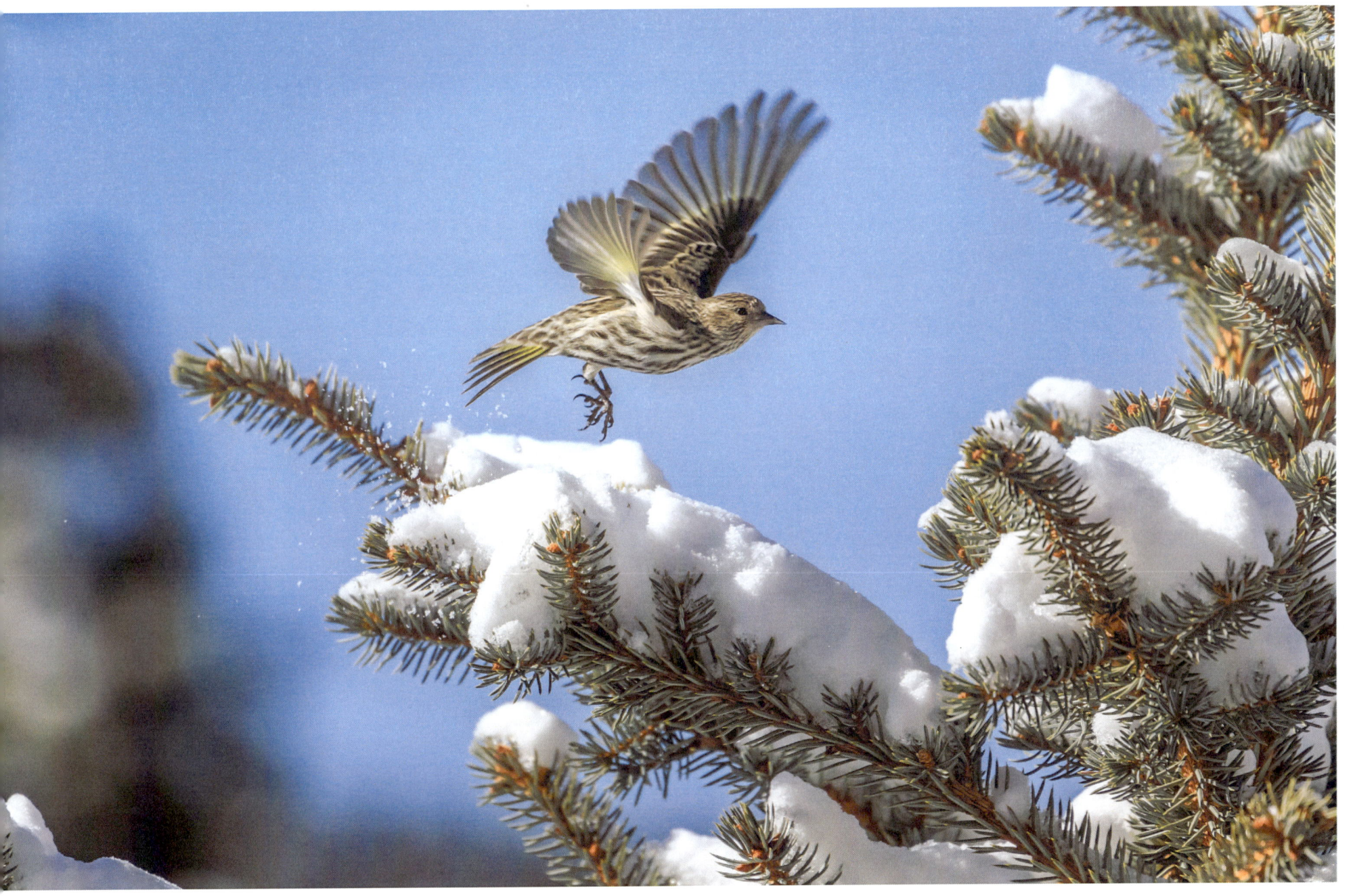

Pine Siskin Just Getting Airborne

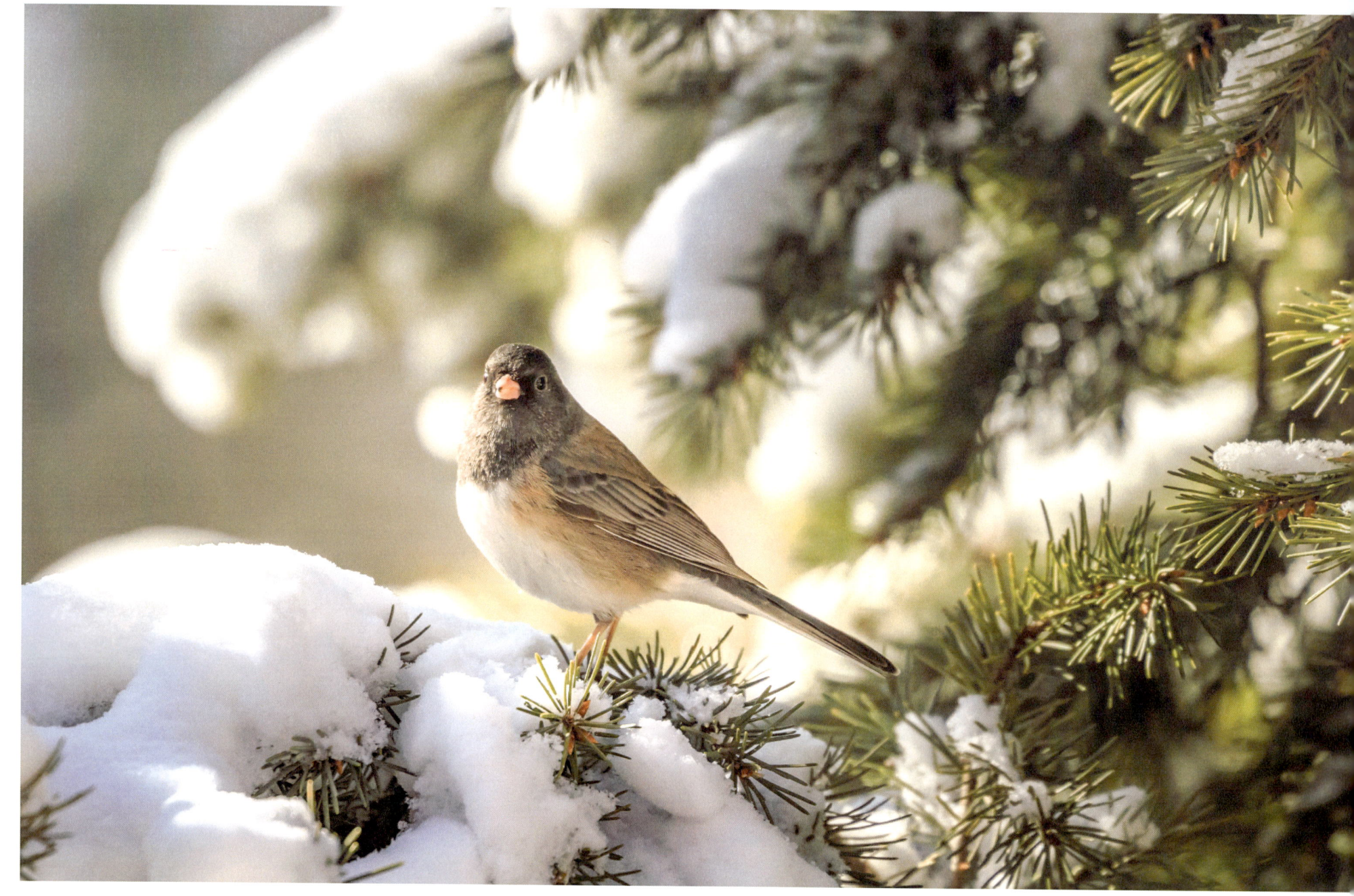

Dark-eyed Junco

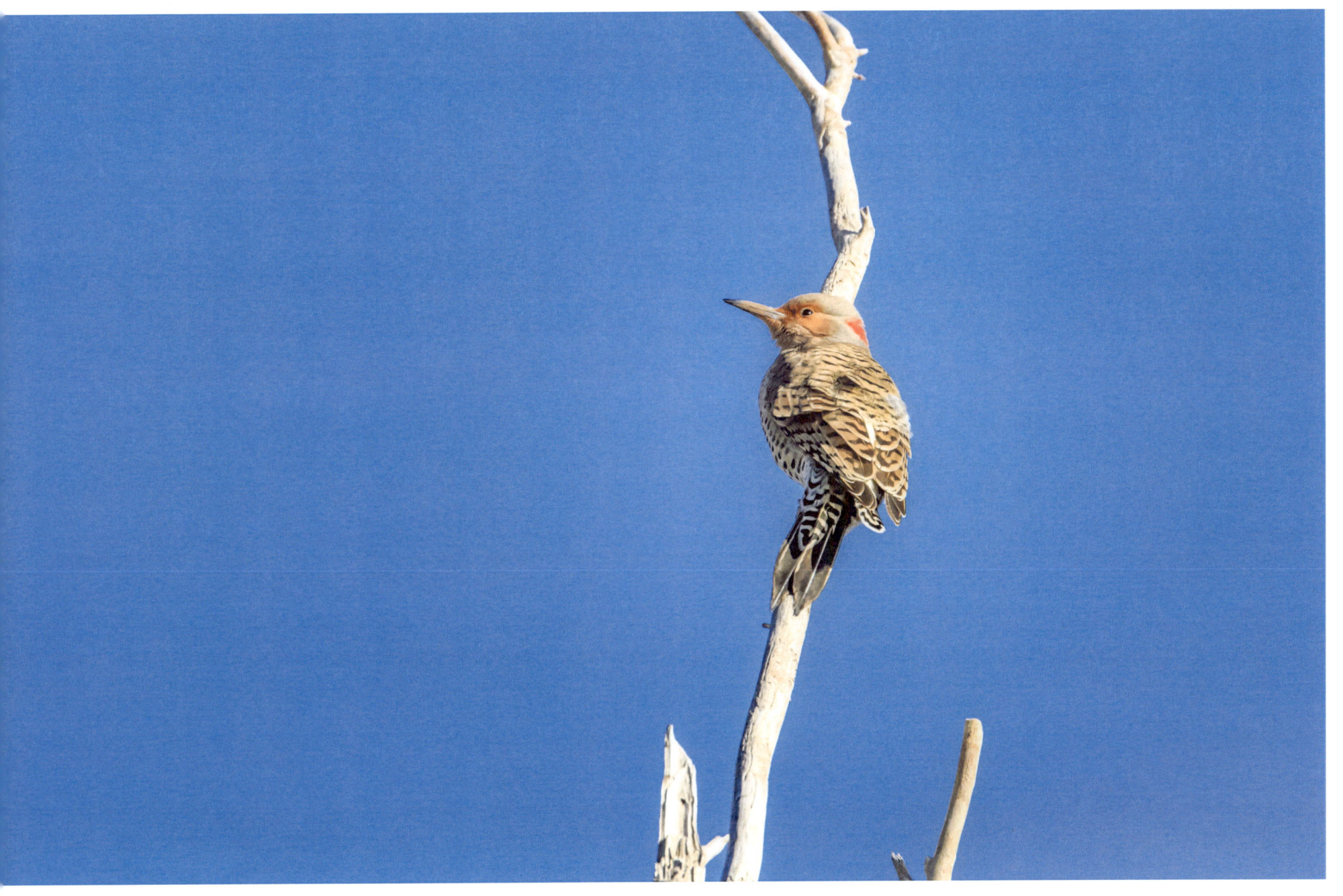

Northern Flicker

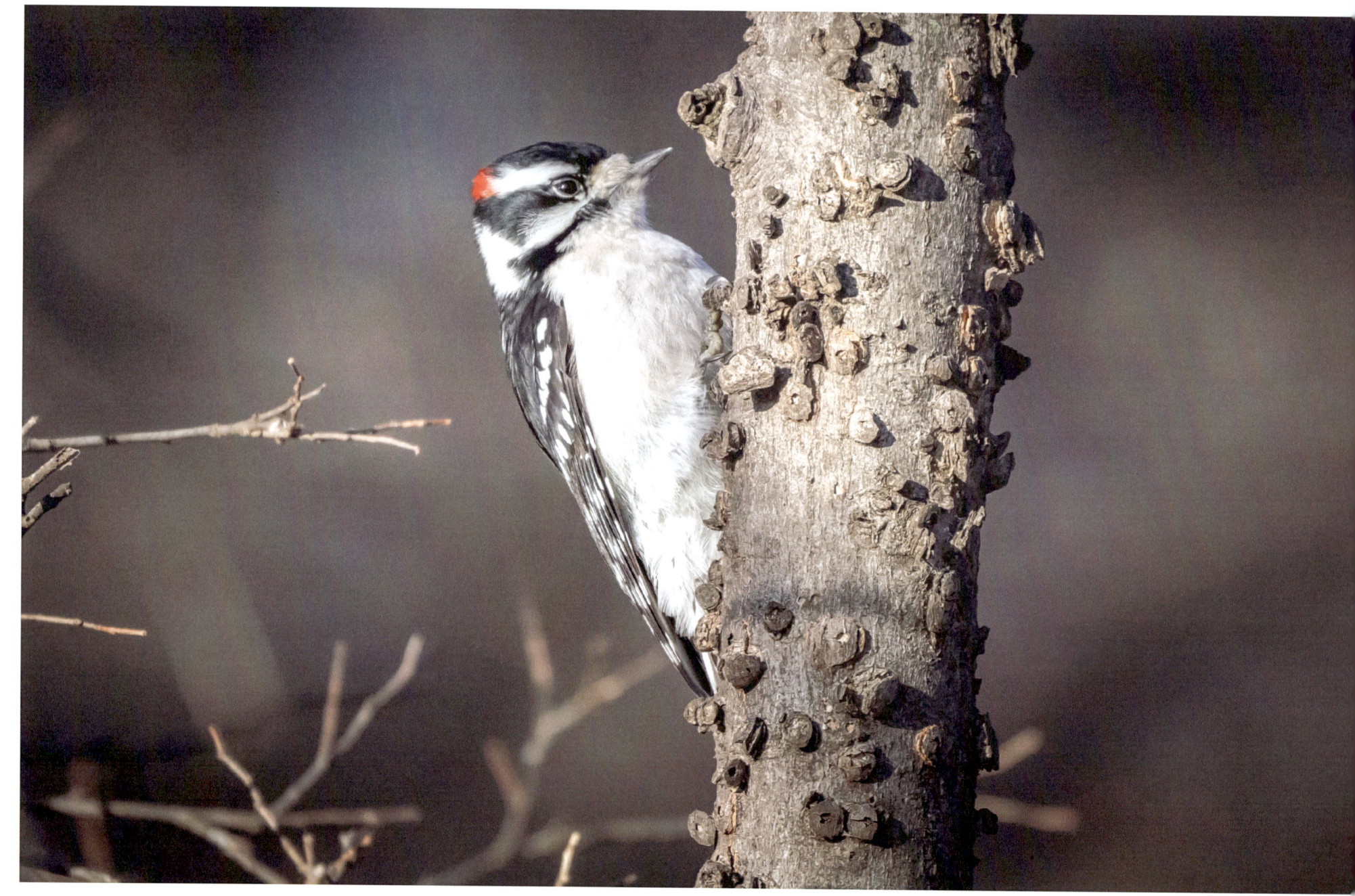

Male Downy Woodpecker at Work

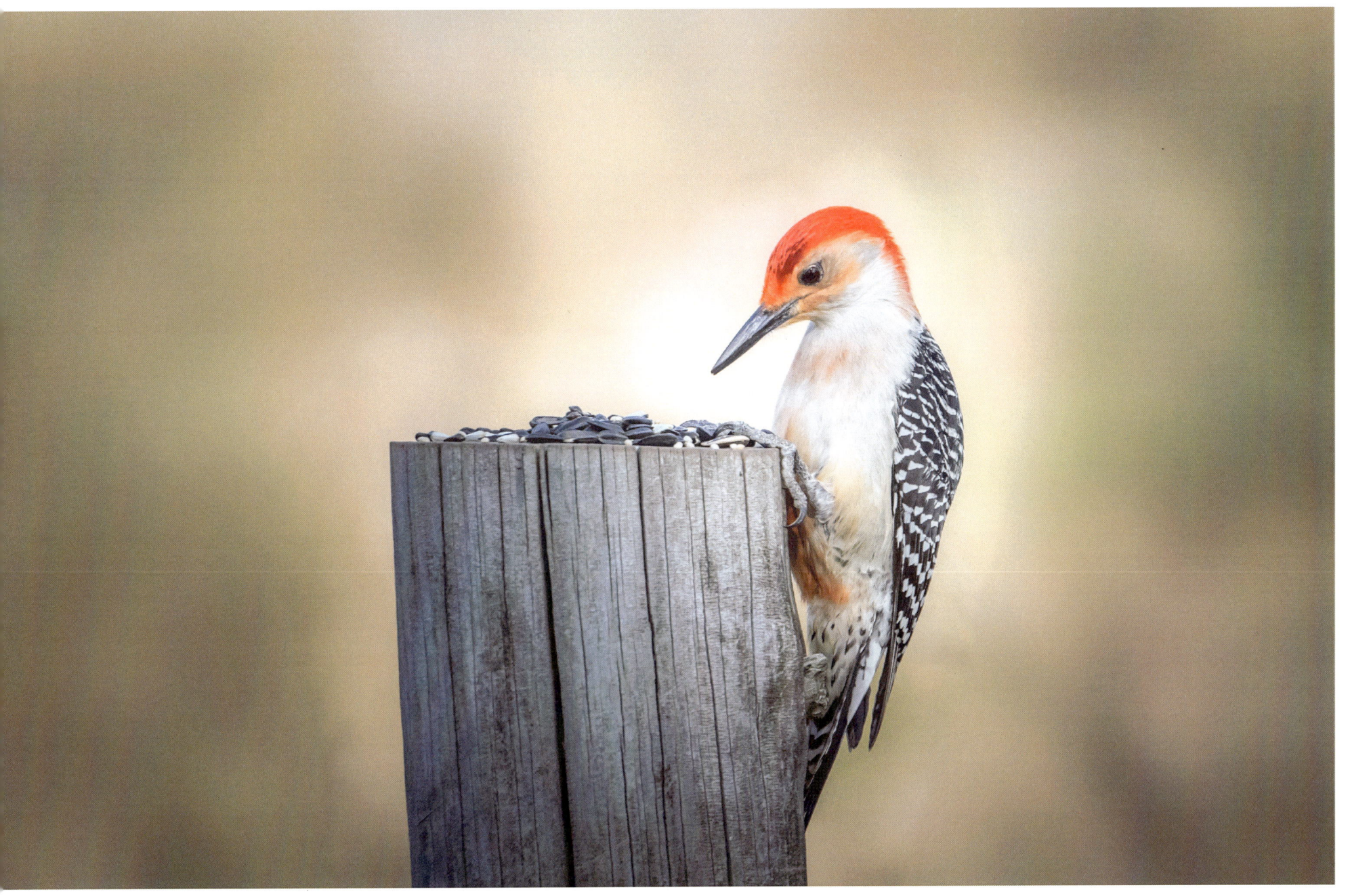

Red-bellied Woodpecker Looking Over the Menu

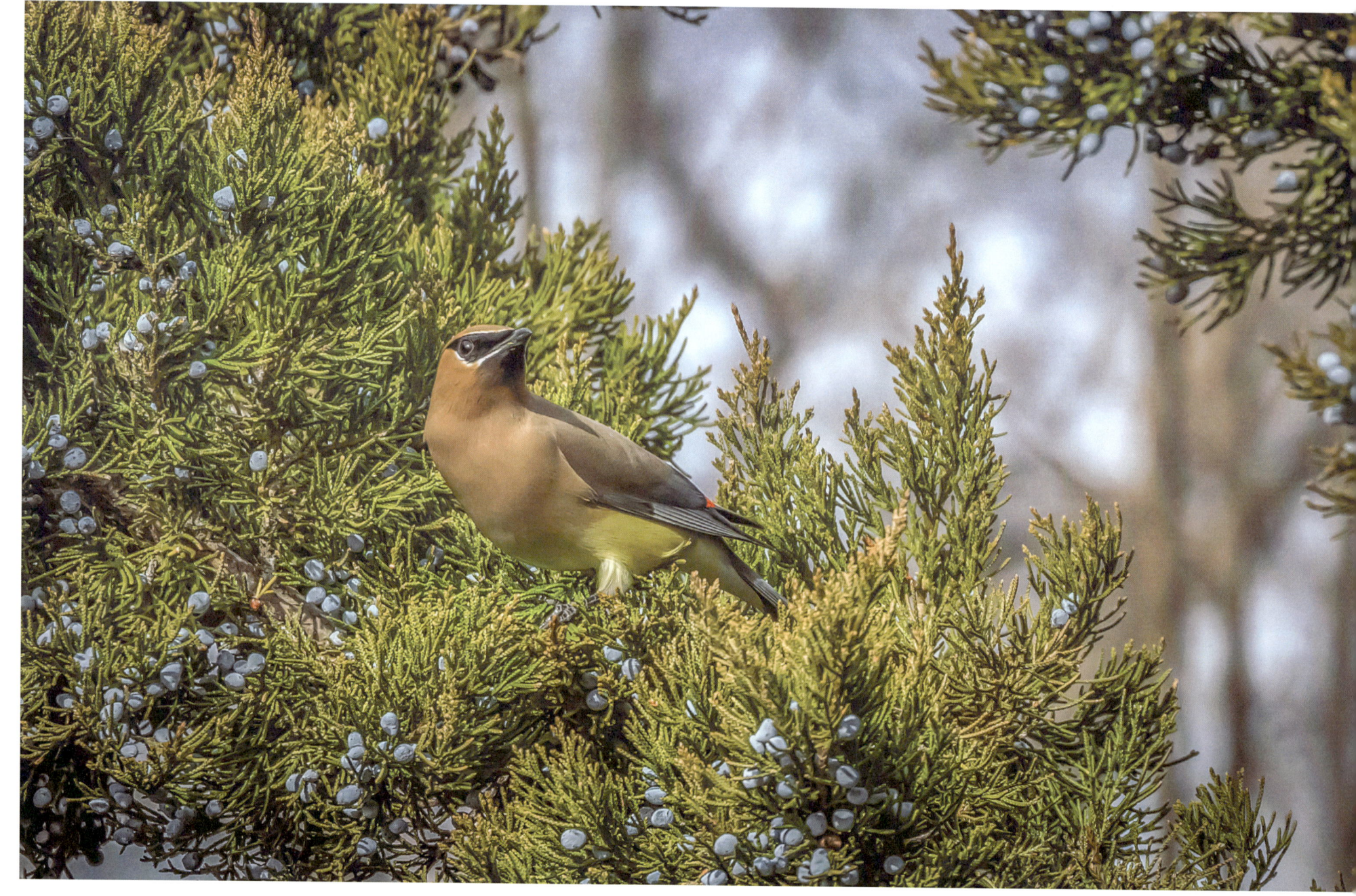

Cedar Waxwing Resting in a Cedar Tree

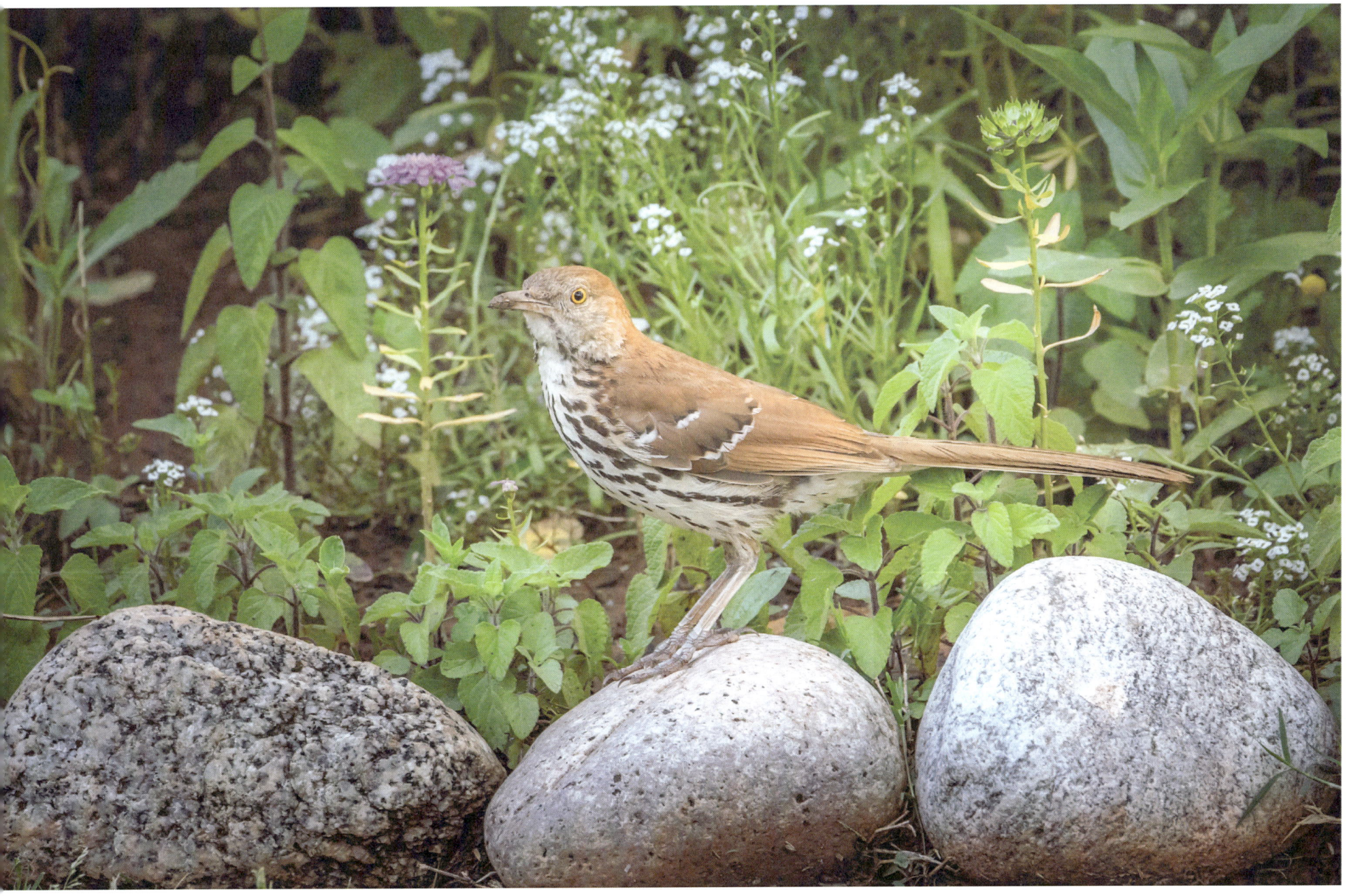

Brown Thrasher

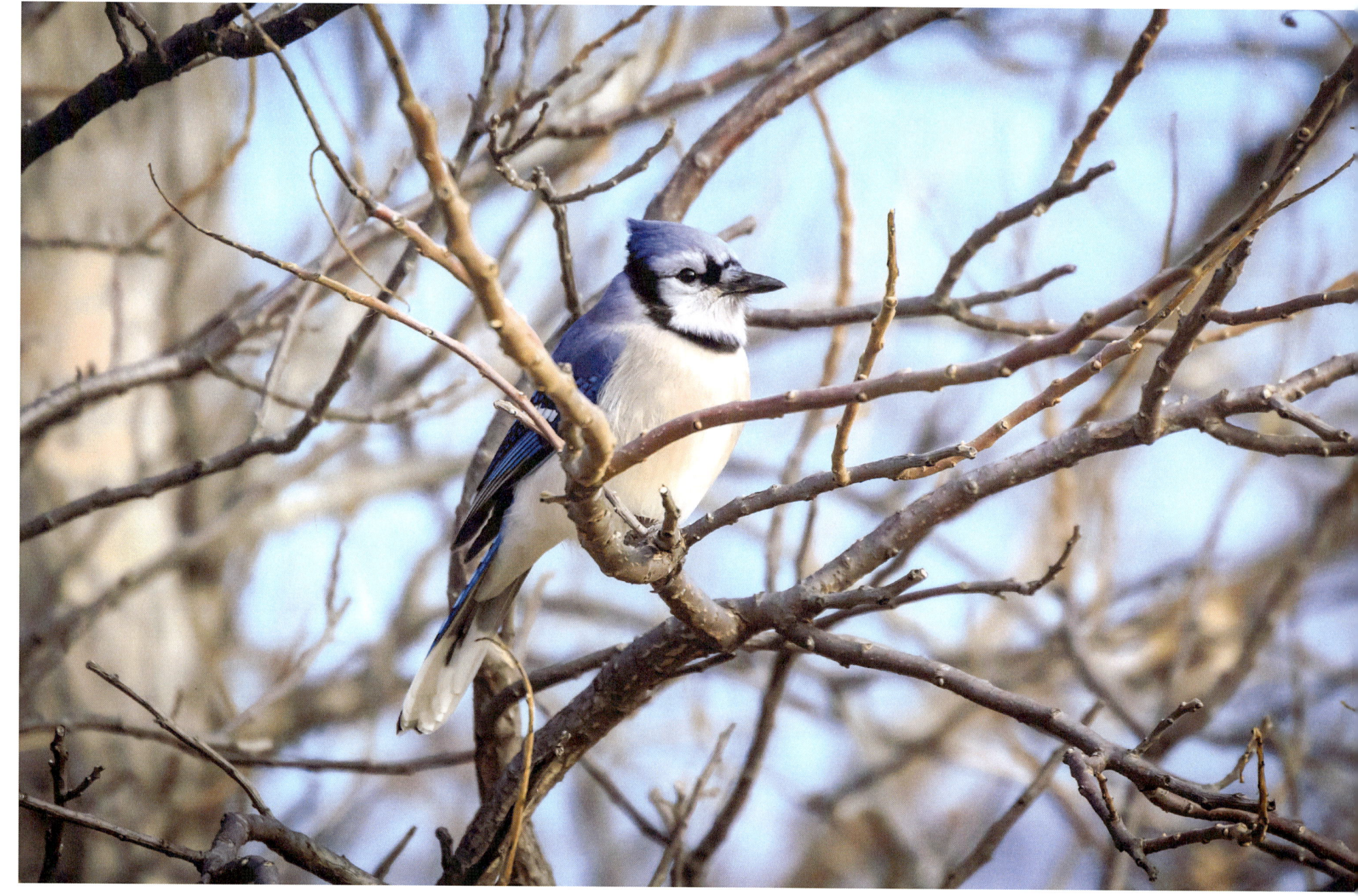

Blue Jay Sitting in a Winter Tree

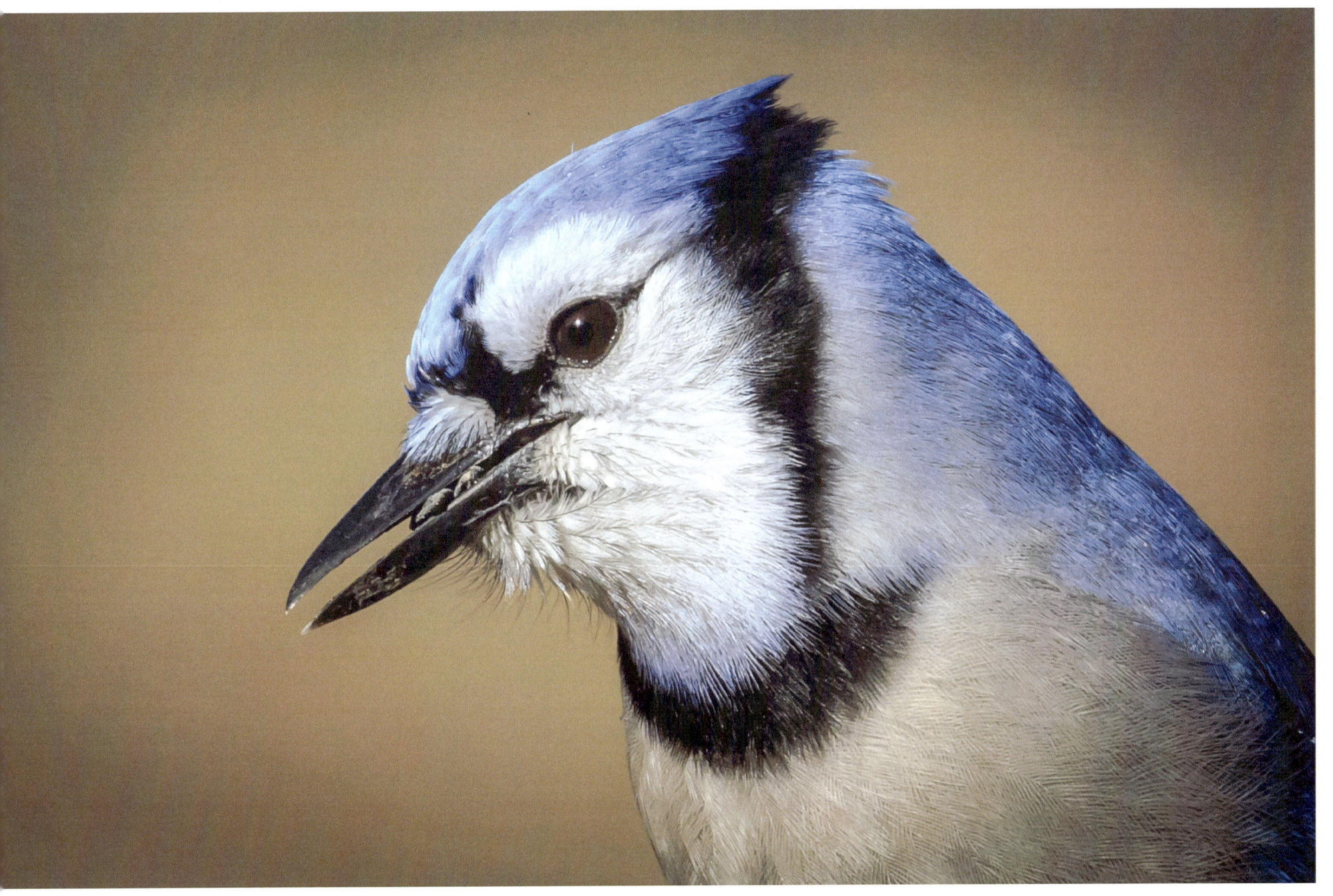
Blue Jay Portrait

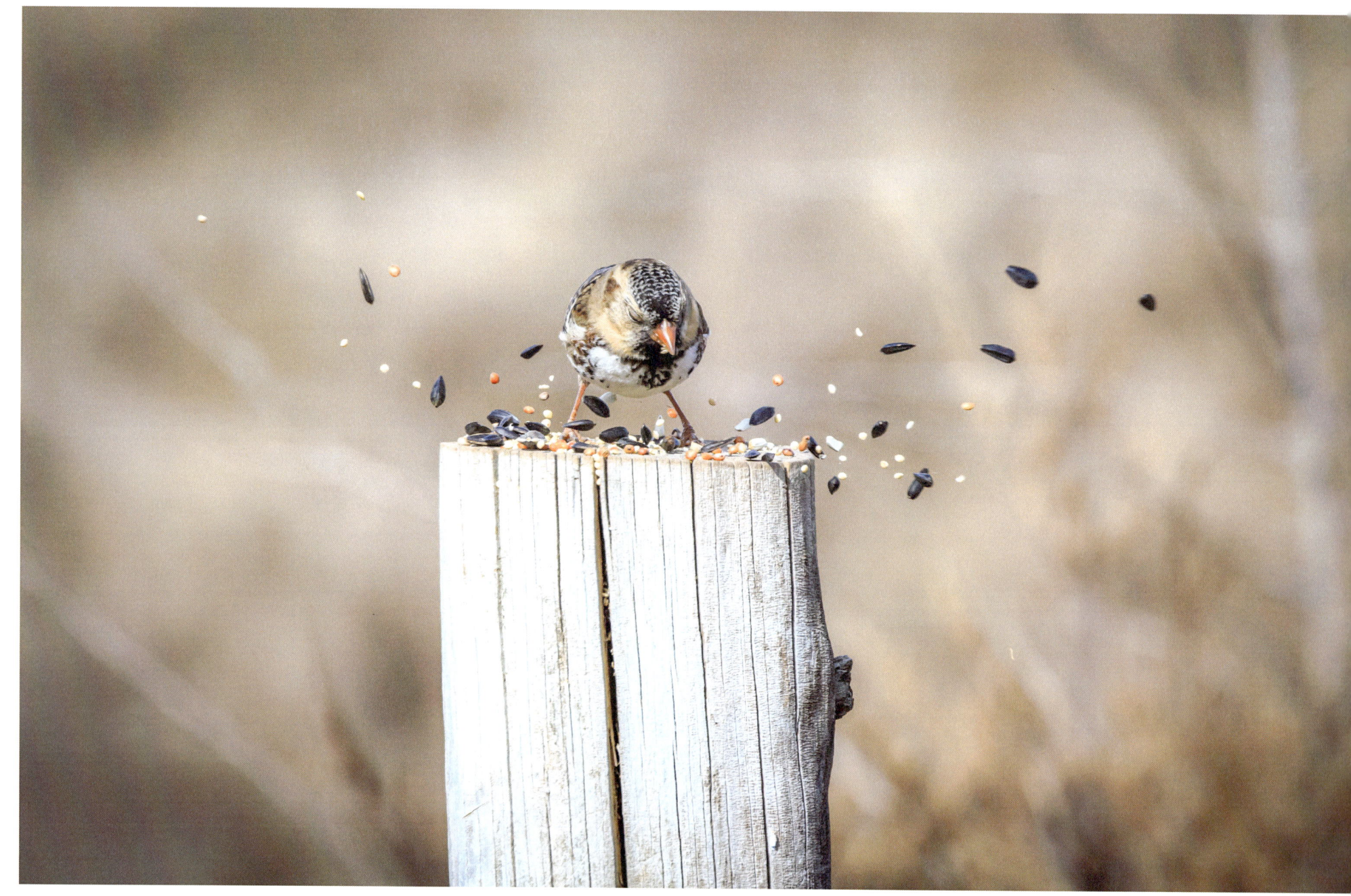

Harris's Sparrow Searching for Just the Right One

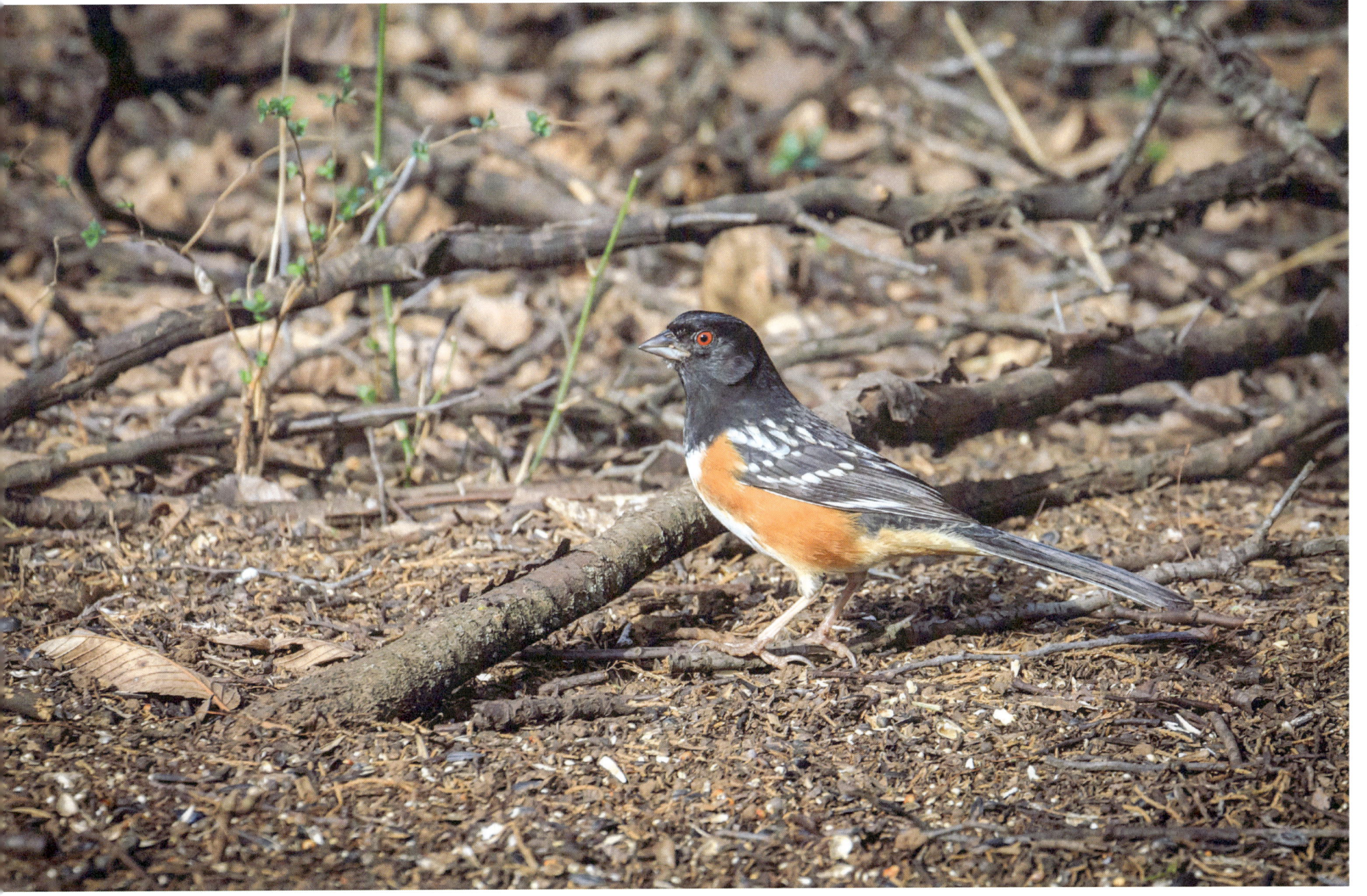

Spotted Towhee

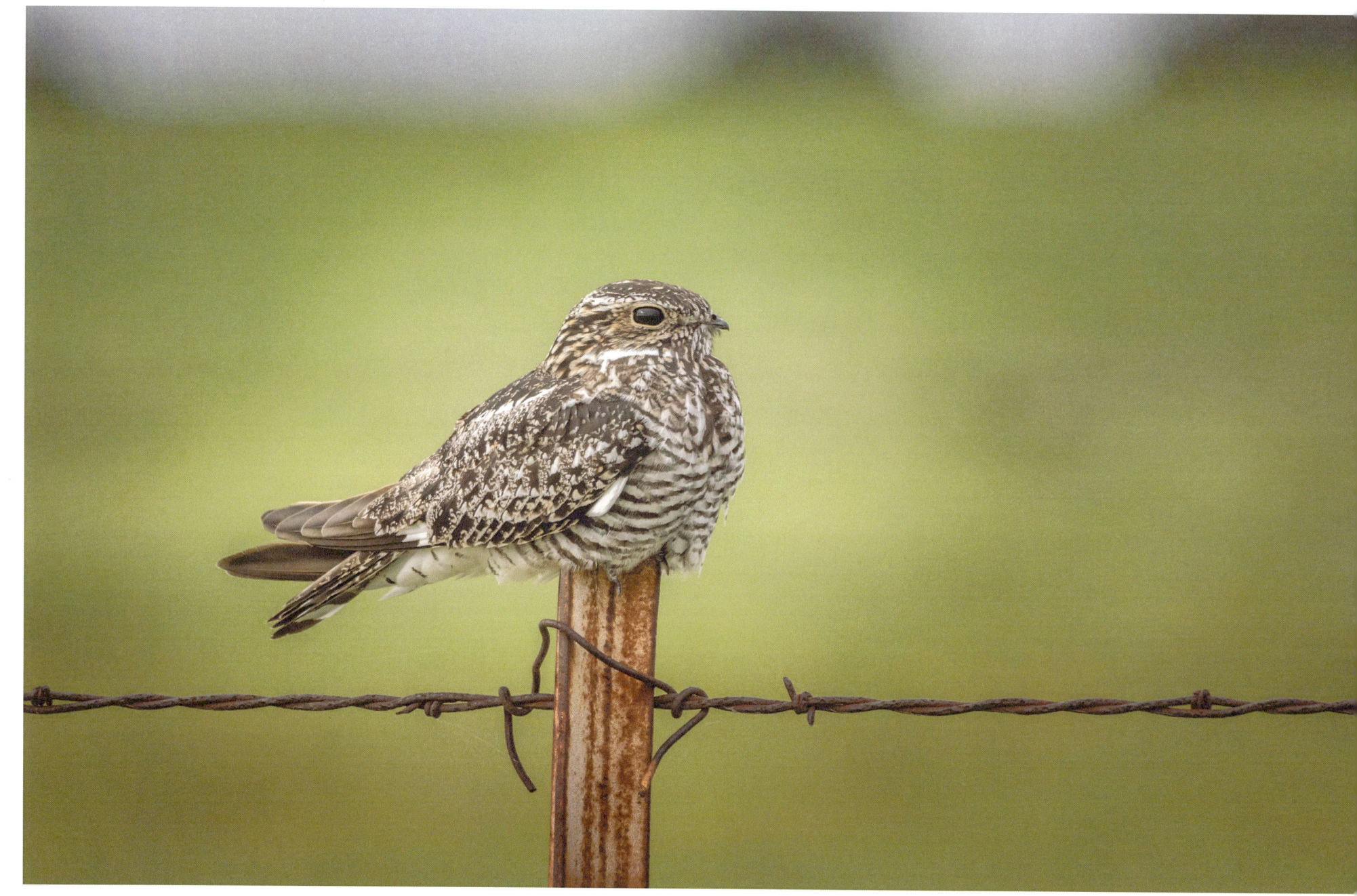

Common Nighthawk

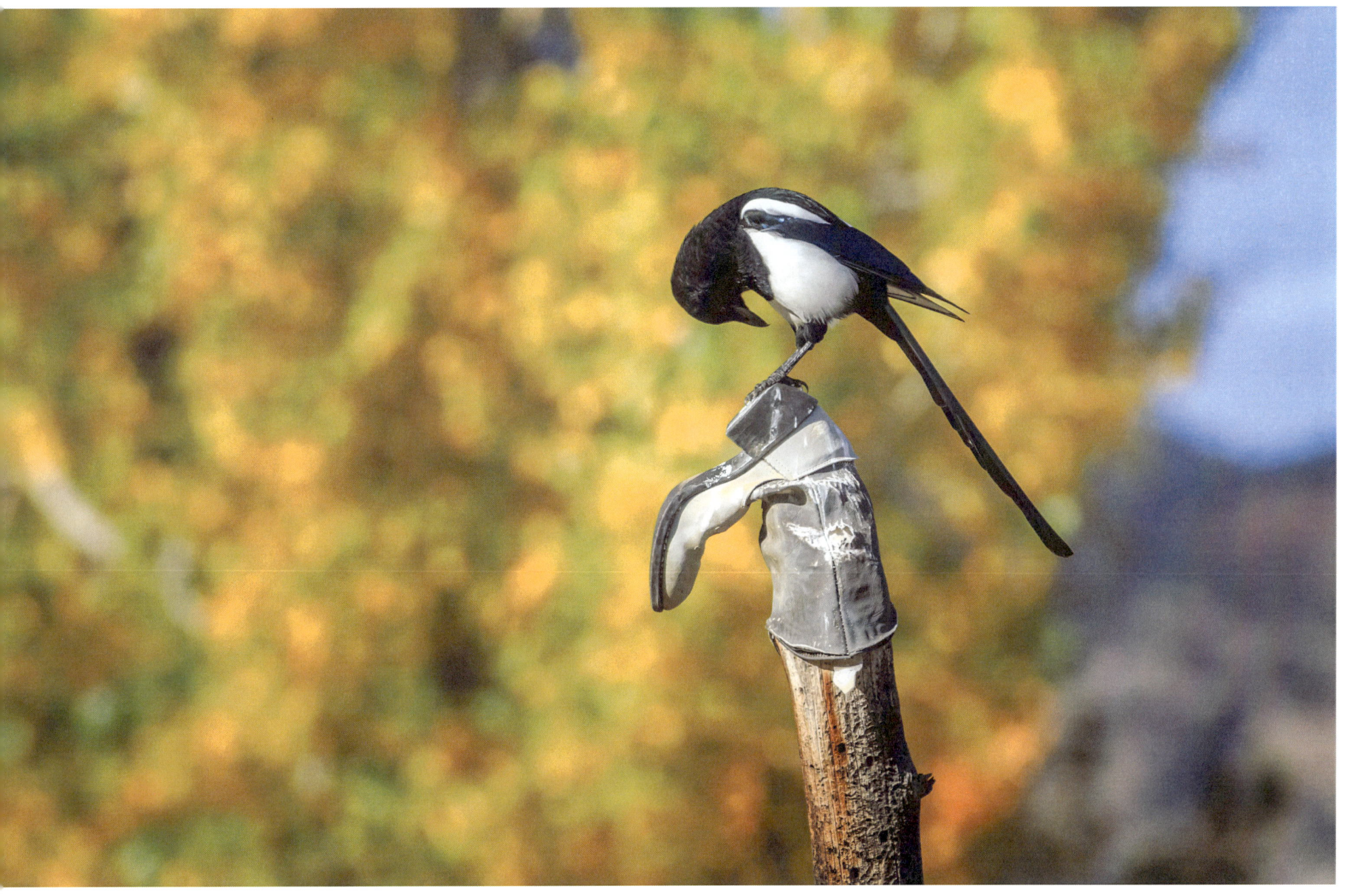

Black-billed Magpie Mimicking a Boot

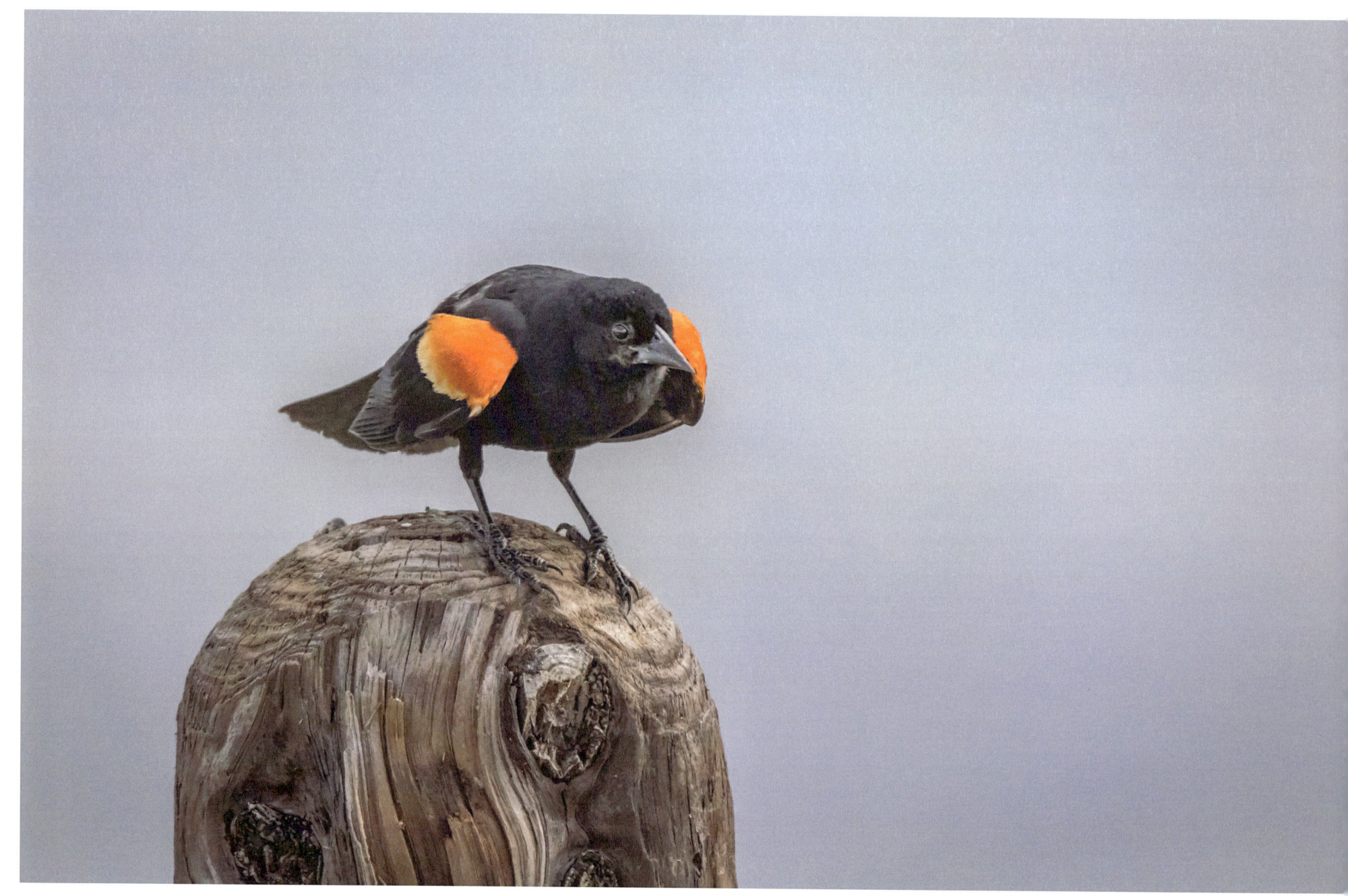

Red-winged Blackbird

Pelicans

Pelicans: giant ducks with a satchel in their outsized bill. The large American white pelican is one of the heaviest of all birds, but it is a master of the air. Their long wings (their wingspan may be nine feet or more) make them graceful in flight, but often they seem to prefer hanging out with friends. Other aquatic birds are often solitary, but pelicans live in large communities with lots of interaction and occasional conflict.

While the American white pelican is the largest and most widely dispersed pelican, the smaller brown pelican lives primarily in coastal areas. It fishes by diving, sometimes from great height, headfirst into water after its prize. It is an impressive dive in which the bird is often completely submerged. As communal as its larger cousins, brown pelicans often patrol the skies in long, low-flying formations; but sometimes a single bird can be found on a lone perch at the end of the day.

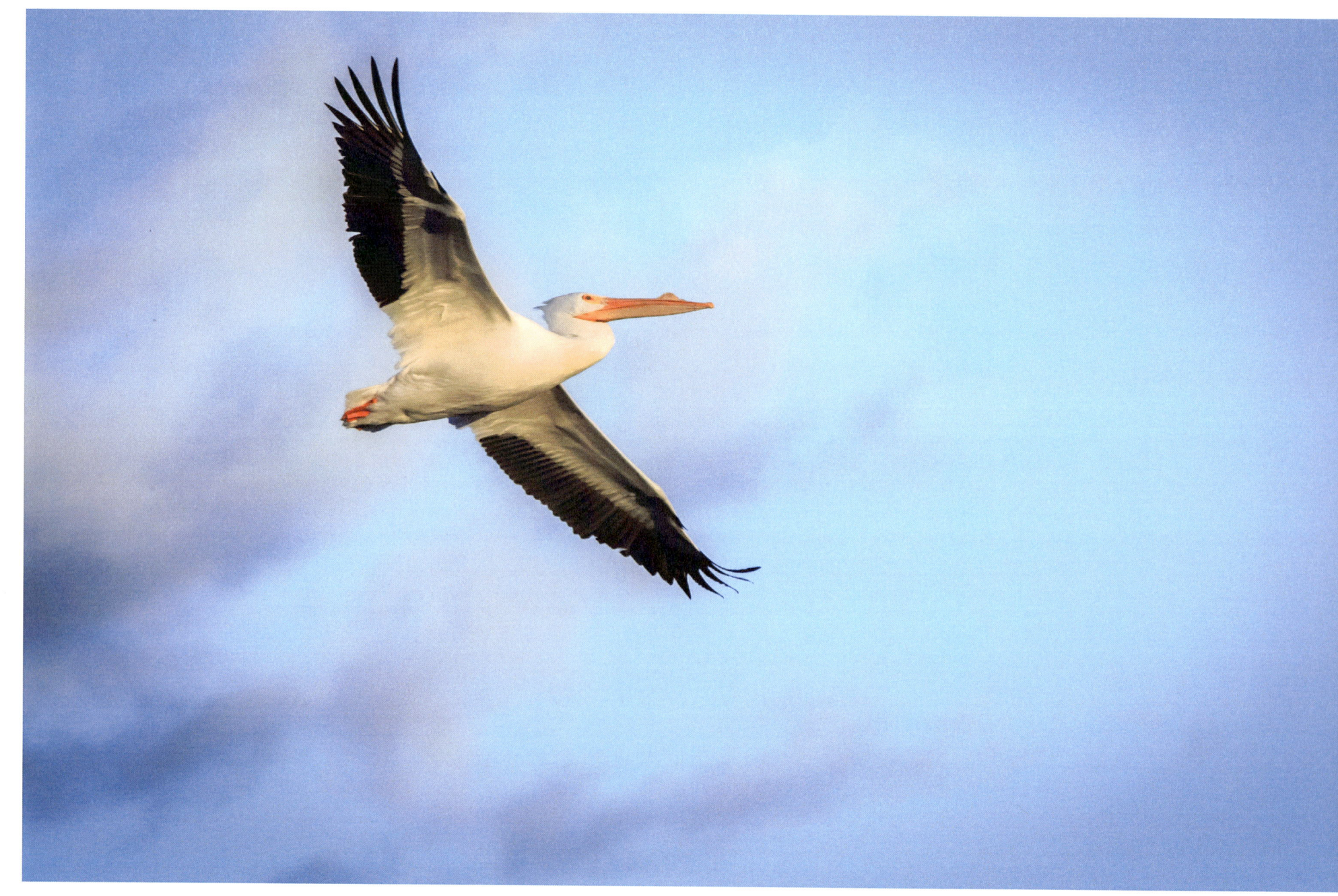

American White Pelican in Flight

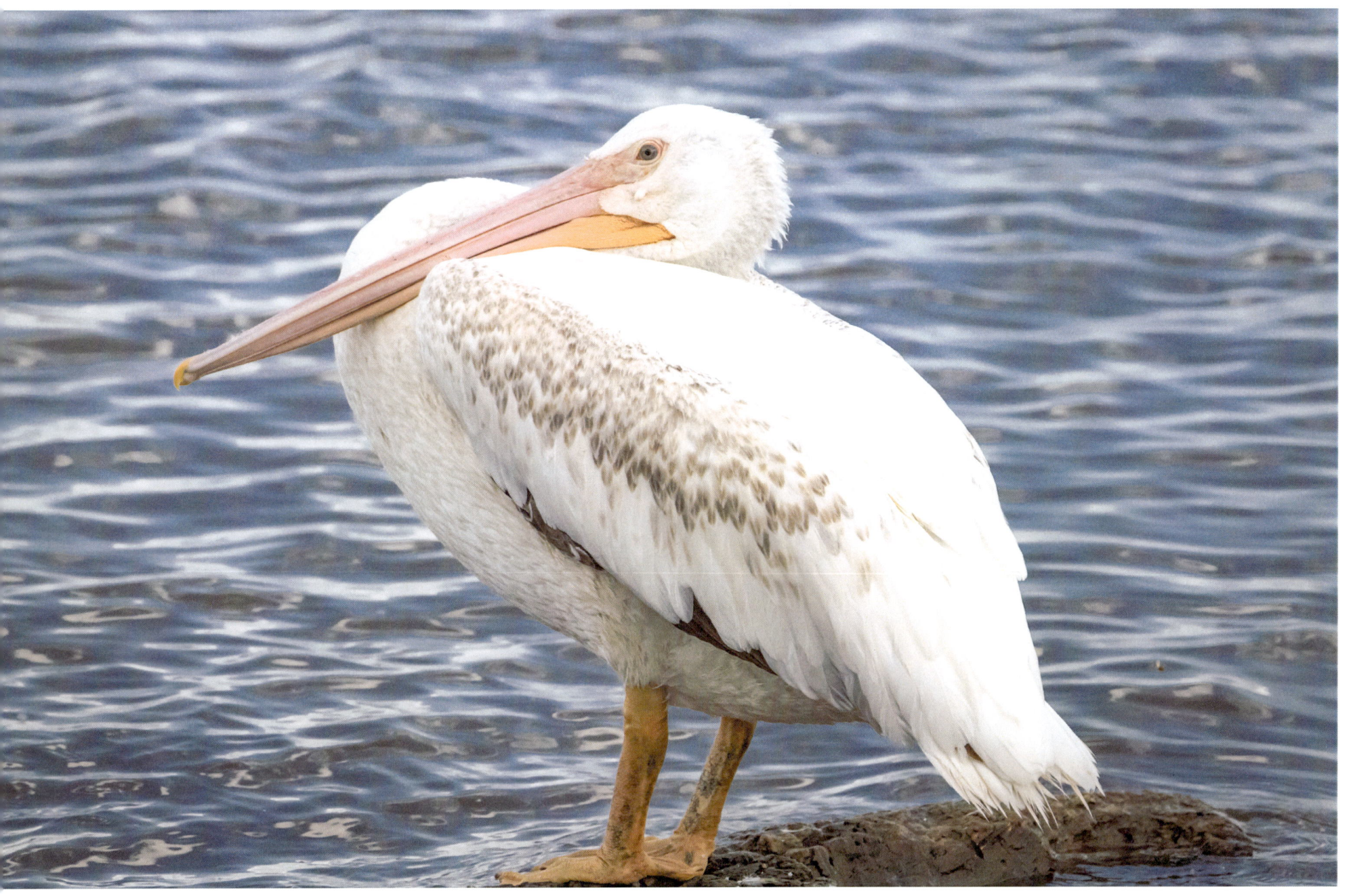

American White Pelican

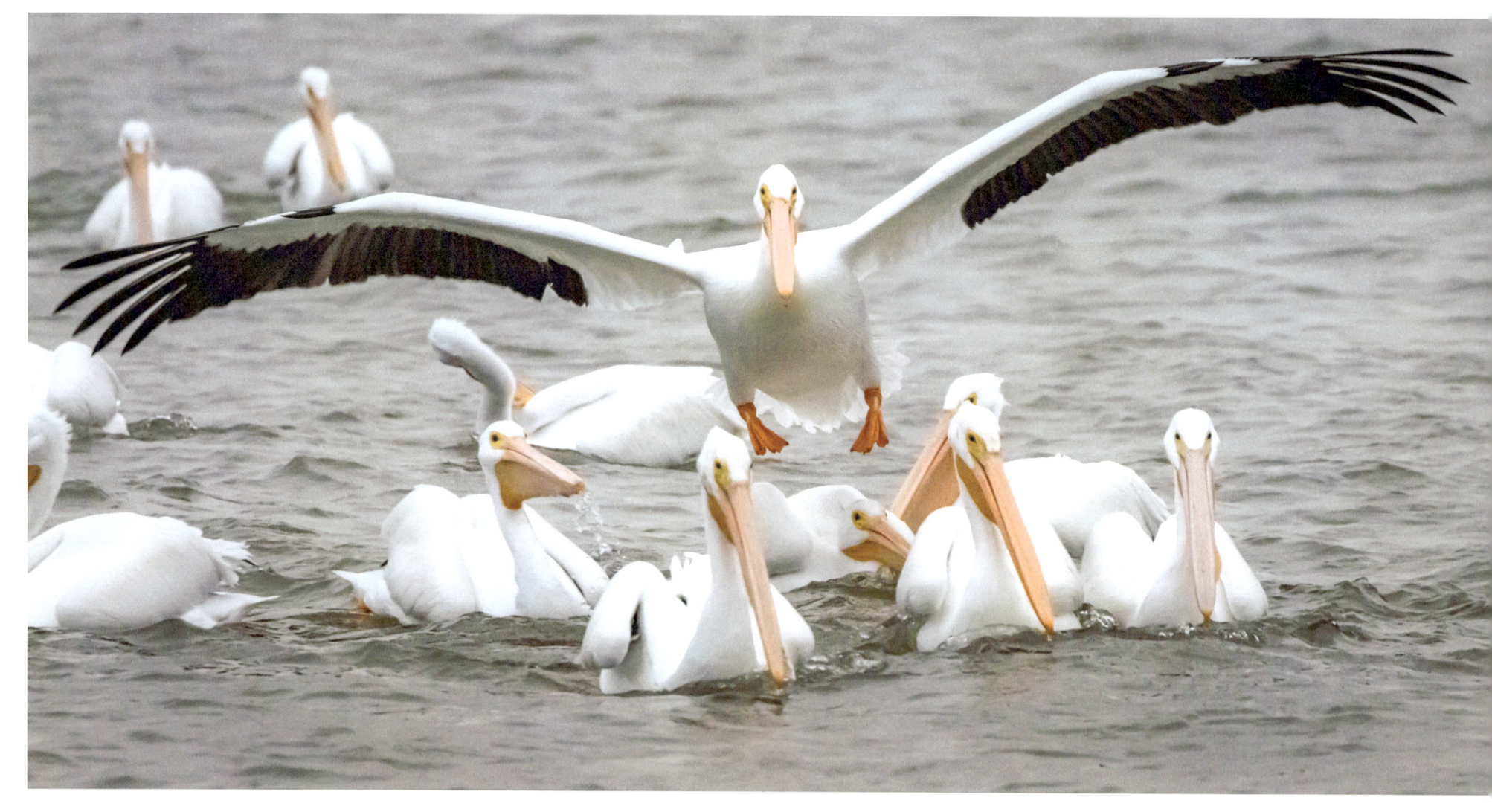

Crash Landing

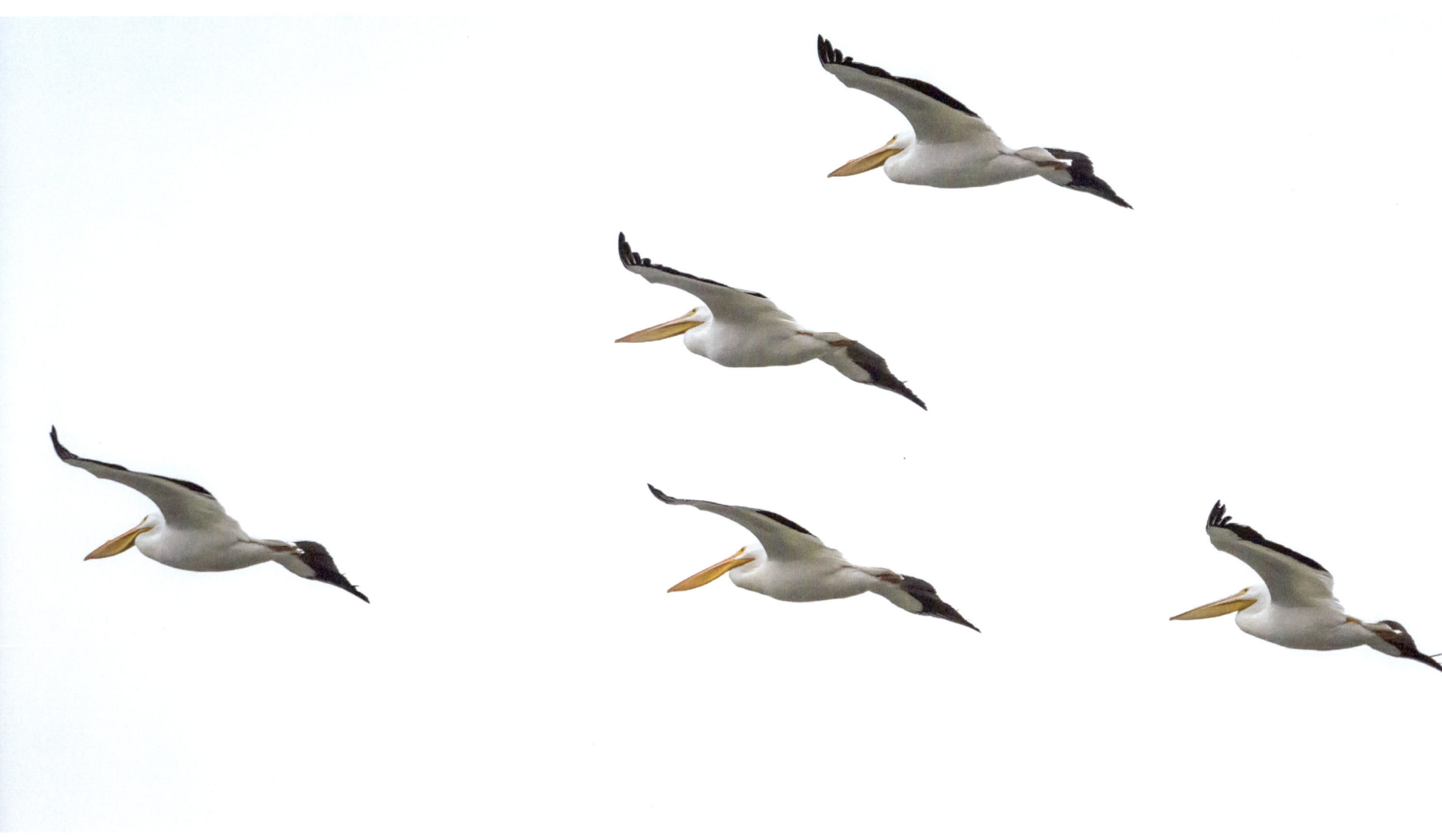

Pelicans Flying in Formation

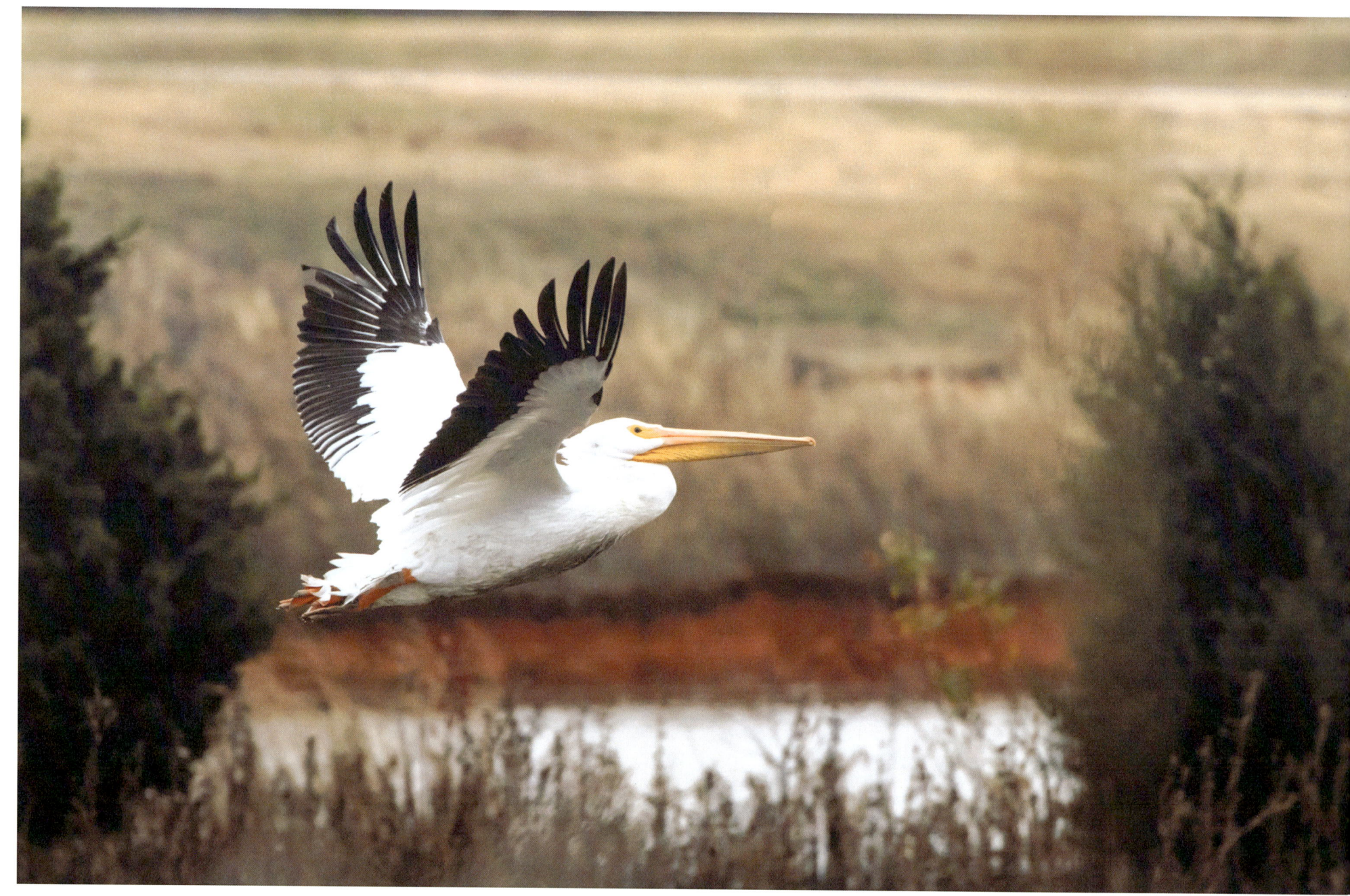

American White Pelican in Flight

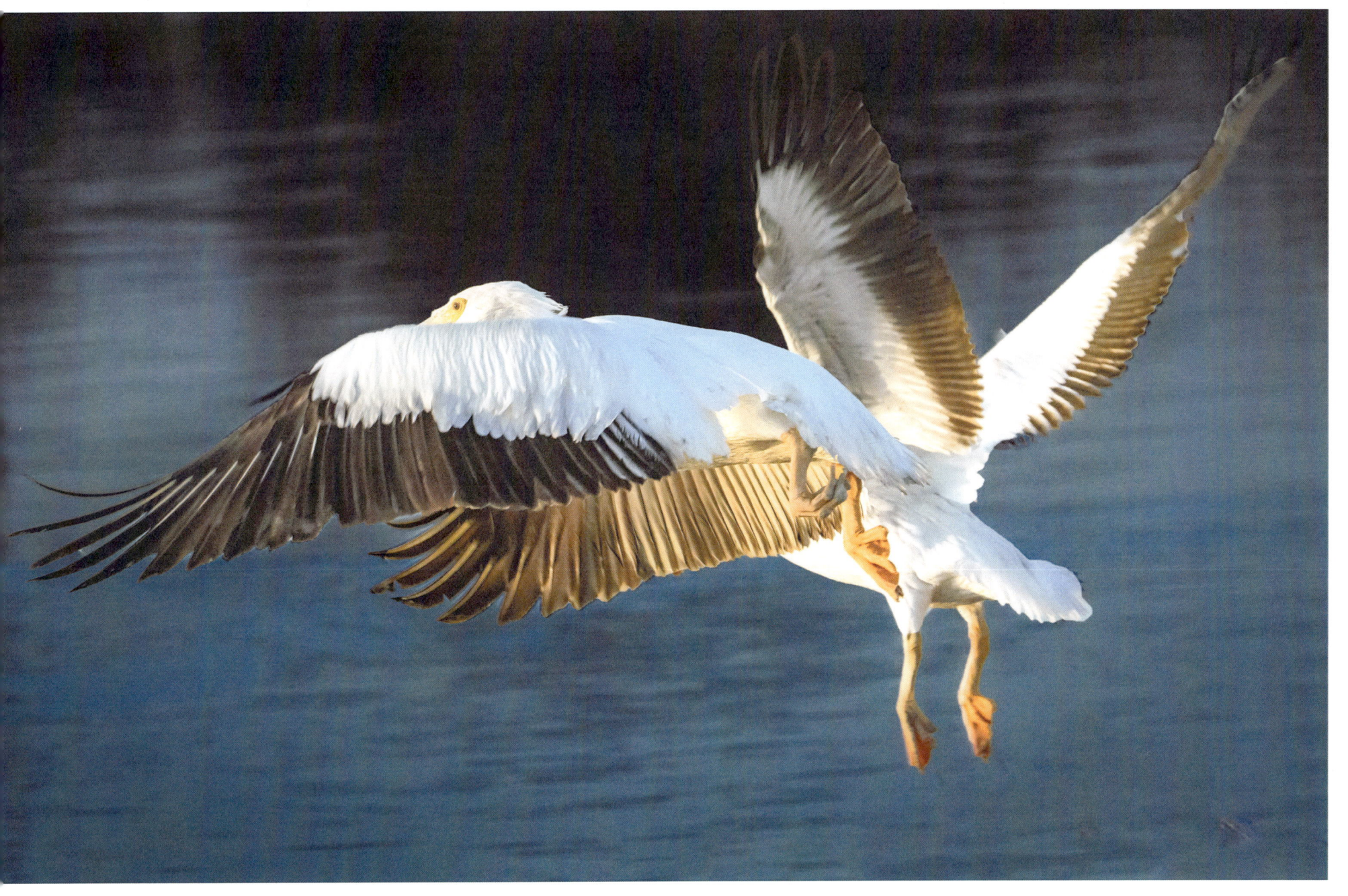

Pelican Dance - Taking Flight Together

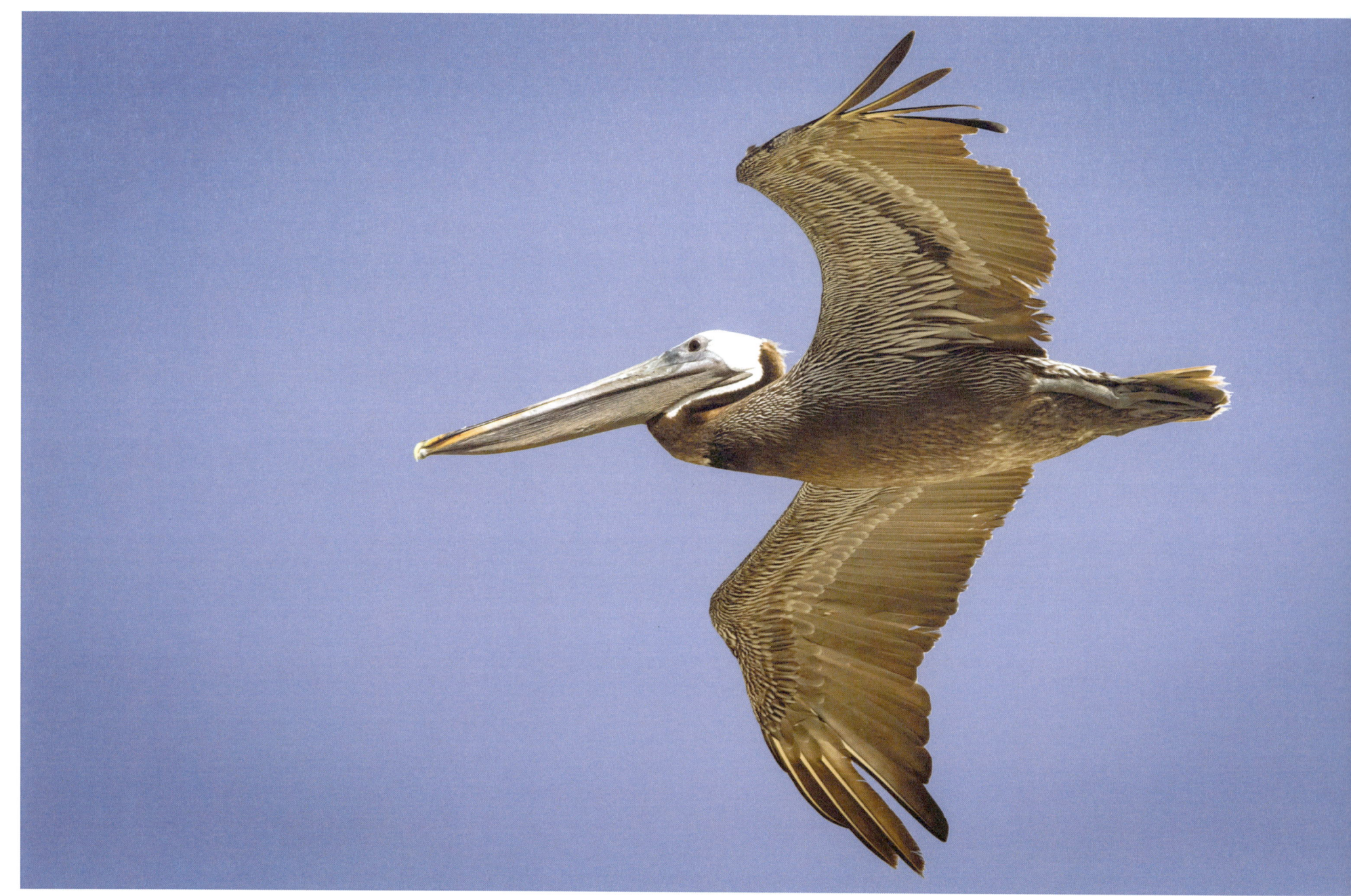

Brown Pelican in Flight

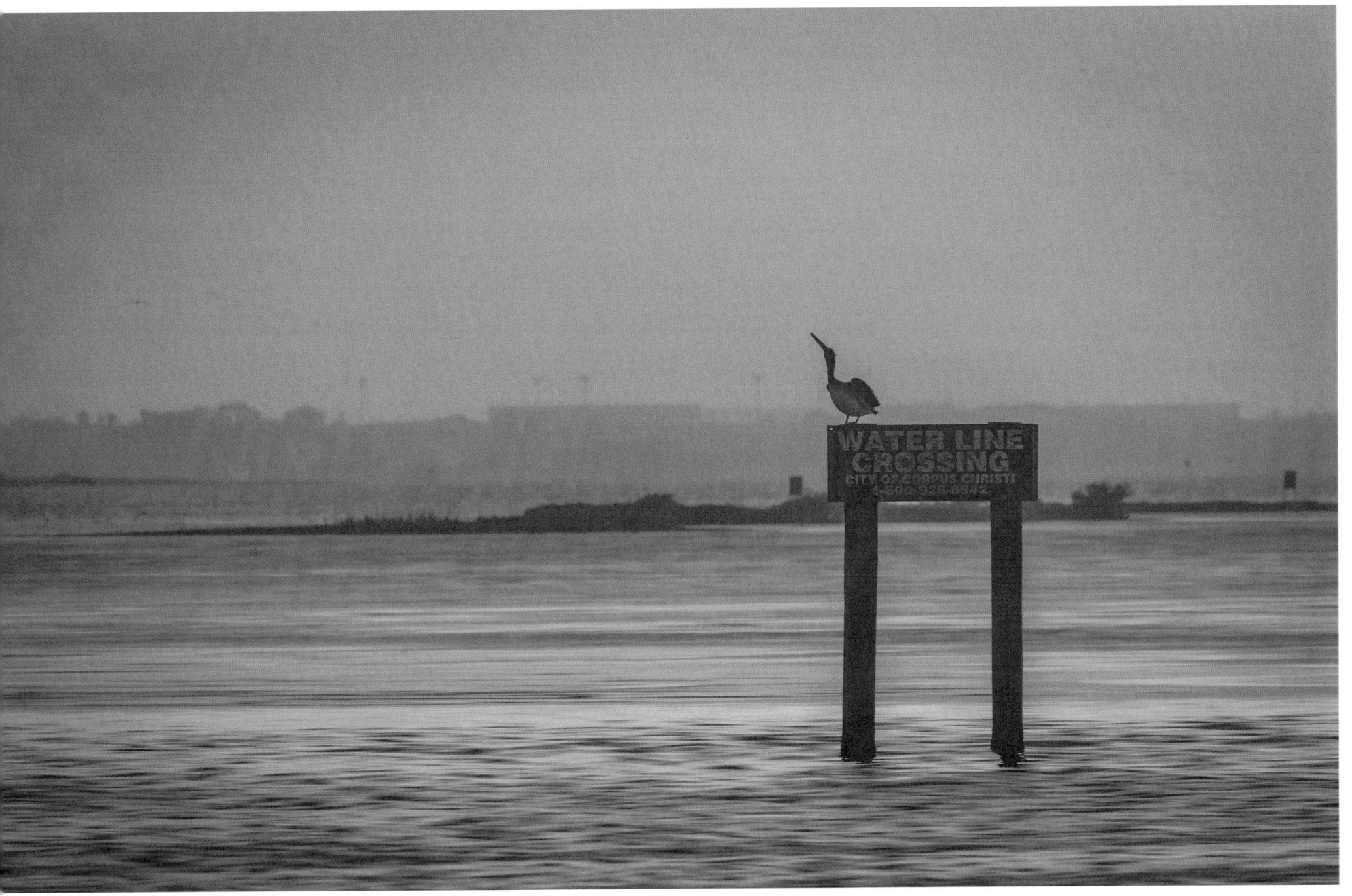

Brown Pelican - Sittin' on the Dock of the Bay

Index of Birds

American goldfinch *(Spinus tristis)*, 72, 73
American kestrel *(Falco sparverius)*, 63
American white pelican *(Pelecanus erythrorhynchos)*, 102, 103, 104, 105, 106, 107

Bald eagle *(Haliaeetus leucocephalus)*, 50, 51, 52
Belted kingfisher *(Megaceryle alcyon)*, 47
Black-billed magpie *(Pica hudsonia)*, 97
Black-capped chickadee *(Poecile atricapillu)*, 82
Black-crowned night heron *(Nycticorax nycticorax)*, 25, 26,
Blue heron *(Ardea Herodias)*, 22, 23, 24
Blue jay *(Cyanocitta cristata)*, 94, 95
Blue-gray gnatcatcher *(Polioptila caerulea)*, 77
Brown pelican *(Pelecanus occidentalis)*, 108, 109
Brown thrasher *(Toxostoma rufum)*, 93
Burrowing owl *(Athene cunicularia)*, 37

Carolina wren *(Thryothorus ludovicianus)* , 79
Cattle egret *(Bubulcus ibis)*, 14, 15
Cedar waxwing *(Bombycilla cedrorum)*, 92
Common nighthawk *(Chordeiles minor)*, 98
Cooper's hawk *(Accipiter cooperii)*, 60

Dark-eyed junco *(Junco hyemalis)*, 88
Double-crested cormorant *(Phalacrocorax auratus)*, 46
Downy woodpecker *(Picoides pubescens)*, 90

Eastern bluebird *(Sialia sialis)*, 78
Eastern kingbird *(Tyrannus tyrannus)*, 75, 76
Eastern meadowlark *(Sturnella magna)*, 68, 69
Great egret *(Ardea alba)*, 8, 9, 10, 12, 13, 20
Greater yellowlegs *(Tringa melanoleuca)*, 37
Green heron *(Butorides virescens)*, 31, 32, 33, 34

Harris's hawk *(Parabuteo unicinctus)*, 56
Harris's sparrow *(Zonotrichia querula)*, 96
House finch *(Haemorhous mexicanus)*, 84, 85

Killdeer *(Charadrius vociferous)*, 36

Laughing gull *(Leucophaeus atricilla)*, 42, 43

Mallard *(Anas platyrhynchos)*, 48

Merlin *(Falco columbarius)*, 64
Mississippi kite *(Ictinia mississippiensis)*, 61, 62
Mountain chickadee *(Poecile gambeli)*, 83

Northern cardinal *(Cardinalis cardinalis)*, 80, 81
Northern flicker *(Colaptes auratus)*, 89

Osprey *(Pandion haliaetus)*, 53

Painted bunting *(Passerina ciris)*, 71
Pine siskin *(Spinus pinus)*, 86, 87

Red-bellied woodpecker *(Melanerpes carolinus)*, 91
Red-shouldered hawk *(Buteo lineatus)*, 58, 59,
Red-tailed hawk *(Buteo jamaicensis)*, 54, 55
Red-winged blackbird *(Agelaius phoeniceus)*, 100
Ring-billed gull *(Larus delawarensis)*, 44, 45
Royal tern *(Thalasseus maximus)*, 41
Ruby-throated hummingbird *(Archilochus colubris)*, 66, 67

Scissor-tailed Flycatcher *(Tyrannus forficatus)*, 2, 3, 4, 5, 6
Snowy egret *(Egretta thula)*, 17, 18, 19, 20
Solitary sandpiper *(Tringa solitaria)*, 39
Spotted sandpiper *(Actitis macularius)*, 38
Spotted towhee *(Pipilo maculatus)*, 97

Western kingbird *(Tyrannus verticalis)*, 74
Western tanager *(Piranga ludoviciana)*, 70
White-winged dove *(Zenaida asiatica)*, back cover
Willet *(Tringa semipalmata)*, 40

Yellow-crowned night heron *(Nyctanassa violacea)*, 27, 28, 29, cover

www.ingramcontent.com/pod-product-compliance
Ingram Content Group UK Ltd.
Pitfield, Milton Keynes, MK11 3LW, UK
UKRC031637240426
12048UKWH00035B/91